Picture of Hope

A Spiritual Journey from
Rich to Rich's
and
Rich's to Riches

by Rich Kovatch

Find this book on Amazon.com

Picture of Hope –
A Spiritual Journey from Rich to Rich's and Rich's to
Riches by Rich Kovatch
pictureofhope@hotmail.com
PO Box 734, Monterey, CA 93942

ISBN-13: 978-1543291124

Made in the USA
Columbia, SC
21 November 2024

47245828R00214

A Personal Reference

 **A *Spiritual Ride* from a Down-to-Earth Poet**

By **Raymond Brown** on November 3, 2017

After spending a number of months contemplating Rich Kovatch's new book of poems: **Picture of Hope: A Spiritual Journey...** I say, **"Really good!"** and something you can go back to over and over again. It is hard, many times, to find books that relate to your life. In laying bare his own life, Rich proceeds to bring forth nuggets that can fit anyone's life. He sometimes brings a smile and sometimes his emotions are raw – but it is the stuff of reality we all experience. Seeing life from another's perspective gives us an insight into our own life.

The first time you read it start at the preface and read it through (although go to the poem numbers as Rich directs.) By doing so, you will find out a lot about the author and why he writes so and even what drove him to write this book. After that, you find yourself jumping from poem to poem as if you were eating some enticing food that you just couldn't put down. I found it most helpful to use a pen to make notes for myself about Rich's thoughts and how they pertained to me. This is a book that should find a permanent home on your bookshelf.

Forward

My continuous praise and gratitude goes out to my Creator. I call this The Holy Spirit, God, and Jesus. I have no issues with what you may call **this energy** I also call *LIFE*. Something so overwhelmingly magnificent, **I believe** mankind was designed just TO BE. I AM that I AM. (NOT *my* original quote of course), but **pretty solid** I'd agree. **Ha.**

I believe God spoke those words to Moses, an Old Testament leader who as a spiritual base equates to The Law. **Unconditional** - in its *DESIGN* & *FOUNDATION*. But the APPLICATION of its principals — our **WILL** to *FOLLOW* the PATH - DIRECTED **as CHOSEN** ! This means that **WE** *are responsible* to a GREAT degree what our world consists of. **How much exactly** I doubt any "age" of Mankind *will* *ever* **KNOW**. Always expanding to new previously before ideas BEing manifested into a "reality" qualified and quantified INDIVIDUALLY and as a WHOLE also, it is WAY too complicated and inter-twined with strong connections and weak connections all having their affects known as the "Butterfly Effect".

How this book affects you **I believe** will be with LAUGHTER, **DEFINITELY TEARS**, & heart palpitations which I hope WILL HAVE you're LOVE **for others grow** with amazement and splendor bringing you to **ponder new questions** to be considered as to how **JOY** may be **SHARED** and expressed **FREELY**. Plus whatever the "**Universal Consciousness**", God, The Holy Spirit, Jesus, **Etc.**, may have for us all accepted GRATEFULLY and in **PEACE** because the **VIBRATIONS** (Karma) sent OUT will affect the creatures and creation I experience with those same vibrations. **Mine... I not only desire** to be full of **JOY and HAPPINESS** but **KNOW I ALREADY AM full of "Good things"** ! Again, they also will be returning somehow thus I daily input "*My* 2 cents" in to this theater of miracles and wonder. However that may be, I CHOOSE to SEND OUT what I INTEND to be POSITIVE.

I would like to give you all a couple little "heads up" as to this background information for a side-note (fact) , ha, I was NOT an "A" student in English class during High School as I was in most every other class. So you (might?) notice (a few?) grammatical errors (mistakes – no... **"first takes"** not quite in harmony with the ideal goal) - like run-on sentences here and there. **Ha.** And funny, to me at least, is that when I was young I was kind of fascinated with **King Rich**ard the **"LION-HEARTED"** and had this connection and affect that I exactly don't know even has any merit besides what I have created the connection to become. See? Please practice while reading to LOOK FOR and FIND the deep meanings only YOU will discover, then I wish...will SHARE! I would also **enjoy** IF that would include getting back with me at Pictureofhope@hotmail.com. or at P.O. Box 734 Monterey, California 93942.

I have figured out though that my path somehow has to do taking advantage of my lung capacity being conditioned to be efficient in exhaling using my trained to be AMPLE breath (**hot air**?) in the form of a (**Kiai**) – a loudly and forceful but mentally relaxed and focused release of energy, intent and efficiency learned from my twenty years of Okinawan Shorin-Ryu karate participation and instruction. See? Run-on sentence? **Ha.**

This collection of poems actually got started the very moment I first saw the woman I was to marry, the still to this day beautiful, Ronda Baldini. Marry TWICE actually. Ha. And not so much a "ha" now, divorced twice. But as with ALL things we experience, there are as many CONTINUOUS LESSONS to be gleaned from waking up every morning as we can dream and conceive, **believe and ACHIEVE**. She is the most special woman on Earth to me at this moment that God has me closest to (500 miles! Ugh. Ha.) but is now on her own path apart from me and still my best friend, as I am to her. Our paths are united to the degree we choose to unite them which would involve the principles I've expressed in this book to harmonize with a reality yet to be created for enjoyment of both parties and their world.

I believe _my_ life has been the catalyst onto _**my**_ PATH to gain EMPATHY and perspectives as to _**HOW**_ LOVE works. **_Yours is too_ - IF you CHOOSE to SEE LIFE that way. I believe** LOVE is described   - very precisely -

throughout the Bible and specifically around 1 Corinthians chapter 13. Also, by the way, I've described it a bit in numerous poems. **Ha.**

<u>This book</u> actually got started, as did my GRAND AWAKENING to **INTIMACY, LOVE** and everything I saw as "**Good**" or "**Bad**"...the first time I SAW **Ronda:**

I've told this story bunches of *times*.
It's hard for me to write without ending sentences in *rhymes*.
My angel came walking down the stairway after washing her *HAIR. HE*
Verbally spoke **9 words** into my head; "**THIS IS THE GIRL YOU ARE GOING TO MARRY".**   (must have been Heaven's? Ha)

So I wrote her a poem that turned her on to ME and **made her laugh**
Because of *this...*
It said: I'd take her out on a date and it would end in a *kiss*.
So out we went. **Three times and it still didn't** *happen*
Till **Ronda** thought to herself; "**What the hell?**... This is *CRAP n'*

Gave me the KISS I'd been waiting forever *for*.
You're *invited* **to read what happened next in** *poem* **after** *poem* about LOVE plus things I abhor.
Our relationship started and *soon LOVE brought forth our daughter Rose.*
Even though Ronda KNEW I didn't really want **a child**, selfish reasons I *Suppose*.

It was the best thing that could have ever happened.
We were so blessed and happy, the only thing that would really dampen
My spirit was that *my name is Rich* but **extra money was** *rare*.
I must have had ants in my pants and jazz in my jeans that lead me to **Dare**

To walk up to a line and cross it if it looks promising.
I put all my fears, doubts and anxieties in their place I've nicknamed "Thomasing".
I write my **"negative"** feelings down expressively then tear them up to "**Set them free**"!

The *"Good"* feelings I've written down *for this book* to keep alive and Grow so many, many may SEE.

See? **Ha.** One thing I've been taught and **believe** is the **foundation** upon all things lain upon **is: A man's word** is only as good as his backing it up! P.S. Note: I ALWAYS "SEE" the man in the mirror – ME – as the filter for what I speak. God has been quoted as saying that "ALL men are liars" which means I AM TOO , but in perspective, it is again...PART of the process to "FIND **PEACE** – (**NO LIES WITHIN** THYSELF) and "**HOW LIFE WORKS**"

I believe this starts with what I believe is God's **WORD**. I also know that a " *lie* " WILL come back TO HAUNT YOU , karma stuff, although there is "A WAY" to overcome, which is up to YOU to DISCOVER. **Jeremiah 29:11** states that there is - *by design* - "**GOOD**" intended **towards us. I BELIEVE THAT. *SO our "Gift" is when we SEE positive stuff and DO positive stuff*.** As the saying goes; "It's not how many times you fall down but how many times you GET BACK UP"! "Trips" aren't even considered to be mistakes AFTER they HAVE BEEN overcome – *only UNTIL* – because *ONLY* **THEN** WILL we "SEE" it was **but part** of the conditioning PROCESS. *****see poem #27. This possibly might be seen as the "**Butt**" part where most of our "**PAIN**" is said to be "happening"? **Ha?**

Same goes for a crazy doctrine in my present opinion that there is NOT EVEN AN "**EVIL**" POWER in this world. Before the situation resolves itself **HARMONIOUSLY**, these things must be and **WILL BE SEEN as EVIL.** I even spent hours recording how many times in the Bible it says God "**Creates EVIL**". **94 times** by my count in 2012! Interpret that as you will, but...come on now...believe what you want, but to me the *fact* the *word exists* means it has some essence of value. P.s. I have the list available upon request. **Denial is not TRUTH.**

So like too many young couples we didn't share the financial burden of raising a child. This led to issues you will read about. Even sad things have a funny side to them. Laughing is encouraged while reading these little ditties. Y-2k was approaching and I was moved to quit, but only temporarily for 4 years from my karate teaching and practice to read the Bible and many other sources involving spiritual **thinking towards GRACE, MERCY, KINDNESS and JOY.**

We decided to move away from cold Mishawaka, Indiana after both our moms died within a month and my dad only lasted right on average about 14 months without the **LOVE** of HIS life to ***SHARE his with*** daily. (actually, NOW, I **believe** that is what happened to my marriage relationship. It died for the same reason).

But the "**Miracle**" of "**Life**" as **I understand it** allows for ANYTHING to happen. (Maybe except a 3rd marriage to Ronda? Not likely but see previous sentence. Ha.) We "Love" each other still...just **differently now.** Life means change. **Life is change through choices made.** This could be seen as selfishness...depending...read on. **I believe** that Miracles only happen when HARMONY between **ALL** entities involved brings about their SHARED CREATIVE IDEA within LOVING, POSITIVE INTENTIONS and THOUGHTS aimed at growth in **JOY** for **Go**d**...US!**

An important bit of information that always has been a huge factor in my relationship with Ronda's is that her dad had a serious head accident and was hospitalized when she was around three years old so she NEVER HAD the MALE SUPPORT that fathers bring to the family but did have aunts and uncles and a cousin in towns nearby. She still has her one and only brother and very minimal older relatives still living here among us in our realm while I still have three and a sister; so we have totally **different dynamics** and **different paradigms about life** and everything in it. Thus HOW our differences and issues became highlighted in our marriage and lives is brought much insightful light to these pages.

I want you to **keep an open mind when reading these** and I certainly don't expect you to agree with some of them because, heck, I've mentioned that these journal MY JOURNEY and I DON'T even believe _exactly_ as I did before. Mostly my view on "**Hell**" as the Catholic "**religion**" wants us to believe and HOW IT HAS CHANGED MY APPROACH TO OTHERS HUMAN BEINGS, and life in general! I hope it will be *very apparent* my positions about Life and Love have been transformed.

We moved to Las Vegas, Nevada to warm up and experience lots of sunshine and light. Then new poems with new spirit started coming out. Mostly because I did NOT listen to Ronda AND The Holy Spirit who BOTH were saying DO NOT buy a house for 2 ½ times what we were leaving. Plus I KNEW there was going to be a BIG HOUSING BUST *but I insisted* on buying the house *right next door* to my guitar buddy from Indiana.

The WEEKEND we signed, the market CRASHED. It was MOTHER'S Day weekend 2007. It didn't take long for things to go south. My 4 different jobs kept laying me off due to the bubble bursting affecting everything, construction jobs first. We lost the house after 3 years and THANKFULLY (by Grace only paid during the 1st year then allowed to stay there for 2 more)! Plus the stress was **BIG TIME**. A shame and total BULLCRAP as far as I was concerned because the "Bank" - (THIEVES) got our government to pay the full price I tried to pay (at taxpayer's expense) ...PLUS sell it AGAIN! And for only $100,000.00 this time which is what we left and what I could afford paying for everything by myself like I had been doing, but of course that was not God's "PLAN".

We ended up separating because I could not physically deal with both hands in severe carpal tunnel symptoms that made sleeping basically NON-EXISTANT and its HEALING properties vanquished into oblivion. The pain ran from both hands bottle-necking and crashing my party at my neck and shoulders (were lots of people hold secondary stress also). Plus a lower back that would also hold stress and get injured from karate falls during workouts, and back-breaking work 8-10 hours a day on a **buck rivet HAMMER GUN** to assemble aluminum truck bodies together...which I didn't seem to communicate the **"HELL"** of experiencing it. I figured it up one time that I personally could be hammering tight nearly **1 MILLION** RIVITS **/ YEAR** ! ! ! And I worked there nearly **12 years!**

She had her own issues which did not get out of the darkness and into the LIGHT where I wanted them to be dealt with properly and with the BEST POSSIBLE RESULTS.

This led to our second divorce. SOMEHOW, the _very next day_ our daughter called me to see if I might be interested in moving out to the Monterey Bay area to temporarily help her out since going to school full-time and working enough to pay the bills as a single mom would, understandably so, seem to be too much to handle. Up until then I had only visited three times in California. It was to be basically a full-time job that I was **very happy** to be **in position to** serve and **enjoy**.

So off I went to be grandpa to my only grandchild from my own loins, though I do have **Joshua**, a step-grandson I guess he is called from Ronda's first marriage of quick duration – which also gave odd color to _our own developing_ marriage and _intimacy level_.

I had barely got my bearings and still working on my **Balance** of this **NEW LIFE** and my new surroundings **when they all changed again** in an instant. **Yup. Another woman. Ha.** But no "voices" this time. Only our own saying "Hi". The occasional chance meetings became less occasional and more for just friendly reasons. Her name was the exact thing I've been lacking for SO LONG…**JOY**! I was in my "Garden of Eden" so to speak. * see poem # 124. Ha. I had beautiful surroundings and a new beautiful woman to hang around with. The local saying goes "Another Day in PARADISE"! And **what a joy the days had become**, for me at least.

I was inspired to start writing again with a **brand new level** of **Joy** never experienced before in my being. **I believe** I became **overwhelmed** so **G**od had a surprising an **abrupt** about-face in store for me on the 4th of July, 2016. On my way back home from a 4 day fishing trip to "**Hell Hole**" reservoir in northern California I **believe** God (as the Devil) screwed with me. I got pulled over because of some words I had on the back end of my truck cap window while playing Hide-n-Seek with my granddaughter and **Joy**. **Joy** told me I should get rid of those words but I was too busy to care, because I really didn't think I needed to …

thinking people CAN M.Y.O.B. as my sister used to tell me which means Mind Your Own Business. **Ops!** Ha. And **UGH!**

One of the four words caused some person vibrating from fear caused through intentionally and socially manipulating purposes (which by the way is the definition of *witchcraft* – although witchcraft does not necessarily denote an energy or vibration NEGATIVE or contrary to ONE'S PERSONAL WILL since I've personally been told that by someone who said **she IS a** "WHITE" witch**! Thank God. Ha**!) to call the police to check me out. I know...another "rough" sentence. **Ha.**

Side note: I am a bit saddened that I never got to experience ANY of THAT MAGIC she claimed to be ABLE TO PRODUCE. **Besides** the **spirit** of **"JOY"** I was also wanting **to connect** with **some 'MAGIC' some**how. CALMING DOWN of our souls was first on my agenda. **My bad! Damn!** Ops. Wrong. I **_DID_** experience **a bit** of **magic. Quite a bit actually** but *didn't appreciate it, so* **I believe I screwed** up the path I thought I was on. *see **poem # 119**. The **last bit of magic she did on me,** which I can't say was not even funny on any level, except *NOW*, of course, **ha,** to make me "**DISSAPPEAR**" from her everyday visual world! **CRAP** !

I KNOW though that more magic must be in my future still **but** from where and who is still in the future... *see # 120. This takes the ABILITY to en**joy** the pleasant "**feelings**" I DESIRE . One must **LEARN TO EXPERIENCE - FIRST -** the "**FEELINGS**" **as though** it **ALREADY IS! THAT** *is the trick* I **BELIEVE:** TO BELIEVE IS Faith *in progress* MEANING ACTIONS. **JUST DO IT.** Do "WHAT YOU **CAN** DO "... *see poem #122. **One MUST** own *HARMONY* with their *intended* vibrations. *see poem #132.

PROOF IN POINT: I AM very happy **_THIS MAGICAL BOOK_** has been created mostly due to my meeting **Miss JOY** and experiencing a new **JOY** daily. The breath of **new life from getting this DONE** is what I have lately learned TO ENJOY.

So, back to **my "Independence Day"** which became a literal and PHYSICAL happening. I was pulled over. Asked to get out of the vehicle which I knew was NOT GOOD. *I knew even* clearer when he slapped me in **_cuffs_! Ha.** I asked what the heck? I was told I might have supposedly been kidnapping someone because of my **dirty (STILL** and *stupidly* by me by THIS time) was the reason. I knew "CRAP just HIT the FAN" **big-time! Yup.** That situation was **not** an issue **but when** he checked out my driver's license **he didn't like** that it was from Nevada still and my plates were California. I told him the dude at the D.M.V. didn't "Make me all legal" like I had gone there AND **ASKED FOR!** I put my trust unwisely in the DMV employee that probably didn't give a hoot and maybe even does it on purpose? Ha. Ya. Funny dude. All for my "Good" though. Ha. NO GRACE TODAY. It's independence Day for goodness sakes! Nope. **He didn't care** since he could impound my truck, and MAKE $$$ for the state, which he did.

I had to ASK for permission to get some provisions, like some clothes, food and water I had because I had no money for a motel since I now had IMPOUND FEES to pay A.S.A.P. (thank you very much you frickin' punk-ass pig...bastard!. Only in my mind. I still love him, just not appreciating his actions at the moment. **Ha.**) plus I NOW HAD TO FIND someone to sign for it to get I out or another $65.00 / day.

The next **day was hell** walking around in over 110 degree weather. Finally after asking about a hundred people for help one empathetic man came through at the very last moment. I had basically given up hope for that day *just seconds before*! *Amazing co-incidence again*? **Ha. NO. Designed** for my **benefit.** Ouchie! Ha. I MUST CONFESS though, immediately when I saw **the lights** "come _on_" to get "**My ATTENTION**", I FELT an **OVERWHELMING PEACE** that somehow "THIS DAY TOO...SHALL PASS" and I WILL "**come _out_**" even BETTER for the experience.

I got back *that evening* and my duties **ended abruptly** for reasons I *didn't quite follow*. Also my getting to *friendship level* with **Miss Joy** ended very abruptly a few weeks later. **These *3 events* threw me for a loop** for a long time. But **eventually I figured out it was to give me plenty of time to get this book finally together and published. Hard** times is when the **GOLD** gets brought to the top for forming (creating) something more PURE now that some DROSS has been **BURNT OUT** during the PURIFICATION *PROCESS* GOD has *DESIGNED*, THANK GOD. (ha) *see poem #27. One of my **Top 2** favorites. **My other is #119.** But MANY are very near and dear to my heart. All actually, depending on la-de-da? Ha. Ha. Ha.

Now I want to thank Kevin Smith, the owner of PIXELS in Monterey, Ca. for the **Grace** he extended towards this endeavor. Also my special thanks goes out to Quinton McKee my award-winning graphic designer, editor guide and final catalyst to "**get it DONE**"! Also the kind folks at the Pacific Grove and Monterey public libraries where the editing took place.

It has been my pleasure to watch how the ***Devil of disbelief*** hindered my progress due to the fact I had a certain due date which I desired to have my first copy delivered to *someone special*. I choose to believe whether that date is achieved or not, **G**od's WILL...WILL BE done for my good and hers.

So here it is! Please read each poem with an open mind understanding I have grown a lot in how I see things. **I believe** you will be able to clearly *SEE* the shifts *in attitude*.   **Possibly your OWN?**   EnJOY ! ! !

Rich Kovatch
2-22-2017

Rich's Poems
in chronological order

Note: As of the TRUE REVELATION GIVEN TO ME **in Dec. 2012**

"Unsaved" = UNLEARNED **of the** TRUTH **of** PEACE
"Unsaved" = UNLEARNED **of the** TRUTH **of** GRACE
"Unsaved" = UNLEARNED **of the** TRUTH **of** MERCY
"Unsaved" = UNLEARNED **of the** TRUTH **of** FORGIVENESS
"Unsaved" = UNLEARNED **of the** TRUTH **of** LOVE

"UNSAVED" DOES NOT MEAN "UNREDEEMED"

Date written:	Title:	Please use / Give out As God leads	Written for:
1) 02-14-99	Valentine's Day		to Ronda
2) 02-14-99	Valentine's Day		to Rose
3) 04-20-99	To My Sweet Wife	(mature readers only)	Married couples
4) 04-21-99	Response poem	(mature readers only)	for laughs at work
5) 04-27-99	The Sinner		UNSAVED people
6) 04-30-99	The Holy Spirit		to God
7) 05-01-99	Confirmation Day		to Catholics
8) 05-09-99	Mother's Day		my mom, maybe yours too
9) 05-11-99	The Senior Citizen		old UNSAVED folks
10) 05-12-99	Your Heart / Part 1		a girl at work /drug abusers in bondage
11) 05-13-99	Today's Young Man	(mature readers only)	a kid at work (ASKED for a poem!) & teenagers
12) 05-19-99	P.J.	(mature readers only)	dude said OK to write him one TOO
13) 05-23-99	Your Heart / Part 2		same girl at work—a softer message
14) 05-28-99	What Time Is It?		UNSAVED people
15) 06-06-99	Graduation Day		encouragement to High School Grads.
16) 06-25-99	To Today's Average Person		my parents, Catholics, weak Christians, and Pre-Tribber
17) 08-05-99	Anger		a rough Marriage/ family ties
18) 08-08-99	A Holy Marriage		Newlyweds & Married couples
19) 08-17-99	Oh, So Now You Want To Talk		kid at work - child died & UNSAVED who don't hear
20) 08-23-99	Words	(for mature readers only)	a rough Marriage
21) 10-19-99	A Glimpse of the Mind of Christ		confrontational guidance for Christians
22) 11-23-99	Thanksgiving Thanks		a Thanksgiving Day Prayer

Rich's Poems
in chronological order

Rich's Poems
in chronological order

55) 12-25-01   My Christmas Poem 2001   everyone
56) 03-29-02   The Intentional Will Of God   everyone
57) 05-25-02   A Wonderful Ride   Barbra Davis – Mom's bus driver partner
58) 11-24-02   Absence Makes The Heart...   to Ronda / Married **couples**
59) 01-01-03   Vanity : Wow!   everyone
60) 02-13-05   Touched By Love   everyone
61) 06-29-07   **I Hate My Life**   (for <u>mature</u> readers only)   everyone
                   (suicide note: INTENDED FOR my *carnal nature* only!)

THANK YOU JESUS! PRAISE GOD! THANK YOU JESUS! PRAISE GOD!
For your;
  Mercy, Compassion, **Wisdom,** Faithfulness, **Patience, Correction,** LOVE
= *<u>Provider</u>* of my strength and courage to *<u>Finish</u>* MY race! To <u>Your</u> Glory!

62) 01-17-09   God Is Wise...Me? Not So   to Ronda / **Married couples**
63) 07-17-09   Rejected   to Ronda / **Married couples**
64) 11-28-09   The Gift   Christmas poem for all / **UNSAVED**
65) 06-07-11   Rose's 25th Birthday   Rosie
66) 07-08-11   Happy Birthday Tammi   Tammi Lowe's 50th birthday
67) 07-09-11   Depression   everyone
68) 07-11-11   The Human Race   everyone
69) 07-12-11   What the Hell   everyone
70) 07-16-11   The Devil Redeemed   false church
71) 07-17-11   Jesus' Doctrine   false church
72) 07-21-11   Lost Sheep or Goat?   false church
73) 08-07 11   Though I...and have not Love   false church
74) 08-20-11   Choose You This Day   false church
75) 09-03-11   Communication Breakdown   false church
76) 09-11-11   I Want to Die   everyone
77) 09-17-11   Creatures of Habit   everyone
78) 09-18-11   Common Sense   false church
79) 09-24-11   Godly Sorrow   false church
80) 09-26-11   Well...Focus   Christians
81) 10-08-11   Only Two Kinds   false church
82) 10-23-11   The Character of God   false church
83) 10-30-11   The Saddest Thing   false church
84) 11-12-11   I Demand My Rights   everyone
85) 11-13-11   One is the Loneliest Number?   false church

Rich's Poems
in chronological order

Rich's Poems
in chronological order

#1 VALENTINE'S DAY

TO MY RONDA :
My life with you has been nothing
But happiness and bliss…
That's why you have that brand new ring
And no more your title "miss".

That's not to say our days before
Were not filled with sorrow
Which tested our love right to the core.
Still, we'll be one yet tomorrow.

For sixteen years you've been my girl
I have not seen one better.
You represent my shinning pearl
And the Lord told me to net her!

For the first time that I saw you
He talked to me this way…
I heard Him say it right on cue…
"You'll marry her some day!"

Though little did I know it
That before this day would come,
Would be a day that we would split
And make us both go numb!

I thank God His unending wisdom's better
And He had seen it all unfurl.
He knew we would get back together
To love our baby girl.

For through it all it surely proves
That love will conquer all,
And overcome the devil's moves
Even when we fall.

Children of God; that's what we are
And we will never waver
To fulfill the reason He received His scars.
His love for us…we'll always savor!

I'll end this poem with this last thought;
I THANK THE LORD YOU'RE MINE!
For a Holy marriage is all I sought…
My God-sent Valentine!

Love:
Rich Kovatch
2-14-99

#2 ROSE'S VALENTINE POEM

Today's the day when we all hope
That there is someone out there
Who loves us as we are within our scope
And tells us that they care.

Valentine's Day should be like all the rest
When our love for one another shows.
We'll try to give our very best;
So each day our love surely grows.

For every day is very special, that's easy to see
And should not be taken lightly.
Stuck in our personal problems we should not be,
Then our love for others will shine through brightly.

Now let me focus on my love for you.
Each day it gets much stronger.
When love is shared between us two
It will last that much longer.

We surely know that when we give
Ourselves to one another
We find the reason that we live:
To love our friends and every brother.

You are my girl, my only one.
I thank God you came along.
My life is now so filled fun
And to a family we both belong.

My hope for you is that you know
With every passing day,
My love for you will surely grow
And in my heart you'll always stay.

No matter what you say or where you go
This fact will still be true
That every day you're sure to know
That our love for each other grew.

Stay with this thought my dear   FROM: **DAD**
Because you are so fine,   WITH **LOVE**
And to me pooker, please stay near   2-14-99
My sweet baby Valentine!

#3 To My Sweet Wife
(Mature Readers ONLY)

What is love? One often asks.
It is to rise to certain tasks.
To give thyself to others' needs
Including taking thy husbands' seeds!   p.s. I hope you snicker!

For when we give unselfishly
It opens our eyes so we can see
That love means comforting your married mate
And not demanding that he wait!   p.s. I hope you snickering again!
                                          I think you are!
Because one never knows the timing of God.
To us it usually seems so odd
When He will call one to His side.   This poem was written
For to His will we must abide.   on a card that said:
                                          "I don't know which I like more…
                                          Your hugs or your kisses!"

We have no rights to call our own.
His endless love we should have known
Means to serve His children when we can
And make ourselves His biggest fan.

                                          On inside page:
                                          To help me decide, maybe you better
For life is short, and sin is sure,   give me a hug and a kiss…Sorry, still
And Jesus Christ the only cure.   can't decide.
To strive to do His perfect will   Better do it again.
May often seem a bitter pill.   Dang, it's still too close to call!!!
                                          Okay, one last time…

But *if* we look beyond ourselves
We'll see the Spirit in which He dwells;
Which is *COMPASSION* and *GRACE* and above all LOVE
To do without question His will from above!

                                          LOVE, RICH
                                          4-20-99

#4 Ronda's Response Poem
(Mature Readers ONLY)

Richie dear, you are so sweet
You're little poem accomplished its feat
Even though it was a little corny
It made me very, very horny!

I can't wait to get home from work
So I can give you your **husbandly perk!!!**

Not really. She did write me a short poem, but I thought
This up real quick at work to **just to make everyone laugh.**

They all did!

Love is silly some**time**s.

#5 THE SINNER

My friends in Christ, I need to say
What is on my heart today
About the message we are to give
To those that are lost in the lives they live.

Of those who study His Holy Word,
A lifestyle that seems to be so absurd
To a world that surely doesn't know
That with this commitment we truly grow.

To be indwelled with the Holy Spirit
And seek His truth, so we can hear it
Within our minds and in our souls.
Then we will know for whom the bell tolls.

It's to spread the gospel, and in our way
Show the world how to live day by day,
And to prove that surely once and for all
That we can recover after we fall.

Because we all know that it will happen.
But sin is not a reason to dampen
Our spirit and turn to self-condemnation.
<u>We know in Jesus Christ is our salvation</u>.

We know that when we stay in daily repentance
That He won't give us that dreaded death sentence
Of being forever *without* the presence of God
And be sent to the Lake of Fire to trod.

For all eternity, the lost will be made
To look for some kind of Holy shade;
Unlike those of us who will live for certain
In a heaven FULL of LOVE and no more hurtin,

#5 THE SINNER

While remembering the life on earth they spent
And cursing God as their only vent.
It's all too late and oh so sad
The wondrous life they could have had.

For warnings were given many a time
To those against God who were committing a crime.
If only they'd have believed in their hardened hearts.
It wouldn't have been so hard if they'd done their part.

All that He asked was that they just turn around
And see the redemption that they could have found.
For God would have joyfully forgiven their sin
If they would have *only listened* to Him !!!

Rich Kovatch
4-27-99

#6 HOLY SPIRIT

Holy Spirit, fill me more.
Please open up the door.
Come inside, fill me up.
Do it quickly! Hup, Hup, Hup!

Come inside, jam in harder
Even if I'm soon a martyr.
You're my guide whose taste I savor
From whose holy ways I'll never waiver.

You entered me and you know when;
The day I became "Born Again!"
Your presence truly makes me happy
Though some wish I'd shut my yappy!

But I can't stop from being verbal,
My last 25 years were total herbal.
You rescued me from his deception.
Now I have life... a new conception!

I'm in your family and it's the best.
My message is for all the rest
That knew me before I came to you
And all the things I used to do.

This is my personal testimony
For they all know that it's not phony.
I truly am a different man
Who's trying to do the best I can.

To do my part; now that's my mission.
I'm to be one who's gone a fishin'
To throw out seeds to my fellow man.
If they don't take, I'll try again!

It's not my job to make them grow.
I'm just happy being able to throw!
The power is yours to do the rest.
I'll just try to do my best!!!

Rich Kovatch
4-30-99

#7 CONFIRMATION DAY

Danny K. this is your day
Bright and sunny, the first day of May
When you verbalized your confirmation
Into our Lord's blessed new creation

Of those who believe in Jesus Christ
And His promise by personal sacrifice.
He died on the cross for me and you
And said He'd be there to see us through

The many tests He must put on us
Before we can get on heaven's bus.
For we're to prove our love for Him
And keep His light from going dim

'Cause we all know who we're to fight
Who causes things to not go right.
When life gets rough and things look grim
And show to all He lives within

To spread His love in things we do.
His holy words our eternal glue
That will keep us stuck to His side
And in His love we will abide

To help our neighbor if he should fall
And answer any and all who call
For help or trust or companionship
And pick him up if he has tripped

With humble meekness and above all love
Which is not from us but from Him up above.
You are young and I'm sure you know
That in His ways you are to grow

And show Him that He is the one
You lived for till this life was done
While knowing that you'll be by His side
When He comes back to marry His bride!

Uncle Rich Kovatch
5-1-99

#8 Mother's Day

It's Mother's Day 1999
And once again I'll try to rhyme
Some words of honor from me to you
Since that's what the Bible says I'm to do.

You showed your love when we were good
You had trust in us, you knew we would
But loved us still when we were bad
Without too often getting real mad.

I forgave you for the time I got
A smack from you that gave me a knot.
On my leg or my butt, you tried to groom
Our attitudes with that wooden spoon!

You were just following God's rule.
Deep inside I knew you weren't cruel.
You were teaching us how He wants us to live.
If we deserved a lickin', you were willing to give!

He says spare the rod and *spoil the child*.
I thank God your *temper was mild*;
Or I'd have received spankings, so many more
That would have kept my *rear end real sore*!

Now let me focus on things you did
That weren't for me when I was a kid
But for others that needed someone there
To love them too and show them you cared

#8 Mother's Day

By showing me how to give of yourself.
It showed me the real meaning of wealth
Is giving from your heart whenever you can
To God's most precious creature, your fellow man!

The other thing you taught to me
Was how _those actions_ helped me _to see_
That God lives in you and shows His face
While we live here in this confusing place.

He made it on purpose to test our will
Too see, in our hearts, are we willing to fill
Our days and nights with His purpose for us
And if in Him we are willing to trust.

To help the lost and those in despair
And if daily we are willing to dare
To give them His word and plant daily seeds
'Cause that's what the world certainly needs.

More moms like you who'll raise their kids well
So all those lost souls will be able to tell
That by raising a child with discipline and love
A good man will be guided from Him up above!

Rich Kovatch
5-9-99

#9 The Senior Citizen

Life is like the sands of time.
Most go through it without reason or rhyme.
Like an hourglass that drops its sand
Most let life fall through their hand.

They think that since they've lived so long
They surely know what's right from wrong.
I'm sure some do, as I have heard,
<u>The ones who follow His Holy Word</u>!

For they have learned what is the truth
From reading the Bible and the book of Ruth!
It talks of love and sticking around
Those in their lives until they have found

Just how to make it back into His flock
And know with whose anchor they are to dock.
Like the little sheep who's lost its way,
Whose hair has turned from brown to gray

They've never heard the Shepard's call;
Probably never heard the words of Paul,
Or Mark, or Matthew, or even Luke!
When one would speak of them, they'd nearly puke!

They thought they knew the world around
And thought they stood on holy ground,
But when it shook and started to quake
It made their tempers start to bake.

They knew not <u>WHO</u> was at the door
And what their call was even for.
For one had put scales upon their eyes
And clouded their minds with constant lies.

The one who says that it's all right
To get upset and start a fight
With ones you love and those so dear,
Or even those you think are queer!

#9 The Senior Citizen

But it's not right to say mean things.
Just look at all the hurt it brings.
The way it makes a person feel...
Sooner or later it's with guilt they'll deal

It's Satan who is "The Great Deceiver"
Who constantly badgers the willing receiver.
Whose purpose is to cheat, steal and kill
All God creation that follows their own will.

Because it's God's will we are to follow with pride
Knowing that He's their right by our side,
Above us, below us, and all around
As we live in His will that we have found.

For in one's heart one can tell for sure
As for all that hurt...LOVE IS THE CURE.
And seniors have been around long enough
To know it's so when things get tough.

They may be carrying a staff in their later years.
They've had many a laugh, cried quite a few tears.
I hope they know what it means to repent
Before all their years are used up and spent!

They've been through it all at least once or twice
And should know better than to just throw the dice
And hope that God will extend His loving arm
Before their last day and they've "bought the farm!"

'Cause then it's *too late* to change their ways.
God gave them oh... so... many long days
To reflect in their souls the paths they've taken
And see all the mistakes they have been makin'!

God extends His grace till He knows it's so
On which way a person really wants to go;
Whether they're 5 or 10 or one hundred and seven,   Rich Kovatch
And if they really want to make it to heaven!!!   5-11-99

#10 **Your Heart / Part One**

Can you hear your heart today
And what it's trying to convey
About the world in which we live
That's mostly take and rarely give?

You might want to ask yourself
About the state of your mental health.
Is it strong and healthy and clean and pure?
And do you think you can endure

The pain you bring upon yourself
When your main worry is of your wealth?
You take that pain off of your mind
When you give to others of your time.

To focus upon the things you need
Is only vanity and selfish greed,
And that's not the way you are to think.
It often cause one to drink

To escape or drown that pain inside
From which we all do try to hide.
We try to conquer it on our own
But we all reap what we have sown!

If we don't live within the rules
And pay attention to all the tools
Our Father gave us in His Good Book
Because we neglect to even look!

The world and all its wisdom teaches.
But don't even listen to what it preaches
Cause it's too hard to live that way
And God WILL forgive your sins today.

But that's only half true and I'll tell you why.
The Devil wants the whole world to fry.
When you leave out repentance, which is a condition
To make it to heaven, DEFY the Son of Perdition!

#10 Your Heart / Part One

He's deceived the whole world; some time it took
To even pervert some versions of the "Good Book."
He's taken out words of encouragement
So we'll give up when our energy is spent.

He'll tell us to quit...and commit suicide,
And that God is not there in which to confide...
You're problem's too big and nobody cares.
To take your own life he constantly dares!

He does it in ways that people know...
Drugs, alcohol, cigarettes, and lack of dough.
But in subtle ways too...he is the master!
In words that are said; maybe even from our pastor!

The Devil is crafty, he knows how to destroy.
And he doesn't care which method he opts to deploy.
All words have power; they'll bring life or death.
If they're bad enough you may even try crystal meth!

You've heard "Sticks & stones may break my bones...
But names can never hurt me!"
Just listen to all the names you hear in your homes.
Do they help you become "All you can be?"

To find the truth there's only one source,
And that's the Holy Spirit...of course,
Who talks to us when we want to find
How to obtain our peace of mind.

Our reference guide for all that we hear
Is His Bible which we should keep open and near
To search for the truth written from Him up above
Whose number one rule is to Love, Love, Love, Love!

Rich Kovatch
5-2-99

#11 Today's Young Man
(Mature Readers ONLY)

Today's young man is basically lost
Little does he realize how much it will cost.
He does not see the things he does
Will send him to hell and that is because

He's willingly ignorant, refuses to see
The real man that God wants him to be.
He's got scales upon scales that cove his eyes
And Satan wants to keep him there till the day he dies.

Unless he's willing to look at his peers,
To open up his heart and unplug his ears
And listen to what God's saints have to say
About the state of the world today.

They tell him it's evil and it's all a big plan.
The Devil wants to take with him all that he can
Into the **Lake of Fire** down below
Not understanding you'll reap what you sow!

He lives in a world that's ruled by his head.
Thinks constantly about how to get chicks into bed.
He constantly hovers around the young girls,
Seeking to uncover their sweet precious pearls.

I understand the feelings that are driving his soul.
When I was young, that too was my goal!
I wanted to find a beautiful mate
To get down to business and go procreate!

That desire is normal for this modern man.
When he can't fulfill it, he uses his hand
To quell the fires that rise up inside
Until he finds the one who'll be his bride.

#11 Today's Young Man
(Mature Readers ONLY)

He looks with his heart and not with his heart.
If he sticks to that plan, with God he will part.
It's unsafe, dangerous and certainly wrong.
Those evil influences are ungodly strong.

The chances are great he'll catch a disease
Like syphilis, or clap, or more S.T.D's.
If lucky, the symptoms with medicine fades;
But no one can stop the onslaught of AIDS!

My hope is that this young man will turn to the Lord,
And turn from the hate and the Devil's discord,
To find peace and security and true happiness,
And to know of his purpose.Then no more to guess.

It's his personal will that must turn the tide,
And figure out to God's will he must learn to abide,
And follow Christ Jesus' plan for success
To save him from his life that's been such a mess.

It matters not how bad we were!
The blood of Jesus is our only cure!
Believe in Him; for He forgives!
And he who does...forever lives!

Rich Kovatch
5-13-99

#12 P.J.

P.J.'s a dude I know at work
Who's usually rude and quite often a jerk.
He said I could write a poem about him.
I'm sure he thought the chances were quite slim

That I would take the time and effort it needs;
But he doesn't know me when I'm plantin' seeds.
When opportunity knocks, I'll jump right in,
Even though writing this may be a sin.

I'll have to repent after writing these words.
He said he'd just use it...to catch his birds' turds.
So I'm not too worried about what gets said.
I just hope some of it sticks in his head.

I really don't know him too closely for sure
But he has a sickness and I know the cure.
He's lost touch with his heart, his thoughts run wild.
From God he's apart and he acts like a child.

A glimpse of his mind I saw on the floor.
I hope what I say doesn't make him too sore.
What I read on his lunchbox was dirty and funky.
It says, "I'd rather be spanking my monkey!"

It clearly shows his bad attitude
That's sinful in nature and basically crude.
And he doesn't care what one thinks of him.
A total reversal? The chances are grim.

But I'm not one who gives up too easy.
Even with one who's horny and sleazy.
I'm hoping this poem helps him stop to think
How much his attitude really does stink.

It should foster kindness, and love, and affection
To change his direction...not cause an erection.
Now I'd better stop while I'm still alive
Before an evil thought he does contrive.

I heard a saying, I hope it's not rumor...
That God really does have a sense of humor.
'Cause inside of me, bad thoughts I have none.
I was just trying to have some good clean fun.

Rich Kovatch
5-11-99

#13 Your Heart / Part Two

You asked for words of encouragement.
For the Love of God please to be sent,
So you could see when times are tough
Why things you do are never enough!

The first thing you must comprehend...
Why peace of mind is so hard to defend.
It's all in the attitude that must be right
That keeps God's Love within our sight.

When one learns about the truth,
The search for it is not uncouth.
Why Christ was born and died for all
Who'll turn to Him so not to fall

Into the traps that Satan sets
In hopes that all mankind forgets
That through pain and sorrow is how we learn.
When we seek comfort...to Him we turn.

And who is Him? Are you confused?
'Cause if you are then Satan's amused.
If Him to you is not our Christ;
Your soul the Devil did just heist!

'Cause his great plan to comfort you
Will keep you guessing, "What should I do?"
He'll distract your mind so you can't even tell
He's sending you down that wide road to Hell!

He'll tell you to take another drink
Then of your problems you will not think.
Or take a snort or another hit
And surely soon you will forget.

#13 Your Heart / Part Two

These things may bring you pleasure now
But in the end you'll "have a cow"
When you find out they were a sin.
And turn from them you must begin.

To find the peace and warmth within
You must trust that Christ will win
The battle that rages for your soul
Once you learn to take control.

You'll understand the Devil's tricks,
And that in God's plans they will not mix.
When you open your eyes and see the light
You'll learn exactly just how to fight.

With truth and love you are made strong.
You'll know to whom you do belong.
Through all these things you will endure
When you keep your heart clean and pure.

He'll show you things that you have faced,
And to what sins they can be traced
So in your heart you can repent,
His Love and comfort will then be sent.

Then you will grow as He has planned
When you've been watered from his hand.
The Word in His book is what He gave
So _ALL His children WILL_ be saved!

It's filled with stories of grace and hope;
Of how and why we are to cope,
By learning the lessons that have been passed.
From generation to generation, down to the last.

#13 Your Heart / Part Two

It's up to you to do your part;
To listen to what is in your heart.
Is it to live but for yourself?
Does His book belong up on your shelf?

Or in your hands and opened wide
So you will learn what is inside
To get the blessings it does bestow
In Revelations for those who know.

So in the end you will be sure,
To end the pain, He is the cure!
And you'll know the reason it has to be;
FOR ONCE YOU WERE BLIND...
BUT NOW YOU SEE!!!

Rich Kovatch
5-23-99

#14 WHAT TIME IS IT?

What time is it? The question is.
Should we go by our, or maybe His?
There is a difference and I'll tell you why
So you and I don't have to die.

Do you know what I'm talking about?
Or do I have to start to shout
The truth out loud so all can hear
Around the world both far and near?

It's the message the whole world has to hear
But doesn't listen to because of fear.
It has to do with sacrifice,
And most the world won't pay that price.

It's only because of ignorance
And lack of good old common sense
That people fail to see the light;
Don't care to learn what's wrong from right.

My people die from lack of knowledge.
They'd rather believe what they learn in college.
It fills their minds with silly lies
So belief in God's word slowly dies!

Social science and health and evolution
That brought the world to revolution.
Beliefs that mankind can find the answers
While only bringing on human cancers.

If you live your life for your own gain
You carry on the sins of Cain
Who killed his brother Able because of pride
And the pain he felt way deep inside.

#14 WHAT TIME IS IT?

He hadn't learned to find the joy
God created for every girl and boy
When they look inside their heart and see
The way God intended them to be.

When they live their lives within the rules
They understand they've got strong tools
To help them overcome the Devil's tricks
And choose the path the good Lord picks

That's guaranteed to give them life
And find their right husband and wife
To raise a family that worships God.
And unlike Cain...not end up in Nod.

The land of Nod is still here today
Where greed and lust is still the way.
It's all for one and one for me!
Get off my case and let me be!

A place where God's Spirit dwelleths not.
People worry about whether their bodies are hot.
A world whose focus is for pleasure now!
As long as they get it... they care not how!

The time is right for Judgment Day.
If you have ***love in your heart*** you'll **hear** what I say
'Cause that's the thing we need **to spread**
To get God's plan **to move** ahead.

He's going to end the way it is.
The exact time known is only His bizz.
For no man knows the day or the hour,
But that doesn't mean we have no power

#14 WHAT TIME IS IT?

To recognize the time of the seasons.
In His word are plenty of reasons
The children of light will know it's Nye;
For His Spirit will shine out from our eye

To pierce the souls ***who want to know***
Is it okay to stay or time to go?
To leave this wicked world behind;
The way to God they want to find!

And that's through CHRIST...the only way,
Who died for us. He had to pay
To redeem our sins. He was the Lamb
To save us all from being damned!

He's coming back soon, *this time a Lion*
To see who loves Him and who's really tryin'
To be a witness and a watchman too
To the truth of His word that's coming true!

In the world's it happens often.
Wake up now before you hit your coffin,
'Cause then it will be too late to save your soul
Once they're lowering you down into your hole!

You've had your chances, and many have tried
To get you the word. They may even have cried
And prayed to God he'd open your ears
And end their sorrowful streams of tears

Because we cry for those of this world
Who won't repent *before* **that** *day's unfurled*
When Christ says, Come, and be with me bride,
It's time for you to be by my side

#14 WHAT TIME IS IT?

And we'll destroy this evil system.
While many will cry because they missed 'um
As they get thrown into the "Lake of Fire"
While wishing they had ended up somewhere higher!

But God gave them time to sort it out.
Instead of smiling...they had to pout
And failed to get back into His hand.
They had their heads stuck in the sand.

They could not see and did not hear
The message that THE END WAS NEAR
So they'll burn in Hell for eternity!!!
They should have just got on a knee

And prayed to God to forgive their sins.
'Cause when one does, the healing begins
And the scales fall off their blinded eyes
As they read the Word and become more wise

And understand why it took so long
For them to see what's right from wrong
And turn to God for wisdom and strength;
To run the race the entire length,

And avoid the pitfalls that will surely come.
Still hit the obstacle but not be dumb
To realize that with strife we learn new things
And see the blessings that overcoming brings.

We grow in spirit when we do well
And stay far away from the gates of Hell,
And give glory to God for evermore,
And thank Him forever that
He knocked on our door!!!

Rich Kovatch
5-28-99

#15 Graduation Day

Graduation day has finally come.
So do you think the hard part's done?
No more pop quizzes and no more tests.
Soon it will be time to leave momma's nest!

So take that flight now, just spread your wings
To see what fate tomorrow brings.
 "You'll make your own bed", your elders will say;
<u>And in it kid you'll have to lay!</u>

You'll have to learn to play the odds.
Just don't start worshipping Idol gods,
Like money or sports stars or even fast cars.
And for goodness sakes ***please stay out of bars!***

I'm telling you things you need to know
So your young mind can start to grow
From these words you'll read and those you'll hear
Given by those who love you so dear.

The world is rough and will eat you for lunch
If you start hanging out with the wrong kind of bunch.
I know you're young and you've got wild oats to sow
But I don't want you to hear *"I told you so"*.

So listen up now and don't be a fool.
Don't think that you are so hip and so cool,
Because attitude determines just where you will go.
You need to learn quickly just *who's* you're real foe.

It's the Devil, my friend; don't think that I'm lying.
Don't wait till you're on your death bed and dying
Because you don't know when that time will be.
Avoid saying, ***"That will never happen to me"***.

#15 Graduation Day

That's arrogance and denial and above all pride.
Don't wait too late to listen to those who've tried
To tell you that the best mindset is to be humble.
And listen to yourself when you start to grumble.

By knowing why you say such things
Is called *maturity* when that little *bell rings*
That opens up your mind to the obvious truth...
That *"I was plain ignorant while I was a youth"*.

And good thing that ignorance can be subdued
When one refuses to be a tough guy and crude.
Its definition is only "a lack of knowledge"
That one can reverse with a few years in college.

Just be careful with what gets put in your head;
And in what direction your spirit gets led.
Remember to stay close to who gave you your life.
You'll need His guidance to find a good wife

Who'll love you back more when you're willing to give.
Who'll show you the *right way* to make it and live.
She'll understand it's God who's first on the list,
And she'll help you see options you might have missed.

A family's the unit God wants you to be in;
So when you have sex, *it won't be a sin*.
And if offspring is what comes out of your bond
Then Love will be present and God will be fond

Of **what He sees** and where it is going,
And the love that's shared and how it is showing;
Knowing your family will all stay together
No matter how gloomy becomes the weather.

#15 Graduation Day

Because God hates divorce, that's stated in scripture.
Just look at the world and you'll see the sad picture
Of *what happens when **children** come **before** marriage*.
It usually turns into chaos and utter disparage*!*

For when it's not built upon **"THE SOLID ROCK"**,
And by leaving God out ... you're just a big jock
*Who's asking for trouble, that **you'll surely find***
And in your walk with God ... you'll get way behind.

So far back maybe you stopped and gave up?
You'll see you're *not* a big dog, *you're just a pup*
*Who **needs** to be **disciplined** from our Great Master*
And pick up the speed and walk much faster

So when He comes back He'll see that you have tried.
You'll know **"The Way"** because **He'll** be your **guide**.
He's showed you He loves you though you've made mistakes.
If you live in ***repentance***, that's all it takes!

I hope you've taken ***to heart*** this long poem
'Cause in it I've given all that I owe 'um;
That's to spread the good word that ***God wants you saved***,
And to do my part to see that you've behaved!

Rich Kovatch
6-6-99

#16 To Today's Average Person

I know I wrote you a poem this year on Mother's Day,
But since that time it's clear there's so much more to say.
Since on this day, June 25th, when you turn one year older
It's that much more vital that this gift comes out much bolder!

I said I saw the **Lord** in you by how you've been so kind,
But now I pray for you today **His message** you will find.
A Christian is to help along his brother when he falls
So he can hear our **Lord**'s sweet voice **every time He calls**!

Our **God is LOVE**, a **Ho**ly **Love**, and when we drift from that,
One has to wonder if on our brain we happened to have sat!
When someone **mocks** or **hinders words** that praise our **Lord** above,
One has to wonder if their reactions are coming out of love?

When we are filled with the Holy Spirit our focus always changes
From what our flesh desires now, and into heaven's ranges.
We'll see the fault our tongues let loose in words that criticize
And recognize that we've just sinned from thoughts our minds devised.

Our struggle is to quiet our will and do **His** from on high.
As we grow we won't be perfect, but our goal is to always try
To say and do all things in love as He directs us to
Since we were born under Satan's rule, but now we're born anew!

When one is **"BORN AGAIN"** of Love, **he learns the simple truth;**
That he must change the way he thinks, he's practiced since his youth.
Brought up in religion that depended on what someone else has said
And if you don't **"COME OUT OF HER" you'll receive her plagues upon**
Your head!

For we're to listen to **God's** *own voice* that's *written* in **His** book.
When someone else tells us words of wisdom, ***IN IT* WE'RE SUPPOSE TO**
LOOK
SO **God** can tell us if it's true or even if it's not!
He'll see that we're not cold or lukewarm, but surely that we're **HOT**!

#16 To Today's Average Person

Our mission when we're saved **is to spread the news** that's needed
And **God will show us** how it's received **just by how we're greeted!**
I have to say we're in the time when milk won't do the trick.
I have to feed you now the meat and I hope you don't get sick!

Because if we listen to what today's churches are preaching daily
It's full of milk and perverted words and sounds like Alice Bailey.
And if you don't know who that was, or even if you care,
A **"BORN AGAIN"** spirit would want to know and **take that step to dare!**

We're in the time when you can choose what will happen to you;
If you'll try to save yourself or listen to you know who!
He's telling you know to run to Him to seek His true protection.
To do that, **FIRST, WE HAVE TO WANT,** then **ASK HIM FOR CORRECTION!**

He'll show us what we need to know through people that we meet,
And send their message as the key to make us move our feet,
To take that step in **FAITH** and **LOVE** to seek **His Holy Pro**mise.
If *we* hide in H*im* our salvation is <u>sure</u>; we won't act like doubting Th**om**as!

It is God's wish for all to be saved and not just to stay lost,
But it's up to us to choose our path and count what it will cost.
The gate is narrow and **you should know exactly what that means!**
If you believe you'll be "raptured out" before the Tribulation, you're
Living in your dreams!

Because all through history it's not been that way - **a lack of
Persecution?**
The Lord is calling His people **out** of their **tradition** and into restitution.
A life of repentance for every sin that we do commit,
And admit a life without God we just can not permit!

For if you're deceived by your church or even in your ways,
You will regret it very soon in these upcoming days.
And when persecution and trouble and strife are closing in on you
You'll be lost, worried and wondering "What is this I'm going through?"

#16 To Today's Average Person

You'll have to fight the Devil's ploys with the **TRUE WORDS** of the **Lord!**
THAT is what you'll need to know; IT'S your two-edged sword!
It's the **_only way_** you'll be able to live **without** great constant **fear;**
When evil is surrounding you and the Devil is so near!

You must be clean to walk with the Lord,
Deny your flesh, get humble, walk toward
Your <u>Savior</u>, <u>Redeemer</u>, your <u>Lord</u> and your <u>God</u>.
Then upon your arrival at Heaven's gate, you'll receive His smiling nod!

Now, you know that I love you and I always will,
But I had to give you this tough, true message still.
Give totally your all to our **<u>God Jesus</u>** up above
And you'll hear my words and be comforted and surrounded by
His Love!

Rich Kovatch
6-23-99

#17 ANGER

I'm angry with the great deceiver   Rev. 12:9, 13:11-18 (**7, 8, 14**)
Who's blinded my wife, but not me... **"a believer."**
He's trying to get me to lose faith and hope
By ripping my heart out and seeing if I can cope.

He knows where the soft spot is in me;
It's with those I love...my family tree.
I can't say for sure that any are saved.
Except for my daughter, by the way they behaved

When I told them I'm not the man I once was   2 Cor. 5:17
Whose most pressing concern was to keep a **"good buzz."**
But now that I'm living to spread the **"Good News"**   Luke 17:5-10 Rom. 15:2
It's depressing that so few listen...it gives me the blues!   John 16:22
                                                  Rom.9:22Cor. 7:8-11
Oh, they may now let me talk in their ears
But it's quite obvious that no one really hears
Since I don't see them perk up and get filled with joy.
I don't seem to help them...it's more like annoy!

'Cause I tell them the truth, not just sugar and spice.
We've got to act like men and not fragile mice,   Phil. 3:12-21
And take control over things in our lives
When Satan tries to divide us from our wives!

Using love as our foothold we thrust forward full speed   Eph. 4:15
Speaking truth from the bible, the only weapons we need!   Heb. 4:12-16
<u>As our battles are spiritual and not of the flesh</u>   **Eph. 6:12**
If we want our actions and our results to mesh!

I see it all over including here in our group;
Men on one side...women in their own troop;
As we struggle to keep them close to our side   Rom. 15:1
And we know in the end it's in us they'll confide

#17 ANGER

When they learn as we have that alone we are weak.   1 Pet. 3:7
As our power fades...God's is hitting its peak!   2 Cor. 12:9-10
And they find it's in unity where power is found.   Eph. 4:1-24
Christ is our guide and to Him we are bound.   Eph. 4:15

For in him truly all things are possible   Matt. 19:16
To him that believes...his cup is past full;   Mark 9:23, 10:27
Spilling out hope and safety to all those in peril
That think that Satan has got them over a barrel.

For the **"Living Water"** is the **Word of our Lord**.   Jer. 2:13, 17:13
That is our offense...our two edged sword   John 4:10-15, 7:37-39
That we'll use to defeat all who come against God.   Eph. 6:17 Heb. 4:12
He'll be pleased we endured till the end & give us the nod   Heb.13:16-22

To enter **HIS KINGDOM** as **"children of Love"**   Rev. 3:20-22
Who kept looking for His coming above...   Rev. 1:2-3, 16:15
Knowing how, what, when, where and why;
Because we never failed to continue to try!!!   **Heb. 12:1-10**

Rich Kovatch
8 - 5 - 99

#18 A HOLY Marriage

A holy marriage is one that comes
From our Father *in heaven leading His* chosen ones
Together from different walks of life
To join together a man and a wife.

But I've got serious troubles in mind;
I'm wondering if mine is really that kind
From all the thoughts that come my way
While enduring my marriage day to day.

I'm aware that the Devil is alive and well.
From what I'm writing it's not hard to tell
That he's the Master of Confusion.
I'm wondering if my marriage is but an illusion.

I study Gods' word to try and find
Comfort and hope so that I don't walk blind
In my *daily struggles concerning the things*
That devoting myself to someone else brings.

Now this next thought that I need to write
Is the one that causes the hardest fight;
Which is: how do I balance between the two...
When one makes me happy and the other one blue?

My first concern is that I'll be of Christs' bride.
But here comes the kicker: does that border on pride
When I think of *myself* and *my* eternal life
As more important than my human wife?

I know the God puts us all to the test...
That's why I continue to give it my best;
Because I have a duty to my wife and child...
To lead them in truth and not let them grow wild.

#18 A HOLY Marriage

But here's where it really gets hard for me;
That my life's but a shadow of what it's suppose to be.
I want to be holy...be an example to all...
Show Christ lives within me so that others might answer His call.

I'm the **"Light of the world"** when **Christs' light shines through me**.
I'll walk into darkness so that others might see
That **through *His* strength & compassion**...that's far greater than mine...
I will overcome all problems that come down the line.

Now here's where I need His guidance right now;
I want both to succeed but I don't know how.
My walk with Him and my family on Earth
For us all to develop enough to accomplish Spiritual birth.

We've all been conceived and are in development stage.
Right now my marriage is rough; I'd like to turn the page
To where we start seeing things eye to eye;
To live for each other and to ourselves...just die!

For the Spirit of Love is to give of oneself.
To care for your partner is to bring yourself health.
As the other one grows and matures in Christ;
You'll be doing exactly what the Bible advised.

Already I feel better after just writing these words.
I hope my wife doesn't think this advice is just for the birds.
But for her and all others that might read these verses
Who need to get out from under some curses.

Because a curse is the opposite of a heavenly blessing;
Which we all will receive <u>when we start confessing</u>
Our weaknesses and failures in honesty to our partners in love
And <u>decide together *as one*</u> to find guidance from above!!!

Rich Kovatch
8-08-99

#19 OH, SO <u>NOW</u> YOU WANT TO TALK

You people seem to live your lives as though you know the score
But little do you often realize I**'m** knocking at your door.
When things go bad or someone dies is when you start to wonder
Why the lightning hit so near to you, but you never heard the thunder.

I**'M** <u>ALWAYS</u> NEAR though you don't care as long as things go your way
I**'m** not important to your daily life, YOU DON'T LISTEN TO WHAT I SAY.
WHEN I WARN YOU about the things you do that are not good,
You go and do them anyway; did you know I knew you would?

I**'ve** seen your life from the first day; and I**'ve** also seen your last,
I know what is to be your destiny; I also know your past.
And that is why I am your God and you are just a man.
I have it all under control...and for you I have a plan.

You should be glad that ***I, your God***, am **full** of **Love** and **Grace**
And that I sent my ***<u>only</u>* begotten Son** so you can see my face
For all who have seen my son ***JESUS CHRIST have*** truly seen **His Father**
And ***HE IS THE ONLY*** *WAY TO ME* , but you must want to bother

To listen to the words **He**'s said and change your selfish ways
And become a brand new creature; clear your mind out of the haze
That Satan has surrounded you in; this world of material things,
And set your sights on the rewards that living for others brings.

For if you will only believe in **Him** and trust there is a way
Then you will surely find comfort there tomorrow and today!
And learn the truth of why things are so very hard to take.
Why bad things happen and friends may die and why you heart must
Ache!

You know you live in a world where evil lurks and lunges,
Where sin abounds and pain is great and into darkness it plunges.
But there is a way to overcome the trial and tribulation
And keep your feet on solid ground and work out your own salvation

#19 OH, SO <u>NOW</u> YOU WANT TO TALK

I know your heart and what you need is almost always different
From what you think that you deserve, for I know what is imminent.
On the path you choose to walk each day, it's up to your own will.
<u>I will not force upon you my way, **you must go your own way still**</u>.

<u>FOR **WIDE** IS THE **GATE** AND **BROAD** IS THE **WAY** THAT **LEADS** TO DESTRUCTION</u>
You must remember *who* it is that *fosters this corruption*
Which causes you to harbor hate and vent your anger violently
<u>INSTEAD OF ASKING *ME* FOR ANSWERS</u> while you wail and weep then
pray silently.

But now that you've been touched so hard down deep inside your heart
You finally see that you are weak but you still must do *your* part
By *ASKING ME* <u>to give you help in making it through **this** day</u>
AND LISTENING WITH ALL YOUR *HEART* TO WHAT *I* HAVE TO SAY !

Rich Kovatch
8 - 17 - 99

#20 WORDS
(Mature Readers ONLY)

Words are cheap, they have little value
When they're spoken by that special gal you
Love and cherish and even marry.
The one you sweat and slave for and tarry

All day at work to get her things
While hoping for blessings that making her happy brings...
Or are suppose to anyway when things go right
But rarely receive when the day turns to night!

She loves me she says; I hear all the time.
She shows me by keeping our home looking fine;
By doing the dishes and laundry and chores...
And windows and cooking and cleaning the floors!

But men need to have special time with their one
To forget all the day's troubles and just have some fun...
And get close to their wife in her heart and her soul
Then eventually her body; their most intimate goal.

Because a man and a wife must have a strong bond.
To be held close by each other, they both need to be fond
To have a relationship like Christ and His bride
Where we know what she's feeling way deep down inside.

I long to give her the desires of my heart
Although sometimes the horse gets in front of the cart!
But I don't understand how to get her to feel;
How to open up her heart to me; and to me that's the big deal!

Until that day gets here I'll continue to **struggle**
With how do I get time to get down and **snuggle**
And "be one" with my wife in spirit and in soul
When our marriage in Christ would be **under control**

#20 WORDS

(**Mature** Readers **ONLY**)

__With both of us being willing to give to each other.__
Wish she'd act like a wife and not just a mother!
'Cause her duties are twofold; to our child (ren) and me
To make us both (all) happy and to set our minds free

To find all the wonderful things Christ has for us;
And to do it with joy and without any fuss;
Knowing we're doing exactly what God wants us to do...
Finding strength in the Lord, starting each day anew.

I'm getting tired of staying up night after night
Not being happy at bedtime, having to get up and write
All these poems that are my way of dealing
With the hurt and frustration I'm certainly feeling!

I pray that someday I'll find the right words
That will sink into her head and not be just for the birds;
'Cause this isn't the first poem that's been on this subject...
And having to do this I'm starting to object!

I notice my mind is very creative this late;
__Maybe what I should do is take her out on a date!__
Then we could focus on just one another
And she'd be only my wife and not just a mother!

Note: (brackets) for you to use if you have more than 1 child
(I only had ONE child) and would like to recite it to your woman.

Rich Kovatch
8-23-99

#21 A Glimpse of The Mind of Christ

The Mind of Christ, according to me
Is to see the temptation, and then to flee.
To recognize from where comes the attack
Then have the **wisdom** on how to fight back.

And when I say fight that doesn't mean
That sparks will start flying, though that's how it may seem
When the problem to deal with is **anger** or **rage**
And the only one that displays it sounds like he belongs in a cage.

And because the Devil works hard in situations like that,
I have to step back and let **Christ** come to bat,
And let **Him** pick the right pitch to hit **His** home run.
So all comes out well when it's all said and done!

The first thing that happens when someone gets mad
Is their voice level raises and that's really too bad
Because others are watching and may come to the conclusion
That being a **Christ**ian is just some sort of delusion.

But they don't see half of what's taking place.
All they see is some mad guy up in my face.
But do they see me staying calm, but standing in truth
And not breaking down when the Devil lets loose?

Now, when I'm attacked saying I'm this way or that
I'll let it blow over until that airbag goes flat,
And not fan the fire with comebacks or demands
But stay focused on the spiritual issues at hand.

And quite often it doesn't seem to go over too well
At least right away, as far as I can tell.
But I keep the faith that the truth will shine through
And that we both realize just what we should do.

And when it's all over, there is one thing for sure
No matter what happened...**it's Love that's the cure**
That will overcome obstacles, **no matter how big**
As I _use_ the Mind of Christ and **don't flip my wig** !   Rich Kovatch

10-19-99

#22 Thanksgiving Thanks

Thanksgiving is the time of year
The Lord is happy we rejoice and cheer
For all the harvest blessings He brings
That makes us feel like Queens and Kings.

A time when **families come together**
And usually not hindered by the weather.
When Indian Summer may just have ended
We add to our family those who we've befriended.

A time when our thoughts turn to sharing
With others our bounty, and *a time for caring*
About how others may have gotten along
And *mend* a friendship that might have gone wrong.

It's fall time now and summer is past
And winter is coming upon us fast.
We'll need all the friendships we can foster
So if things go bad, we'll just go down the roster

To see who can help us in our time of need.
A new friendship that blossomed, *if we planted the seed*
And watered it with Love and weeded the soil,
Someone *who'll come through* when we struggle and toil.

That someone is *JESUS* who will pull us through
And **He *may* just *show* Himself...*through me or you***
When we offer our hand to whoever is in trouble.
When we give of ourselves, His blessings are double.

The one who is hurting receives just what he needs
And our minds get stronger as our loving heart bleeds
And we offer our time or sweat and maybe some tears
As we think more like JESUS and overcome our fears!

Because we're all in this together, we must help one and all,
And be willing to pick up our friends or enemies if they fall;
Because someone with love was there when WE hit the ground,
AND WHERE SIN IS ABUNDANT, GRACE WILL ABOUND!! Rich Kovatch
11-23-99

#23 MY FRIEND "PASSED AWAY"

I've lost a friend I've known so long
And I shall miss him dearly.
The bond we had was very strong.
It grew each day, each month and yearly.

He was so kind and gentle hearted
To know him blessed my soul.
It grieves me that he's now departed,
His absence will take its toll.

I'll miss his voice and I'll always remember
It always accompanied a smile,
And if on him a problem I'd render,
For me he'd walk a mile!

♥♥♥♥♥♥♥♥♥♥♥♥♥♥♥♥♥♥♥♥♥♥♥♥♥♥♥♥♥♥♥♥♥♥
But I'm not sad for I truly know
That the LORD has brought him HOME !
And he will reap what he did sow:
But from *G o d' s   L o v e* no man *CAN   ROAM !!!*
♥♥♥♥♥♥♥♥♥♥♥♥♥♥♥♥♥♥♥♥♥♥♥♥♥♥♥♥♥♥♥♥♥♥

I know the Lord will comfort us all
And get us through this rough time,
And once again we'll all stand tall
When I realize my friend's heart *still lives* in mine!

Rich Kovatch
12 -5 - 99

#24 Let's Live In Forgiveness

I say, "Let's live in forgiveness". You say, "What's the big deal?"
I say, "What goes around...comes around. It's like a big wheel.
There's no one alive that doesn't need this kind action.
When we're quick to forgive...there's no stronger attraction!

'Cause we've all done dumb things that makes someone mad,
If they don't forgive us, then don't we feel sad?
There's no one that's perfect...**we must understand...**
When someone falls short... we must still offer our hand

And tell them it's over, let's go on from here.
Especially when it's someone to whom we are near!
Because *if we are unwilling* to start all anew
Eventually, we'd have no friends! *Then what would we do?*

I'll tell you what happens, because I've been there myself;
Our thoughts all turn inward, and that's not good for our health.
We'll drown our feelings with some selfish corruption
That will only lead us **down the road *to our own destruction!***

I'll give you a word of wisdom I've learned;
Turn to our Lord Jesus before you get burned.
'Cause He tells us that...*if we* **will not forgive,**
He will not forgive us! **And we'll pay as long as we live.**

His rules are so simple: You'll reap what you sow!
He wrote you a book so that you'll come to know
That He wants you *to read it so you'll learn* what it takes.
And it's really so simple: *LEARN FROM YOUR MISTAKES!*

Our life is so short, not a moment to waste.
When we turn to Jesus...the good life we'll taste.
Now, I'm not saying that it'll be a breeze
But our perspective will change when we get on our knees!

Then He'll do what it takes to get you to see
How to become the real person you know you should be.
'Cause there's *love* in your heart *you refuse* to let shine.
You're just a branch...you must connect to the vine!

#24 Let's Live In Forgiveness

A branch by itself will wither and die
And it'd be a shame if you don't even try
To get life from the source that comes from the root!
If you knew His word...that point would be moot.

You'd know, **_on your own_**... you will **_not_** succeed.
You'd get help from the Lord to get what you need.
And don't get too worried, 'cause you're exactly like me!
I need help from Him too, to be *all* **_I can_** *be!*

The last thing I'll tell you in this inspiring poem
Is that <u>you must forgive your flesh man</u>, your _spirit_ _man_ must woe 'um
To draw nearer to _the Lord who knows_ your _flesh nature is weak_.
And you'll understand He's forgiven <u>ALL</u> of everything, when <u>HIS LOVE</u>
<u>Has MADE YOU m</u>eek!

Rich Kovatch
12-31-99

#25 THANKS FOR LOVING ME

I THANK YOU Father for Loving me.
When I was blind, you helped me to see
Through all the things that I went through.
You stuck by my side like you said you'd do!

I THANK YOU Father for Loving me.
I'm writing this poem to honor thee.
I long to worship and praise your name.
I hope you don't think this poem is lame!

Because I'm so new to this way of living
I need to learn more ways of giving
My life and time and energy to you
So I'll do the things you want me to.

I've learned so much and I thank you for
The saints you've brought to my front door
Who've helped me to open up my heart
And got me off to such a quick start.

I THANK YOU Father for these days ahead.
As usual, to write this, I got out of bed
Because it seems to be the best time to inquire
About what words your Holy Spirit inspire

That will give YOU the honor and glory and praise.
How to show me, above all others, **YOUR NAME I WILL RAISE**
And get out a message that will help others to see
What a great joy it is to be so close to thee!

I THANK YOU Father for Loving me.
The Love you gave me has tripled to three
Since my wife and daughter have followed this lead
In seeking the relationship with YOU that we need!

#25 THANKS FOR LOVING ME

I THANK YOU Father for Loving me
And most of all for offering your son on that tree
Where you showed you were willing to take on such pain
By giving your Son, so mankind you could gain!

You're the Spirit of Love, shown by Christ in the flesh.
With the spirit of giving is how we can mesh,
Into one body in Christ, through which all things were made.
Then we'll be building on a foundation that's already been laid.

It's when we follow this rule that your will gets fulfilled,
And upon THAT ROCK you said you would build
A great church that will grow through brotherly love
WHEN IT'S WISE AS A SERPENT AND GENTLE AS A DOVE!!!

Rich Kovatch
1-7-2000

#26 THE GRACE IN JENNY

A friend was telling me about the news
Of a certain young girl walking in Christ's shoes
Who found some money and acted in a way
That is not often found in the world today.

She thought to herself, "If this was mine
And I had lost it, I'd probably wine".
Thinking, "Who in this world would be honest enough
To return it to me, 'cause that would be tough".

With the way a selfish person thinks only of himself
They'd say, "Look at this; I've just gained instant wealth!
I'll just stick to the rule: Finders keepers...loser's weepers!
Ha! Too bad for *that* sucker; **I'm buyin' new sneakers!"**

But I'm happy to say, and it brings me great joy
That she was different from the average girl or boy.
It showed me that there is someone who's wiser than most
That's teaching this girl how to move forward, not coast.

Who's taught her that others come before her
And that being unselfish is a way to secure
A life that will bring many blessings her way;
Like the one I'm trying to bring her today.

I'm proud of you young lady, whoever you are
And also of those who've brought you this far
In the knowledge of doing what Christ says is right.
You're not lost in the darkness; someone's shown you the light!

This blessing is not one you can take to the bank,
But in God's last day's army, you've just stepped up a rank
And are well on your way to becoming a leader.
You've eaten up God's word...soon you'll be the feeder!

And *by your example* may you lead the way
In *your area* of influence. Do you hear what I say?
Just keep striving for excellence in all that you do
And God's grace will surround you and those you touch too!

Rich Kovatch
1-5-2000

#27 I Tripped *Again* Today

Oh Lord, I tripped *AGAIN*   today!
What in the world could I possibly say
That could justify the reason I did you wrong…
When I've been doing the same thing for oh…so…long?

Believe it or not I do know why
And the reason truly makes me cry
Because the fault lies deep within
My heart that continues to lie and sin!

I say to you in my prayers at night
That I'm trying to continue on with my fight
Against my flesh, the Devil and the world;
But now I'll tell you what your Spirit unfurled.

It's that *I'm unwilling to make you the Lord of my life*;
Even though you're the bridegroom and I am your wife.
I know that's not something I should take for granted;
But I understand, in me…your seeds' just been planted!

I know that in me it's found fertile soil;
Even though *right now* **I continue to toil**
With the influence the world has engrained in my mind.
As I keep seeking water I know soon you'll find

That the effort you've put in me has not been a waste.
I thank you so much for giving me the **sweet taste**
Of the **Fruit** of the Spirit that **continues to grow**
As **I'm chastened** and the *w inds of ch ange* **continue to blow.**

These things only make me **stand up straighter and strong**
As you show me the things I keep doing wrong
And purge them from this vessel of such impure gold
With the fire of your holiness…so you'll eventually mold

#27 I Tripped *Again* Today

Me into **the image _you_ want me to be**
I know the cost is certainly not free!
I must **give up my will** which is so **hard to do**
And **start doing your will...** and *take on the hue*

Of the *Pure Light of Righteousness* that *shines* through *your Son*.
I know that I'll shine like that too...when it's all said and done
And I'm living in heaven so close to your side
After you've told me I'm worthy of being your bride

Because you had me believe in Jesus and in your Grace
And that He would forgive me as I ran my race
While I learned the wicked ways and wiles of the Devil

And kept the narrow road to *happiness* fair*ly* smooth & level.

Rich Kovatch
1-11-2000

#28 Will Good People REALLY Go To HELL?

Will good people **really** go to hell?
Well brother and sister I'm here to tell
You that God's Word has the final say.
Don't wait to find out on **YOUR** Judgment Day!

The message here is very deep,
I really hope it makes you weep
And brings you down upon your knees
If God is not the one you want to please!

These words alone won't do the trick
But I hope upon your heart they'll prick
Convictions so you'll come to see
That God is their author and was not me!

This story goes all the way back to the Garden of Eden
And upon **which tree** you've been feedin'.
There were two main trees and one fallen angel bent on upheaval
That seduced Eve to eat from the Tree of Knowledge of Good and Evil.

Now the real lesson is about to begin
But one can't understand it until they're "**BORN AGAIN**"
And have decided to eat from the Tree of Life's seed
From which came Christ Jesus to a world in need.

The Tree of Knowledge is **symbolic of The Law**
Which does not bring life; **it just shows you your flaw**
That if you live in the flesh you'll for sure be condemned
For it is corruptible, but God's spirit can mend

The bridge the occurred after Adam's willful sin
The age of disobedience began and the Devil did grin
Because he knew that mankind will follow Adam's path
And thought forever man will be subject to his deception and wrath.

God's word says that each tree will produce fruit **only of its own kind**
& this knowledge of good & evil will be at the front of everyone's mind.
So in that, **Satan knew he had his best tool**
And it would be **so easy** for him **to fool**

#28 Will Good People REALLY Go To HELL?

Men and women into thinking that if only they'd be good
That they will be pleasing God like they know they should.
But here's THE deception that will lead to their doom
That's been passed down to all children straight from Eve's womb!

It goes back to **which tree** man's spirit comes from
And that mankind is marching to the beat of whose drum?
Remember the one tree which God said not to eat of
For in that day thou shalt surely die was the word from above.

Well, that curse has been on us since Adam and Eve
And the *only way* for you to break it is for you *to believe*
That **Jesus** bore the burden to live *His life without sin*
So that a way to be reconciled back to God would begin.

He was born of a woman, but His seed was not cursed
From the law in Adam's bloodline, for in the word He was well versed
Since *He is the Word* come to Earth *covered with skin*
To be tempted in all points with the power to win

The conflict with sin that brings death to man's soul
Which, before Him, mankind found too hard to control.
But through Him, He's given us **HIS GIFT** of great grace
So we can now stay holy and finish our race.

All our righteous deeds are as but filthy rags.
If you depend on them to get to heaven your understanding lags
To the point where the Devil has sucked you in
To believing your race you will actually win!

Your righteousness comes **only** from **relying on JESUS**,
And if what you do is only to please us
So to receive honor and praise or to bring recognition
You're only inviting the Lord's admonition!

Being good in the eyes of the world is dangerous.
It too easily leads to pride and causes much fuss
Between who thinks they're doing the Lord's work the best.
And on these laurels you think you can rest?

#28 Will Good People REALLY Go To HELL?

But I'm telling you **good works <u>won't</u>** get you to heaven!
If the intention is wrong, it's just lots of leaven
That will spoil the whole loaf and bring on destruction
If it's not dealt with by heeding to good words of instruction!

There are so many things of the flesh you must learn.
To Galatians 5:19 I wish you would turn
And read it as if your life was in the balance
Because it is my friend! And just what are your talents?

Do you see them here?
Does it make you fear?
Or does what you do
Start in verse twenty two?

You have to come to this life saving knowledge
And it doesn't take money and four years in college,
But it does take commitment to submit to the Lord
And step out in faith and pick up His sword

And start confessing to whom you truly belong.
Start speaking the truth in words or in song.
For this is the good works; to show others the light;
To tell them if they've wandered to the left or the right.

It must be said with all meekness and love
So they will know it was sent from above,
That your purpose is only to save their lost soul
And you don't want them to get thrown into the bottomless hole!

God is the God of Love, that is true.
But you have to see He's a *God of judgment* too!
Do you think it would be right to let all people in
When some obeyed Him and others stayed in sin?

#28 Will Good People REALLY Go To HELL?

The ones that will get in are but a small flock.
And I'm telling you **they're not the ones who would mock**
The words of the Spirit when He called for you
To answer the door and start living your life true!

The Holy Spirit is calling quite loudly to you
And patiently waiting to see what you will do.
But you must understand that **time has an end**
And **JESUS knows if you're His enemy or friend**!

You **can't walk** in the middle or sit high on the fence.
If you're not boldly on His side you should now be real tense!
Because *lukewarm* believers will be ***spewed out*** of His mouth!
And this is one time you won't want to go south!

Normally it would be a trip that you might desire
Where the constant temperature is always quite higher
But in this sense *the heat will be an inferno*
That will torture your soul forever eternal ! ! !

Rich Kovatch
2-4-2000

Happy 50th Anniversary

#29

Wow, you've made it 50 years!
Even though you consumed so many beers,
Which was your way to make it through
All the dumb things we kids would do.

But with the help of your wife and our loving mom
Who bore **Mike, Ed, Carmela, Richie and Tom,**
And the Lord who showed you that your body was weak...
Be of sober mind, like He did for your son **Richie...the freak.**

I'm sure you agree that your life now is much better
And I'm glad when you saw mom, you went to go get her;
And won her heart over so that you could marry
The girl you loved so much, her burdens you would help carry.

Like supporting five kids in the days of the Cold War
But you knew **the reason you had us for:**
To bring more Love into this world than the two of you had
And produce God loving children that would call you Mom and Dad!

Without a doubt you know we all thank God for you two
And are sorry for all the times we made you guys blue.
And thanks for providing a home filled with so much abundant love.
Certainly *your marriage was arranged* from **Him up above!**

I could keep writing words of honor to you 'till the sun goes down
But I won't, because if you had to read that many *you'd surely frown.*
So I'll show you how much I do love you...
Okay, that's it! This poem is through!

Love, Richie Kovatch
2-18-2000

#30 Ronda's 41st Birthday

My wife today is one year older.
She's the girl I love, I've always told her.
She's the proverbial apple of my eye
So I wrote this poem and I'll tell you why.

God told me Himself this is the girl I will marry
When she came down the steps after washing her hair. He
Made this girl to be my helpmeet
And it took her love to make me complete!

Because a man without a wife is like
A singer in a band without a mike
Who can't tell the world how much to him she means...
Especially when she's wearing her tightest blue jeans!

The funny thing is that the one year has added
A certain charm to her rear end that's now padded
With maybe an inch of new cushion for daddy...
Who's really so grateful she could never be called fatty!

She's kept herself in such marvelous shape.
When she walks in the room I long to close the drape
And make mad passionate love to her...at least for a while.
Although to do it I'd probably have to chase her a mile!

LOVE,
Your husband forever...
RICHIE

This card came on a card that read...
Don't think of it as having another birthday!
Think of it as I do...the anniversary of the day
The world was graced with your presence!

Rich Kovatch
3-7-2000

===== #31 RESURRECTION DAY=====

Today, most of the world celebrates our Lord's Resurrection,
But in their personal lives haven't made the connection
Between <u>what</u> Jesus did, the cross **and why,**
And how we are to pick up our own cross and die!

They all say Christ died, and was buried, and rose from the dead
<u>But the deeper meaning</u> ***never reaches their hearts*** <u>from their head.</u>
While they confess with their mouths the things that occurred
The true message of Love has been lost or obscured.

God's trying to show them that He's given them the tools
To learn how to love Him and what are the rules.
He's given them His Word, in the flesh and in writing
But they refused to study; they were content on just fighting

With whoever God sent them to show them the way.
They'd just tell them, "Oh, that's just what you say!"
But would never take it to heart what He was trying to get through.
They'd say, *"I'm free to love God my way!"* They thought that they knew.

But there's only one way no matter what they say
And God showed us all on that first Resurrection Day.
<u>It's by sacrificing our flesh and picking up our own cross</u>
And by rising to a new life with Christ as our boss!

You must accept the fact that you were born a sinner
And humble yourself; follow Christ to be a winner,
Submit to His teachings; make an effort to learn,
And spread the **"GOOD NEWS"** <u>when it comes up **your turn**</u>!

For that is what Jesus did, His whole life as our lesson.
He did what the Father told Him and there was no guessin'.
He was lead by the Holy Spirit after it came down as a Dove
<u>And He expressed God's will by showing everybody Love</u>!

<u>**He told them the truth and said they should believe:**</u>
<u>**In this life it's always better to give than receive.**</u>
Then you'll receive eternal blessings and life in God's kingdom
If you'll be quick to forgive and God's praises... you singed um'!

Rich Kovatch
4-23-2000

#32 MOTHER'S / FATHER'S DAY

Why is there a Mother's / Father's Day?
Is it so we all can say
How grateful we are you gave us birth?
I'll tell you now what that was worth.

All that did was bring us in
To a world that's full of hate and sin,
And set us on a path that's doomed
Unless Christ's Spirit was installed and groomed!

Now, you know I love you and that's a fact,
But this message I'll try to explain with tact
That being a good mother or father is not in itself
The most important thing you can do for my health.

You could lead me to exercise and keep an eye on my weight
But those things have nothing to do with my eternal fate
Which is determined not by my looks, my brain, my smile or my style,
But if I understood my need for a saviour, or if I died in denial!

You see, most people think their lives start at conception
But truly it begins when they get spiritual perception
And realize that they've **been "BORN AGAIN"**
A BRAND NEW CREATION, at the Devil's chagrin!

For Jesus is the only one who's got the power of creation
And His *Holy Spirit* leads us into all truth with elation
Because He knows we wanted to become a child in love
With the Father we now yearn to relate to above.

We must be "BORN AGAIN", that's what Jesus has said,
The knowledge of God has to enter our hearts from our head;
Because He's Dealt each man a measure of faith first hand
But it's up to us to earnestly contend for that faith and make your stand

So **a parent's real purpose** given by God they should know
Is to train up a child in the way he should go,
So when he is old he will not depart from it.
My prayer for all parents that read this is; its message will hit!

Because they'll both personally hear what God will have to say
When they're brought before Jesus on their ***personal* Judgment Day**
And He asks them why they **didn't follow His Law?**
What is the **"Lake of Fire"** as the punishment they could draw ???

Rich Kovatch
5-14-2000

#33 MARRIAGE VOWS

Today you start a brand new life
As you make your vows to become husband and wife;
And **give your promises to love <u>no matter what</u>**
Even when the honeymoon's over and you get in a rut.

Marriage isn't as easy as it may seem
Especially if you don't keep alive your dream
Of building a family with God at its source
Since He has the answers to all your questions...of course!

When things get tough...and you know they will
He's given you the manual to get you over the hill
That's full of encouragement to give you peace and hope
When you're at your wits end and you don't think you can cope.

The answer is always to show love to your mate...
And tell yourself that your needs and wants can wait
Until God sets the time up *according to His clock...*
Even if it causes you to walk around the block!

He's wiser than us and knows what's best in your case;
And *that **time*** to cool off and think will put you ***back** in your place*
And help you to remember to put yourself in your mates' shoes;
And He tells you that <u>now</u> *is the time* for you *to pay your dues.*

You'll come to realize *that one day* the roles *will be* reversed
And it will be you that needs to be pampered and nursed;
Because that's what a partner is suppose to do
When their soul mate is feeling way down and blue.

You're to be an example for your children to see
That putting others before yourself is the way it should be;
So that God will shower blessings on you day after day
When you see that your children are happy to do what you say!

You're to train up a child in the way he should go;
And the best way to do that is to show them you know
That <u>true happiness comes from helping others in need</u>
And never letting yourself fall into that bad trap called *greed.*

Rich Kovatch
6-1-2000

#34 THE *ROTTEN* TONGUE

Scriptures
To Read

That may sound like a pretty rough title
But it's the one thing the Lord told us to bridle
Because out of the mouth comes the <u>thoughts of the heart</u>.   <u>Matt. 12:34</u>
Learning to control the tongue is only the start.

James said, "The tongue no man can tame"   James 3:8
And "It defiles the whole body" just the same   James 3:6
Because it's like the governor that guides the ship   James 3:4
And if we're not careful it will cause us to slip.

"The tongue is a fire, a world of iniquity"   James 3:6
And if Christ is in you, you'll be able to see
That *your words* are the *essence* of what you believe.   <u>Matt. 12:34</u>
And the good Lord, you know, you cannot deceive!

<u>For He reads your heart and knows what you think</u>!   <u>1 Kings 8:39</u>
Don't let a foul mouth put you on the brink
Of continued damnation for swearing night after night.
Every person will know that His judgments are right!   Ps. 19:9; 119:60
Rev. 16:17, 19:2
Out of the same mouth proceeds blessings and cursing   James 3:10
And speaking with compassion and love we should be rehearsing
When times are good and no pressure is found
So when things do get rough God's own words will sound.

We're COMMANDED from using God's name in vain.   Exodus 20:7 Deut.5-11
When He hears that phrase *it causes Him pain*!
When I hear someone say that I wonder if they're insane
Because they certainly are not even engaging their brain!

How can you use His name with such disrespect?
You're disobeying His word with a total neglect
Like what He says has no meaning at all!   Exodus 20:7 Deut. 5-11
Keep that up and you're not too many steps from a great fall!

#34 THE *ROTTEN* TONGUE

So let's not use words that belittle or hurt
And make others feel worthless or as dumb as dirt.
Refrain from badmouthing or using a racial slur
And you'll be well on your way to making your thoughts pure.

Jesus said, "Be holy, for I am holy" you know;   1 Peter 1:16
And <u>remember you'll surely reap what you sow</u>!   Gal. 6:7
<u>God is not mocked! Don't be deceived</u>.   Gal. 6:7
<u>He promises</u> what you give out…<u>you *will* receive</u>!!!   Gal. 6:7-9

Rich Kovatch
6-6-2000

#35 HEY YOU! PICK UP! HE'S CALLING YOU **NOW!**

Hey you, my brother, why can't you hear
God calling you? **FOR THE END IS NEAR!**
It's time for you to open up your mind
And be filled with the **_joy that you will find_**

When you stop denying Jesus as God's son
And come to realize that they both are one.
The **_only_** way God could save **_your_** soul
Was to shed **HIS OWN BLOOD,** and **that is His goal!**

God created all things through Christ, His Word.
"True and Faithful" He is to the things we've heard.
He shall not lose one that the Father has given
But on the last day **all believers in Jesus** will have risen!

I wrote this for you brother, God got me out of bed
Because of the love I have for you was consuming my head
And to obey Him meant I should write You this poem
Praying these words will take root and the truth will help grow 'um

Into a new creation that has sprouted in you
'Cause that's what the true Spirit of God will do.
And if you truly want to have eternal life in heaven
It's time **RIGHT NOW to start purging the leaven!**

My reason for living is to bring the light to the world;
To illuminate the darkness the Devil has unfurled
By getting people to hate and kill others if they don't switch
To a religion where Christ is not believed in, now there's his real niche!

He deceives so many with his tricks and wiles
That many will die when God opens up His vials
And brings judgment on all those who don't live in the light.
And were **unable to discern what's wrong from right!**

Just the fact that you're reading this is giving me hope.
I think you'd rather talk to me than the Pope
Because we two are friends and you've seen how I've changed.
Now it's time for the thoughts in your head to be rearranged!

Rich Kovatch
7-9-2000

#36 Spiritual Oneness

The Bible teaches that marriage is Gods' most intimate way
To show His children what **True Love is:** *submission day to day*
The husband to his head, who is Christ, His actions should be holy.
The wife, her head is her husband...but this *in no way* makes her lowly.

A woman's need is of security... as **Christ** has given **His Word**
To **His** church, His *dowered* bride, through the prophecies it has heard.
A man's need is of a loving reverence, **like God requires of us all**
To know who holds the keys to life. We all must answer His call.

The husband is not anything unless he gives *his all*
Which is his life, like Christ did for His bride, after mans' garden fall.
Christ, the Head, had to pay for sin to save the weaker vessel
So when testing time is over and done, for eternity they will nestle.

My problem is that *I don't know* **exactly how to give**
To my sweet wife and confidant what she needs most to live
As God would want her in *her role as Queen* **unto her King**
While she shows committed effort, like she said she would, when she put on
That ring.

When one gets married they offer themselves as a living sacrifice
To their partners which our all-knowing *God provided as a teacher and a vice*
So we could learn how hard it is to truly learn His ways
As we **keep** *diligently seeking how Love will overcome our daze.*

The Law was our schoolmaster... *but now we can better understand GRACE!*
It showed how man can never measure up to finding that perfect place
Where we will not fail to show perfect submission to the Holy ways of Love
Until the Kingdom of God comes *upon us* **and** *we* **love as He does above!**

That day won't get here until Christ *personally* **guides our spirits, but until that**
Day arrives,
We've been given the gift to follow the path *if we will open up our eyes*
And **SEE The Way, The Truth,** and **The Life** which is *Jesus living in* us
Then He will show us our mistakes *when we forget to trust!*

So since Christ lives in both of us, it's together we're to follow
The pattern He set before us, so in our flesh we will not wallow
As we learn to live in the **Spirit** of **Faith** and **Hope,** and **Joy,** and **Love**
Then we'll function as one Holy body, like the bride and our husbandman
Above.

Rich Kovatch
7-30-2000

#37 **So,** You've _Got **Problems**_ ?

So you've got problems? Well join the crowd.
And what might they be? Let's name them out loud.
There's never enough time and much want for money.
But I'll tell you some more that aren't at all funny.

When there's **sickness** and **death** and **hurt all around** us
It's amazing the things we find for reasons to cuss.
"I don't have enough" or **"That should have been mine".**
When we don't get our way, how often we wine

And act like a child who hasn't grown up,
Like two people getting married but still need a pre-nup.
There's a lack of true love there, of faith and of trust.
And if a relationship isn't protected, like iron, it will rust.

But the biggest problem you've hinted at I can see
Is that **you don't know exactly _who_ you're supposed to be.**
You haven't figured out why you were born
And why your heart - in two - has been torn.

The thing you call a family
Is **_not_** one in the eyes of the God. As far as I can see
It's a man's version, what **_YOU_** think is **O.K. ...**
Even though you never had a Wedding Day.

How do expect for things to go right
When you don't know how to resolve a fight?
One that starts because of **selfishness**
By you or her, **or both,** I would guess.

I'll tell you what you need to do
Is to seek Godly counsel to see you through.
It can be found in people like me.
Or better yet...get down on your knee

#37 So, You've Got Problems?

And **ask God for forgiveness and wisdom from Him**
And **confess to Him** that **you are in sin.**
And **ask Him to guide you,** let Him **show you the way**
So **you can _start_** honoring His holiness **_today_.**

You've told me you believe in our Lord Jesus Christ.
Do you believe Him now that your heart's been cut up and diced?
Do you believe He cares and has a way to repair
Your "so called" family? Do you have the faith to even dare?

To trust in Him one hundred percent
And try to understand just exactly what He meant
When He commanded you to **"study to show yourself approved",**
So when TODAY'S Judgment Day comes you won't stay removed

From His ever drawing presence and love for you sent from heaven
Because you preferred to fill your life & thoughts with self-rising leaven?
Have you studied enough to know what I've just said?
Or are too many of Satan's deceptions still filling your head?

This poem for you is getting a little long
But the message it's conveying must be strong
To help you see God's plan for you in your life.
First of all, **The BEST** for you isn't a girlfriend, but a **wife!**

My friend, I've been exactly where you are today
That's why God has given me the guidance to say
Please take the time to humble yourself
And get Godly counsel from someone who's been there...like myself!

I'd hate to see the Devil win
By persuading you to continue in sin
By telling you to make excuses and hide
Because **that's why** he was removed from heaven - **it's called PRIDE!**

#37 So, You've Got Problems?

AND PRIDE IS EXACTLY THE OPPOSITE OF HUMILITY
And a life where you do what you want is not how God wants you to be.
He wants you to sacrifice yourself like Christ did
For the benefit of others; *like maybe...your kids!*

The most important responsibility you've got now to do
Is to **BE THERE _EVERY_ DAY** for them and see this thing through.
Because excuses won't cut it, and they'll feel lost
If their daddy on earth doesn't properly evaluate the cost.

Now it won't be real easy...repentance never is.
You'll reap what you sow, Will you follow your mind or His?
One will bring trouble, and pain, and sorrow, and strife
And **the other will too,** but He'll give you a new life

Where He'll give you **The Comforter** to help get you through
The tough times you'll have, **but your perspective will be new**
When you put **your** needs *after* God's, your wife's, and your offspring's;
You'll experience the joy that following His wisdom brings!

Rich Kovatch
11-12-2000

#38 DO YOU <u>BELIEVE</u> IN JESUS CHRIST ?

Do you <u>BELIEVE</u> in **Jesus Christ** our **Lord**?
Or when someone talks about **Him** do you get **bored**
And tune out whatever message God has to say
Even though it's relevant to your life today?

Do you even know what it means to **BELIEVE** ?   Romans 10:11-15
If you don't then the Devil has deceived
You into trying to figure out your problems on your own
Even though most often *your solutions* cause you to moan and groan!

He guides you into the knowledge of your worldly friends   1 Corinthians 1:7-31
Who don't even realize that their advice tends   1 Cor. (all of chapter 2)
To *keep you in the dark* because it's the wisdom of man   Corinthians 3:18-20
That will not solve your dilemma like the Word of God can.   James 1:5-6

Believing in Jesus means you'll trust **His Word**   Ephesians 1:12-14
But the truth will not have power until it is heard.   Ja.2:21-27; Heb.2:12-15
Do you believe that **He wants you to find peace**   Luke 2:14; Matt.5:2-12 (vs.4)
The first thing He may have you do is pray, and not cease   1 Thes. 5:17-19

Until you hear from the Holy one who loved you so much
He died on the cross so *your heart* He could touch.   Mark 15:24-38
If you think **about** Him and the *reason* He came: John 3:16- 21
To show you - for answers you must *BELIEVE* in *His name*.   Mark 16:9-20

His name should <u>easily</u> make you break down and cry   Luke 23:33-46
As you start to ponder why **He was put on that cross to die**.   John 19:14- 30
It was for **YOU** and **ME** while we were yet lost!   Romans 5:8-10
Have you ever even thought about just how much it cost?   Luke 14:25-35

Imagine you have to solve the problem of sin.
It's so big a problem I'm sure you don't even know where to begin!
Well, **God knew** when He created **YOU** that you'd experience Hell Matt. 23:24-39
If He didn't provide to you <u>someone</u> who was eager to tell   Rom. 10:10-15

You about the <u>power of Jesus to save the lost sheep</u>.   He. 1:2-3; Ro.1:16-22,9:15-24
And **His Word says that <u>ALL</u> God <u>gave</u> Him, Jesus <u>will keep</u>**!   **John 10:28-29**
But listen to me - **HIS SHEEP KNOW HIS VOICE**   John 10:26-27
And it's in **"The Potter's"** timing as to IF and WHEN your choice   Matt. 10:32-4;
                                                                      John 3:18-20

#38 DO YOU <u>BELIEVE</u> IN JESUS CHRIST ?

To answer His knock happens on the door to your heart   Rev. 3:20-23
Because with <u>**YOUR**</u> **SOUL** He doesn't want to be apart!   **John** 3:14-21, **(vs. 3:16)**
But He can NOT live IN you if HE doesn't open your door   John 5:27; Rev. 3:16
And you become so <u>eager to hear more</u> !

His voice will come to you from the people He's put around you   Eph. 4:11-29
That **KNOW** what **His Word** *for you* **will do;**
That's make your heart melt & become like the potter's clay Jer. 18:4-6; Isa. 29:16
So you can be molded by the message He's sent you today.   Rom.9:20-24

The evangel of Christ crucified, entombed, and risen is the most important
Message you'll ever hear
Because you never know **if your last breath** on earth is far away or near !
And the **TRUTH IS this** life you're given the most glorifying **CHANCE**   Heb. 9-27
To show the "Light of the world" to this **"present evil age"**
And *enjoy our EONIAN Dance!*   Eph. 5:16

Rich Kovatch
12-20-2000

#39 "I'm Not Hurting You..."

There's a phrase I hear all the time
That happens to be my wife's favorite line.
She uses it when I make known of something I disapprove.
I state it... she debates it. It's always the same unhealthy groove.

This specific topic has to do with *her* health
Which is an important determining factor of her wealth
Towards our marriage, our family, to God and our life.
I long for a happy, loving and healthy wife.

She smokes cigarettes and she knows it's not right
But she can't see why it might cause a small fight.
The phrase I hear is **"I'm not hurting you!"**
She doesn't understand how it hurts you know who.

I'll tell you exactly how it hurts me and why
Because it's sin and may easily cause her to die.
God commands us to glorify Him in our body and spirit.
His word says that if we defile it, He'll destroy it! I wish she would
Hear It!   1 Cor. 6:19-20

Of course that won't stop her from entering Heaven.
She'll just make it there sooner, because it's leaven!
Sin is the reason that we suffer and die
But it will hurt me deeply if her smoking becomes the reason I'll cry!

Now I'll get to the point I originally intended;
It's that when we got married...it's me she befriended
And we two became one...in spirit and in flesh   Eph. 5:31
To nourish and cherish each other with reverence, this way
We will mesh   Eph. 5:29, 31

#39 "I'm Not Hurting You…"

Into a Holy and pure _relationship_ that will bring glory to God
Whose sacrifices _to each_ other would smell like sweet incense, not
Fishy Like cod.
One where we gain strength from our partner in love.
And most certainly that strength comes from our Father above.

It takes _courage_ and _faith_ to _overcome_ our shortfalls and fears,
But when we have trust in Jesus, we'll make it through our tears.
We know it hurts when we decide to pick up our cross and die,
But we choose to do it anyway _out of Love_ for our mate and God,
That's why!!!

Rich Kovatch
1-10-2001

#40 It's My **Right** To Choose

Today's world has the spirit of the Laodicean Church
Where everyone wants to stand upon their own perch
And squawk to then world that it's their right to choose
Even when it's **_someone else's life_** they will lose!

The story of mankind has been told from the beginning of the ages.
It's been foretold from God in the Bible, written on its pages
That men and women would grow increasingly wicked and vile
And not even care about other people's lives with wicked guile.

There'll be a total lack of respect and affection
And people will demand the right to go their own direction
No matter who gets in their way or who may get hurt
And they'll even start treating their own unborn children like dirt!

They'll **refuse** to even **accept** that there **is** a **life**,
And unborn children they'll sacrifice and put to the knife
Like women have done since way back when, to Molech
And in the process it's **their _own_ lives** they will probably wreck

Because when a woman has an abortion **something dies** inside
And no matter how hard they try, **the truth will not hide**;
And every year when that date rolls around
Her conscience will heat up and **the truth will be found**;

And be brought out in the open that **she's made a mistake**.
God will strongly desire her to **ask for forgiveness, _that's all it'd take_**
To get back on the right path where **all life** is sacred.
He's promised... He'll _forgive_ all who _admit_ what they did

Was morally wrong and mortally fatal
To that little child they'd have had in their cradle.
A new life that would show them the value of giving
If they had brought to term the child that was living

#40 It's My **Right** To Choose

In her womb safe and secure where God entrusted the mother
To provide for her child like she'd do for another
That's already been born and depends on her love and support;
Not scared that she'll terminate the process because it's okay with the
Supreme Court!

There may be a ruling that gives the woman the right
But the right thing to do is to do right in God's sight
And not be influenced by your selfish desires
But give birth so you won't end up in Hell's fires!

Rich Kovatch
1-15-2001

#41 Gideon's Army

Do you know the story of Gideon and who he was
And that God chose this young man because
He was the least in his family and one full of doubt
Who didn't know what the power of God is all about?

An angel of the Lord appeared to him; the Lord Himself he did perceived
Who called him a mighty man of valor. This at first he didn't believe.
But the Lord instructed him to deliver Israel from the hands of the
Midianites
And he would succeed in this thy might: because God had sent him into
The fights.

He started to understand and trust in the Lord
That he would have power when he picked up his sword
As he obeyed God's commandment to first offer a sacrifice.
He did all he was told without having to think twice.

But wait...soon after that day when push came to shove
His flesh intervened. He wanted reassurance from above.
He tested God to prove that His words were true
By setting out a fleece and controlling the dew.

Believe it or not, Gideon still had doubt
So he set it out again and asked God to turn it about,
And do the exact opposite of the miracle just done!
After God did that too, Gideon's trust was then won.

Once again Gideon's flesh took over as he gathered all that he could
To do battle with the Midianites because he thought that he should.
But God told him there were too many, too much chance for pride
To creep into Israel's mindset and forget who's driving this ride.

#41 Gideon's Army

So twenty two thousand volunteers God sent on their way
When Gideon proclaimed: All that are afraid leave...the rest, you can stay.
But still God sensed even more pride in the ten thousand still willing
So He sent them to drink water; to see with what water their mouths
They were filling.

I'll pause for a moment to give you some insight;
There were first thirty three thousand willing to fight,
But of this number, most were there only because of duty.
See, twenty two thousand were more worried about their _own_ booty!

The ten thousand left were brave for sure
But God saw that their motives were far from pure.
They knew their mission and that they would win
But the PRIDE that would grow from their own works was sin.

We're saved by _GRACE_, not by works that we could boast.
When pride swells up, God puts us in the fire to roast
And burn up that unrighteous thought process
So further down that road we won't continue to digress.

The three hundred men that drank the water with care
Kept an eye out for the enemy, they didn't fail to beware.
The water symbolizes God's Word, which is food for our hearts
But we're not to lose focus on where comes Satan's fiery darts

So we can withstand the attack and know how to defend,
Whether they hit us straight on, or from the rear end.
The True Water of Life _was shown_ us as JESUS, The King
And what a blessing a life in submission will bring.

#41 Gideon's Army

But once again Gideon's flesh became fearful
So the Lord told him and his servant to go get an earful,
And be strengthened with this new knowledge of what the enemy had
Planned.
Then...you will be confident victory will be delivered into your hand.

The enemy occupied the valley; **Gideon took <u>the high ground</u>,**
Which shows us the depth of sin and the height in which believers are
Found.
Then Gideon used his three hundred men **<u>armed only with trumpets
And lamps</u>!**
They shinned their light unto the darkness and blew the trumpets.
They were the champs!

The Light symbolizes the Truth and the Trumpets...The Word.
They yelled, "The sword of the Lord, and of Gideon!" All the camp surely
Heard.
This caused the enemy to turn their swords upon one another and many
Fell dead.
The two princes were slain at the wine press. Gideon then chopped off
Their head!

Could these two princes be like unto the Dragon and False Prophet?
Surely they are, this isn't just a story like "Little Miss Moffitt".
Old Testament stories all have a truth to be told
<u>So since The Great Tribulation *HAS BEGUN*,</u> **God's church will be bold.**

We'll have studied the stories throughout all of time past
And we'll understand; in eternity...only two things will last.
That's surely...God's Word, and all the souls of mankind
<u>Who will be forever stuck to the Spirit they chose to be entwined</u> !!!

Rich Kovatch
1-18-2001

#42 The Sower and The Seed

My favorite parable in the entire Bible
Is the **Sower and the Seed** in which to describe I'll
Break it all down as far as I can
To see if you have any embers I might be able to fan.

To bring back the fire you had in the past.
To help you understand why it just didn't last.
Why your love for God's Word became smothered and lost.
Could be you never really estimated just what it would cost.

These stories are all found in **Matthew 13**
And I thank God Jesus told us what we would glean
If we've got ears to hear and eyes to see.
He told us exactly what will come to be.

He explains it so clearly **and it gives me great hope**
That those seeds that don't mature *QUICKLY* because they're
STILL LEARNING **to cope**
Are *still given a chance* and the worst be averted
If they'll **listen** with **their hearts** and then be **converted**.

It's just that their hearts had waxed gross causing their ears not to hear.
Their eyes they had closed, they didn't perceive what to fear.
The parable *tells us* what Satan *will do…* raise tares among the wheat
In his effort to cause **the kids** of The Kingdom to go down in defeat.

The Sower, *who's the Son of Man*, went forth and sowed from his cup.
Some seeds fell by the wayside, and guess who showed up.
The wicked one stole the Word from the heart that understood it not.
This is the *first group* that God *predestined* to not receive what His elect
Have got.

#42 The Sower and The Seed

Other seed fell upon stony places where it was heard & received with joy.
This brought about a quick sprout and an excitement like when
receiving A new toy.
But **no root** in God's **Word** was able to be formed because, of it, he was
Offended
When it caused tribulation and persecution in his life, the sprout was
Soon upended.

Still other seed fell upon the thorns, but the Word did still get through,
But the cares of this world & deceitfulness of riches stuck to it like glue
And choked out the truth that much evil comes from the lust of money
At its very **root**
And this in turn made this seed wither in the shadow, and thus it bore
No fruit.

Finally other seed fell unto **good ground** and *grew*

<u>Because it understood</u> **The Word** and **The Truth** it *knew*.
And when someone spread false witness he'd get down and dirty
Thus bringing forth **some a *hundredfold, some sixty, some thirty*.**

Now the thing **you must trust** in is the end of the harvest
When the tares grown with the wheat are separated at the Lord's
Request
And the angels will gather the tares to be burned in the fires
Only the carnal works of the flesh, **not His children** who lived life as
Unwitting **liars**.

Then, the wheat will be gathered and put in God's barn for safe keeping.
After the Earth and Heavens are made new, there'll be no more wailing
And weeping.
Then all things will be made new & forever "**The Righteous**" will shine
Forth
To dwell in God's glory from the East to the West and the South to the
North!

Rich Kovatch
1-22-01

#43 YOUR MISSION FIELD

I'll try to write down some words of encouragement
Which I've prayed to God they would be heaven sent.
They begin: once you've realized your future is sealed
He's **GOING TO send you** out to a mission field.

Those **STRONG** in God's word will know - that's a fact,
Though you may get second thoughts when your bags are all packed.
Your flesh man or the Devil may try to stop you from leavin'
But you will find strength when it's God's will you believe in.

You might have to leave behind your family and friends.
The distance and duration most certainly depends
On what God has need for to be accomplished and how
By those who are willing and content to go right now.

The beauty of being one of Jesus Christ's chosen
Is that the whole load **can't be** carried by just the one who's posin'
As an apostle, a prophet, an evangelist, pastor, or teacher,
But He'll show you your field, so God's lost church, you can help reach Her.

His flock is wandering around all over this land
And He's going to gather them in with the help of your hand.
Whether it be by T.V., or radio, or pulpit, or work place
The lost sheep will recognize Christ's peace in your face!

God never puts on you more than you can handle.
Just speak of God's truth, and you'll be His candle
That will bring light to a world that's lost in the dark.
Don't ever be scared to stand up and bark!

Submit to His love and He'll show you the way.
The Holy Spirit will guide you on which words you should say
That will lead out the captives past the gates of Hell
To drink from the **Living Water** that's found only in ***Christ's*** well!

#43 YOUR MISSION FIELD

So whether you're called to stay put or go travel,
Stay happy knowing you've got the power of God's gavel.
Don't be scared to judge evil when it rears up its evil head.
*You're mission **is to do that** so that the lost sheep will be fed!*

Even if it lands you in jail like Silas and Paul,
Jesus will be smiling when you give it you all
And are willing to take it hard on the chin
To speak the *"**Good News**"* to those who are lost in their sin.

Prison time may not sound like much fun
But you know, there's sheep in there too that need to be won.
And they're probably the ones with the deepest despairs.
God may need you to **go *there*** *to show them He cares.*

Jesus will never leave you or forsake you... you've heard
Because to be called to a mission field, you'll for sure know His Word.
He'll give you *only* whatever you'll ***need*** to get by
And when you're in Heaven, you'll know exactly why.

Rich Kovatch
1-31-01

#44 Man Shall Not Live

"Man shall not live"; Jesus once said to Satan.   Matt. 4:3; Luke 4:4
And that's a fact. There'll be no debatin'.
I can show you exactly where it is.
Now let us continue on with this quiz.

"There is no God". There's no need to vote.   Psalm 14:1
I can take you right to that specific quote
And *prove* to you the words *are there.*
Now here's a couple more quotes I'd like to share.

How about: **"Say unto this mountain, be thou removed, and be thou
Cast into the sea"**   Matt. 21:21
With **_NO DOUBT_** at all, it **WILL BE** DONE <u>because</u> **JESUS said**;
"It SHALL BE".   Mark 11:23
Or better yet, **"Whatever ye shall ask in prayer, ye shall receive".**
          Matt. 21:22
Sounds like a really good concept; **"You JUST HAVE TO BELIEVE"**!
          Mark 11:24

Our savior **"WILL have ALL men to be saved"**, we also read,   **1 Tim. 2:4**
For **God will put enmity** between Satan and the woman's SEED. Gen. 3:15
And of **God**, *every* man **SHALL** have **PRAISE**   1 Cor. 4:5
And *every* man, in **INCORRUPTION, SHALL** be *RAISED*!   1 Cor. 15:52

We **_shall ALL_** be changed in the twinkling of an eye   **1 Cor. 15:52**
So there's **NO** REASON to be scared to die.
Sounds pretty assuring doesn't it now
Since ALL men **WILL** stand before Jes**us or bow.** Ps.145:14; Phil.2:10; Rev.20:12

Jesus said; **"With God ALL things ARE possible"**.   Matt. 19:26; Mark 10:27
Okay now, let's keep going, I'm on a roll.
 I thank the Lord that **I AM** <u>PERFECT</u>! 1 Cor. 2:6; Phil. 3:15; Heb. 10:14; 1 Peter 5:10
The Word says, be<u>fore</u> time *was*, Rich Kovatch, <u>He picked</u>.   Rom. 8:29,30

#44 Man Shall Not Live

Now, before you all get up to punch me out,
Let me tell you what this is all about.
Believe it or not, I know where this is going.
It's time for your understanding of **God's Word** to start growing.

I could go on with many more quotes
But some of you would have to start taking notes
To be able to make sense of what I'm saying.
I still hope you don't attack me, believe me I'm praying.

"Do ye not therefore err, because ye know not the scriptures"?

Matt. 22:29; Mark 12:24

I'm trying to put into your mind **these wonderful pictures**
That makes it *sound like* we've got it made
But in reality, speaking words like this, God forbade.   Titus 1:10-13

All these are examples of scripture which I can defend,
But I'll show you what happens when people begin to bend
The **Word of God** to fit their belief.
When I hear them **preach half-truths**, I pray to Jesus for relief.

A half-truth happens when scripture is taken **out of context**.
Then, when someone is not well grounded, they'll get perplexed. All 1 Tim.
So to lose footing in **God's Word** will cause many to fall   All 1 Tim.
If they refuse to *LISTEN* **to The Holy Spirit's true call**.   All Titus

Let's tighten up some loose ends now so to keep your attention:
Like **the rest of Jesus' words** I neglected to mention;
"By bread alone, but *every word* that proceeds out of the mouth of
God".   Matt. 4:3; Luke 4:4
That's every word *held together in HARMONY* and *used to rule* forever
With an **iron rod**.   Rev. 2:25-29

#44 Man Shall Not Live

"There is no God", oh yeah, that's said be **the fool**   Ps. 14:1
Who thinks *his brazen demeanor* makes him **look cool.**
Well, it does, to those who are still in the dark.
Too bad...pretty soon these same people might be accepting the Beast's
Mark!   Rev. 13:17

Speaking to the mountain and receiving whatsoever you ask for in
Prayer is **all GOOD** and **TRUE**
But you have to understand what **HOPE** and **FAITH** are in case **God's
WILL** is that **you're to go through**
Whatever **ordeal you're in** if there's **a lesson to learn.**
And *if* you *DON'T learn* it, **to the same lesson you're SURE TO RETURN!**

You see, we're to **"Live by Faith, and NOT SIGHT".**   2 Cor. 5:7
That way, *we'll learn* to **listen** to **The Holy Spirit** when **He** *tells us* what's **Right.**
We're to **HOPE** FOR THE **BEST**, *but* **ACCEPT** life with **patience** and **trust**
          Rom. 8:24-28
So *if we ask* for something **&** *believe it WILL* come *true*, it won't be a **MUST!**

In *this* **life**, first of all, we're taught *not to worry* about *OUR* needs.
          Matt. 6: 30-34; Luke 12:28-32
Just like **Christ** did as **our example**, because *we're* **Abraham's seeds.**
     1 Peter 2:18-21
We're to FOCUS on showing God's LOVE *for mankind* and *EACH OTHER*
          Matt. 5:16; Eph. 2:10; 2 Tim. 3:17
And have COMPASSION & *GOOD* works towards our sister & brother.
          Titus 2:7, 14; Heb., 10:24; 1 Peter 2:12

We are to believe **our desires** *WILL* **COME** TRUE   Ps. 145:19
But not necessarily in the flesh, but *maybe after* all things are made new
          Rev. 21:4-5
Because we know *the flesh is corruptible* and *what we've sowed we'll be
Sure to reap.*   Gal. 6: 6-9

But **"in due season"** may not be soon, **and for sure** *won't be cheap* **!**!**!**

          Rich Kovatch
          2-16-01

#45 MY TRUTH FOR TODAY
(Mature Readers ONLY)

I've written so many poems on life and marriage,
But unfortunately I find that I'm still disparaged
Because the seeds I've thrown out haven't taken firm root
With my wife who keeps giving my advances the boot!

The hard truth is that *I have to keep looking inside*
My own heart to see if to anyone I've lied;
Like to myself, or God, or especially my wife;
And *is it the reason* that I keep seeing strife?

I'll start with the basics on when marriage was started;
Back in Genesis 2 when a man from his parents then departed
And God said he would cleave unto his wife to make him then whole
Because the *two would become one to complete each others' soul!*

Now, the two became one, and it says in Paul's letter   1 Cor. 7:3-5
That the man has not power over his own body, but the wife…he should Let her
Be free to render due benevolence unto him at her own leading.
It's just a shame that her timing keeps my heart constantly bleeding.

The same letter states she's not in control of her body;
That the man has that power, but he shouldn't be shoddy
With that responsibility and desire to help her become happy and Whole.
The trick is they both are to make the desire to please the other…their Goal!

But the problem is that we live in a fallen world, for sure
And that the Devil is quite busy trying to keep us from the cure;
And that's the leading of the Holy Spirit which guides us to truth
So we'll act mature in Christ, not like immature kids in our youth.

Now…*the hard part to that…for me*, is called *submission*
Whatever the situation, circumstance, or condition.
I'm not to act selfishly, demanding my normal desires to be met.
It's just that the place where our desires mesh is where I'd like to get!

#45 MY TRUTH FOR TODAY

(Mature Readers ONLY)

Personally, I feel *there's a spiritual battle going on* between us;
And *it's the reason* why there's strife and the reason we fuss.
I try so hard to stay calm, and I've talked to a friend;
But I'm so anxious for this unholy temperament to end!

What I feel as a husband is a lack of intimacy.
I not only feel...but need! I just wish my wife could see
That *that's not a weakness* on my part as a man;
But *she should be thrilled* I want to be intimate as much as I can!

God gave us this desire as the most pleasurable way
To forget the hard hours and Satan's attacks during our day.
He desires us to get lost gazing deep inside each other's eyes
So every trouble and worry of this hell bound world simply dies!

I can't think of a better way than to hold in my arms
My beautiful wife and soul mate...and be lost in her charms!
We've been put in this world where our wills are to be tested.
What's wrong with jumping in bed and falling asleep with our minds
Well rested?

We should thank God for giving us someone we can feel with our skin.
Because we're creatures made of flesh, sometimes our faith in God
Wears thin
And we lose track of the fact we're to overcome till our earthly days end
And He's enabling us so that *our faith* in Him *won't break*, but only Bend!

We're like the wheat in the harvest that when it matures
Will bend in the winds and all of life's detours
And discern between the chaff that won't bend...*but will break*
This **chaff** is the **pride** and **selfish spirit** that comes *before* humility that
Gets thrown into **FIRE LAKE**.

Just one more thing about the intimacy I need...
It's not just the sensual but the spiritual deed
Of *opening up our minds to each other* & giving our problems fresh air
When we know, NO MATTER WHAT, our partners will always be there!

Rich Kovatch
2-11-01

#46 My Wife's 42nd

Today my wife turns **42**
So out came this poem...right on cue.
And it's going to be like I promised just last week;
One that encourage us to stand cheek to cheek!

I thank the Lord He sent her my way
And that our love for each other grows day to day
As we learn through experience the skills we need
While we listen to Jesus and let Him *lead*.
I thank the Lord He has saved us both
Because now we're both uplifted by our spiritual growth;
And our marriage becomes a witness to our neighbors and friends
As they see Gods' love and commitment and blessings He sends.

Her eyes now sparkle like the stars above.
When we meet her smile tells me how much we're in Love.
How she's happy to see me like I'm her knight in shining armor.
Makes me feel like she's my homestead and I am the farmer.

I enjoy the opportunity to till the ground and plant the seeds.
The hard part is trying to keep out the weeds;
Or at least to keep them in check so the crop will still grow.
What I have to remember is that I'll reap what I sow!

The Lord tells me to treat her with tender loving care,
But so far the job I've done I'd rate as only fair.
I thank God that Love covers a multitude of sins
And she's happy to be with me when each new day begins!

Thank you Jesus for *her warm loving heart*;
And help me to remember to keep the horse in front of the cart.
That means since I'm to lead and power the action
I must make sure there's a strong and constant attraction

For her to follow my lead down the row through the field.
I thank God we both believe that our marriage is sealed
With your approval that we were meant for each other.
I couldn't ask for a better woman to be our child's mother!

Rich Kovatch
3-7-2001

#47 L i f e

Life is so precious, but so few see
What it was given for to you and me.
What is its purpose, have you ever thought?
It's so sad that so many people think that it's all for naught.

When they look around and see pain and sorrow...
So many lose hope for a happy tomorrow.
They just lose sight and get deceived.
A better tomorrow just couldn't be believed.

Then, unfortunately, they make the mistake
Of playing **God** when their own life they take.
It's so sad they knew not where to turn
And had no one to guide them and to help them learn.

That life isn't easy; that part they knew.
But **how to get through it** and why we get blue?
Depression and sadness and rejection are **common to all**
But they're all **useful** and **necessary** to **teach us** how to stand tall.

No one or nothing gets strong on its own.
It takes stress and resistance to cause us to groan.
That's **when** the buildup of muscle and resolve ***grow*** *the fastest*,
Then the *repetitions* and *experience* will **bring out our best**.

You see, it's all in **God's** plan, and He saw from the start
What this world would do to our minds and our heart.
It's not like He's left us alone and hung out to dry.
His **Holy Spirit** is available to find for all those who try.

The **Holy Spirit, The Comforter** will lead us to all truth
Whether we're old and decrepit or still in our youth.
We must be ***"Born Again"*** of the Spirit, **Jesus said.**
And all that aren't are sadly just the walking dead!

#47 L i f e

These are the words of our **Saviour**, not from my head.
He's the **"Bread of Life"** from which all can be fed;
And must be if we're to understand why this life is so hard.
He'll give us the tools, ability & knowledge so our hearts we can guard.

Remember...He said that His children perish for lack of knowledge.
And He's not talking about the secular wisdom that's taught in college.
It's the knowledge that He has the answers to any question we ask.
And believe me it's no problem for Him. He's up to the task.

Why is there famine and death and hate and war?
Why are so many *men* and *women* so rotten to the core?
Why does He allow all these bad things to continue?
Why won't **ALL** people be saved, **but _only a few?_**

Why, why, why, when, where, what and who?
What in the world are we suppose to do?
Who has the answers and when will we know?
Where will I go when I die? **_Will I really reap what I sow?_**

All the answers are written in **His** word, there's no doubt.
And it's not too late for you if you don't know what I'm talking about.
God has His "Chosen Ones" in place, eager to harvest the field,
But the only _ones that_ will be brought in are the ones that _will yield_

To God's call to come unto Him and _accept His Way,_
The Truth and The Life - that's _JESUS_ - do you hear what I say?
You must admit you're a sinner and that you are lost
And **BELIEVE YOU'RE FORGIVEN BECAUSE JESUS PAID THE COST!**

Rich Kovatch
3-27-01

#48 Now I Lay Me Down To Sleep

Now I lay me down to sleep.
I pray the Lord my soul to keep.
If I should die before I wake,
I pray the Lord my soul to take.

A simple rhyme from long ago,
But did you believe it was really so?
Do you recite it still when you go to bed?
Do you know where you'll go when you are dead?

The basic premise is that the Lord will say:
"Welcome to my Kingdom" on that fateful day
Because you lived a good life and showed faith till the end,
And you knew for sure that **the Lord** was **your friend.**

This childhood prayer is meant to convey
Who is The Truth, The Life, and The Way.
The deeper meaning shows that the Lord holds the key
To us finding our final resting place for eternity.

The prayer is said knowing that there is a place
And the consequences of your actions...you'll have to face!
But the only one that determines it for sure
Is: Did you know **Jesus Christ...your Saviour?**

Did you care enough to get to know **Him?**
Or was it more important that you get to the gym
To exercise your body that one day will be dust?
Did you live for the future or a world full of lust?

God reads all men's hearts and you cannot hide
What **was** *really* **driving** your desires **from** *inside.*
Was it to help bring more souls into God's paradise?
Or was it to enjoy this short life and just roll the dice?

Rich Kovatch
4-10-01

#49 Heaven Is Whatever You Make It?

A friend of mine told me the other day
That Heaven is whatever you make it.
But I had to correct him and speak out to say
Heaven is what Heaven is and you'll **have to** leave it or **take it.**

By his pronouncement of this unbackable view
It just showed his hardened heart
By not believing God when He said all things will be new
Including Heaven and Earth when eternity will start.

He gets **his** wisdom from the created beings
That **God Himself has made**
Who raise themselves up as wise men and kings.
But eventually their influence will fade

To another lost soul that thinks up some crap
Which **cannot** be found to be **a fact**
And lulls the lost sheep into taking a nap
So not to hear when someone tells them the truth that's lacked.

The Bible is true and is found to be sure.
It's **the very word of God Himself**.
God has given man's history and most thankfully the cure;
Which is faith in the Savior, which then brings mental health?

There are over 3,000 prophecies in the Bible and most have already
Come true
And almost one third of the Bible is prophetic;
And the ones that haven't yet are just waiting for their cue
Because the word of *God is kinetic.*

It's God's living Word, Christ Jesus in person
And He states: for most people **that fact won't be believed**.
Unfortunately, their idea of Heaven will definitely worsen
When they're on the outside ***because they were deceived.***

#49 Heaven Is **Whatever** You Make It?

My friend said, "Keep your mind open, and don't get stuck on one view"
But **your belief** doesn't make **a fact** change.
When that guy doing acid believed he could fly, out the window he flew.
Unfortunately, **10 stories** was way out of his range!

Or the guy who thought he could drink heavy and still drive home.
The truth is that was not the fact
Because what happened was obvious, like my intent in this poem,
His **LIFE ENDED** when that **BIG TREE** he smacked!

I hope, my friend, that you take **your** own advice
And keep **your** mind open while you search for God's truths.
God promises He'll show you it once, twice, and if need be...thrice.
But He'll still give you your choice - Heaven's freedom...or Hell's noose!

Rich Kovatch
5-08-01

#50 Are You Ready To Die?

You need to know the answer to
One of the top three questions I'm going to ask you;
And that is: Are You Ready To Die?
I said you need to know it and I'll tell you why.

I'll try to explain it simply, in terms familiar to all mankind.
With their knowledge of physics and math and astronomy, scientists
Think they can find
The answer to how life started, the how and the whys
From the clues they see on the Earth, in the waters and the skies.

The popular theory is that of the big bang.
And upon this assumption their presumptions do hang:
That the laws of the Universe have always been the same.
But can they answer from where all this matter came?

All matter comes from matter, a fact no one can disprove;
And energy can't be destroyed, lost or completely removed.
But it must change its form, like from friction into heat,
Unless it's a miracle - and only God can accomplish that feat.

Can life come from a non-living primordial soup?
Or does life come from life in a continual loop?
Has anyone, besides God, ever made an intelligent life form with the
Ability to reproduce?
Do you believe that a golden egg can come from a goose?

When you look at anything, there's _**always**_ **a design**.
They say: form follows function, it's not hard to follow that line.
It will accomplish the task the designer has intelligently programmed in.
And my friends, we humans in our flesh were made to decide about sin.

#50 Are You Ready To Die?

The second question is: Do you believe that there is sin
And do you know how it started and when it did begin?
What's the reason for death? Is there life afterwards?
Would you rather trust God or a world full of nerds?

I know these questions bring you right to the point of strong conviction.
Now please, just try to relax and try not to have a conniption.
I'm trying to get you to listen to the truth, not a lie.
<u>Your soul WILL again see life even after you die!</u>

The third question is: Do you really want to take that chance
And what proof do you base it on? You must...and already have taken a
Stance
On whether you deny God's existence and His requirements for seeing
Heaven.
Please use your mature adult mind and not one like you're still seven!

The best message I have for you is that you still have time
To come to your senses and it won't cost you a dime;
But it **WILL** determine **if** you'll live **for _the next eon_** in Heaven or lose out
While in Hell.
Can you wait to decide tomorrow? Will you still be here? Can't tell !!!

Rich Kovatch
5-15-01

#51 Are You **A Good** Witness?

Lord, am I a good witness of you?
Are you happy with the things I do?
Do I show others the love you've given me?
Am I letting you make me all I can be?

Am I patient and forgiving when others wrong me?
Is my response cheerful or do I have an unrighteous plea?
Do I complain as if I have some right?
Do I emit the light of day or the gloom of night?

Does my tone of voice attract the lost and confused?
Do I let it damped my spirit when I get abused?
Will my actions bring glory to you and make others take note?
Do I follow the advice and commandments of which Peter & James &
Paul wrote?

Do I apologize when I let my flesh win a battle?
Do I admit when I've goofed and deserve a good paddle?
Can I humble myself and take what I deserve?
Am I mature enough to gather up the nerve?

Am I lighting up the path that you have laid out?
Do I show my workmates what being a Christian is all about?
Will they be envious and wish they could have the same peace?
Will they come up to me and ask how to get their pains to cease?

Will they trust the advice I give if I tell them it's from you?
Will I be bold enough to speak out whether they're a gentile or a Jew?
Am I learned enough in your word to trust that you'll guide my tongue?
Will your love flow out graciously to encourage the old and the young?

God help me to participate in the Great Commission.
I feel like I'm a fisherman who can't wait to go fishin'
And be a fisher of men like you told your disciple Peter.
Because to me...in helping save a lost soul...there's nothing neater!

Rich Kovatch
6-1-01

#52 Are You Truly "Born Again"?

This question is not only for the lost sheep
But *for those who say* God's word they keep;
For those who say they practice religion, from Christianity to Zen.
The question is: **"Are you truly Born Again"?**

The practice of religion is just a deception
If you blindly follow a man or an organization's reflection
Of how they interpret the correct way to live your life.
Does it cause your mind to be constantly filled with strife?

Do you live to please the Lord, or a religion, or a man?
Will you make it to heaven by doing the best that you can?
Who guides your conscience, the Holy Spirit or *church rules*?
Does this guidance turn its followers into wise people or fools?

What truth do you follow and from *where* does it come?
Does it bring strong conviction or cause your mind to go numb?
When you sin do you feel sorry you've just done the Father wrong?
You see, conviction is the first sign you're singing the **"Born Again"** song!

The second sign is in understanding the concept of the cleansing of sins.
Of how it gets done and when it begins.
What had been the pattern throughout history and how it was changed
From a daily shedding of blood to Jesus' perfect sacrifice: into eternity it
Ranged.

Have you learned to trust what Jesus has done?
Do you believe His blood can cleanse the sins of everyone
If only they'll confess to the Father that they know they've screwed up,
Then He's promised to forgive all that have drank from His cup?

And **when Jesus said "to the Father"**, he meant God...*not a priest.*
I'm sorry to burst your bubble, but **religious organizations are** part of
The beast
Which is **described the revelation of Jesus Christ**. The last book of the
Bible.
I said I was sorry, but really I'm not, because *a real Christian's job is to
Tell the truth and* not try to *connival*

#52 Are You Truly "Born Again"?

Those that don't study *or even at least read* God's words of instruction
That **will lead** the truly **"Born Again"** to the truth...not to their
Destruction.
Those truly "Born Again" *will desire* instruction and holiness.
**If someone asks you if what your religion teaches *is the truth*, you
Won't say "*I guess*".**

Because the Holy Spirit will lead you unto **The** Truth through His **Word.**
But before it can be believed in it must be heard.
***That's why this poem is being composed; to lead you to explore
So you'll learn for yourself* not to follow a *"religious system"* any more.**

A **"Born Again"** spirit will follow the example the Bereans displayed;
Who studied the scriptures to test if what Paul had told them had
Already been laid
Down in the writings of the Old Testament as a shadow of the new way:
That *Jesus fulfilled the law* and it is now the Old Covenant. We have a
New Covenant today.

We now live under God's grace wherein we're covered by Christ's BLOOD.
We don't have to sacrifice bulls and goats anymore or worry about
Another flood
Because God's promises are true and He's said **"Believe In My Son"**
And that there's not a wide road to heaven, ***but it's a narrow one***.

*We will live by faith **in Jesus*** if we're in Abraham's clan
And we'll have *faith **in God's Word**, not in the Pope*, who's only a man;
Who was born into sin, ***thus not infallible, like he says,*** pride incredibly **high!**
And only JESUS was SINLESS, not Mary too, as **Catholicism teaches
these Two lies.**

There are many more that I could write down...and prove,
But I'll just urge you to ***get off your duff*** and get on the move;
Back onto the narrow road where our ***personal relationship with Jesus***
Won't dim;
Not the continuing deception of RELIGION...an **IDOL ITSELF**...if put
Before Him**!**

Rich Kovatch
7-21-2001

#53 ETERNAL SECURITY

There's a teaching going on that casts a doubt
About what the mission of Jesus was all about.
And unfortunately those that believe it commit blasphemy
Against our Lord and Saviour as you will shortly see.

The teaching is that you cannot be sure
That your eternal destiny in heaven is secure.
They call it the **"sin of presumption"** if you say   Cat. Catechism 1036;2005
That you will go to heaven instantly on your dying day.

They say that it's pride when you speak that phrase.
They say of the path to heaven, there are A **COUPLE** OF WAYS!
One is called purification in a place called **Purgatory**
Where people can still pray for your atonement. A likely story.
Cath. Cat.1030-1032; 1054; 1472

They also teach that you can go straight into the Father's arms
If you've lived a life that was full of good works and plenty of charms
Cath. Cat. 1472-79
That'll please Him enough to say something like "Come hither *my* **child**".
But these are two ways, for too many people, the Devil **has beguiled!**

First of all, the place called **Purgatory is not scriptural at all**.
It came from the Roman Catholic Church shortly after they picked up
The religious ball
And started to run with it as if **IT'S** WORD was infallible.
Unfortunately, too many of their teachings are full of bull.

At the Councils of Florence and Trent they made up this doctrine
Cath. Cat. 1031
And on the Devil's face, just then, was planted a huge grin
Because it was a small step away from completely trusting in God's Son
When He died on the cross after His last words attested to the fact that
"It *IS* Done".   John 19:30

#53 ETERNAL SECURITY

The other doctrine leads you to believe that enough good works

Cath. Cat. 1472-79

Will earn your way into Heaven. It is here the Devil's deception lurks.
It says in **Ephesians 2:9** that *good works* **WON'T** get you inside
And it warns you that if you think they will - THAT is but pride!

Huh, now THAT'S the sin of presumption
If you think you'll get into Heaven upon this assumption.
Good works are a sign that show you've been saved...
Not a means of salvation as if *your own road* you've just paved!

You can do nothing on your own that will get you in.   **Eph. 2:8-9**
The only things you are capable of are evil and sin.
But when one gets "Born Again" he starts learning to submit every
Moment to the Lord
And accepts the truth that you can only enter in on Jesus' accord.

PRIDE comes before the fall. The Bible does say   **Prov. 16:18; 1 Tim. 3:6**
That's why Lucifer was cast out of Heaven on that fateful day;
And *it's his main trick to keep you out too*
If you refuse to humble yourself 100% and accept what Jesus did for You!

Now let me tell you what God Himself has said
And I hope and pray that it will sink down deep into your head.
But it must also be planted and start growing in your hardened heart
So you, by yourself, will begin to study His Word and do your part.

Almost everyone knows what **John 3:16 says** and it cuts like a knife...
That whosoever **believes in Jesus shall** have everlasting life;
And **Hebrews 12:2** says **He's the finisher** of our faith for sure
So that's **not** something we're to doubt...our destiny is secure!

#53 ETERNAL SECURITY

The main word in **John 3:16** is BELIEVE!
We're not to fall for any tricks Satan has up his sleeve!
The word believe is a Verb, which means it's an action
That continues to grow and blossom to the Lord's satisfaction.

Remember, **HIS WILL IS THAT ALL SHOULD BE SAVED!**   Luke 1:71
He did not offer Himself as your Saviour so that opportunity should be
Waived!
He created you to fellowship forever with Him in a place without time!
But it must be done freely, of our own will, just **BELIEVE** it's a **free** Gift…
It **can't** cost you a dime!

A **FREE GIFT** is something that **cannot be paid for!**   Romans Chapter 5
All He wants you to do is answer when He knocks at your door.
It's a ***SLAP IN HIS FACE*** if you think YOU should HELP PAY!
That wouldn't be an action of BELIEVING Jesus paid the **FULL** PRICE that
Day!!!   1 Cor. 6:19-20; 7:20-24

Have you not read Hebrews 6:11-12 and **10:18-25 too?**
God's Word shows you EXACTLY what you are to THINK and DO!
BELIEVE, as an action daily that His Word is True… right to the "t"
When Jesus stated, "All that the Father has given me shall come to me".
                                                             John 6:37

Or have you read **Psalms 31:23-24?** These verses the Devil hates.
Read it closely, Will you dispute what it states?
For the Lord preserves the faithful and **rewards the PROUD DOER!**
Be of good courage & He'll strengthen your heart. **His Word is the cure!**

So **BELIEVE** that you're a child of God and He holds your fate.
Try reading your Bible…like **Colossians 2:8**
**Which _warns_ of philosophy and vain deceit after the _traditions_ of
men!**
TRUE FAITH & BELIEF in JESUS' WORK will stop you from ever doubting
Again!!!

                                                      Rich Kovatch
                                                      8-23-01

#54 EMOTIONS

Emotions are a special gift
That God has given to us **all.**
But there's one thing that I hear that has me *miffed*;
It's when preachers tell us not to trust them or we could **fall.**

I know that's true when your soul is *led*
Buy your flesh or even the world's **ways...**
But if it's God's Holy Spirit that keeps you *fed*
You'll be certain to do right all of your **days.**

For emotions touch us so deep *inside*
In a place where men are taught not to **go;**
That a man is strong if his feelings he can *hide*
And it's wrong to let his emotions **show.**

Why do you think God put in *us*
These feelings that flood our **mind?**
Could it be He uses them to cause a *fuss*
So His answers, *when we ask*, we'll be sure to find?

We are most special to God; His word does *say.*
He's put us above all His creation...we're His pride and **Joy!**
He still longs to touch us through this *way*
Like He so easily could when we were a young girl or **boy.**

But His word tells us our thoughts are to *mature*
And we should no longer think as children **do.**
When we surrender our wills to His ways our actions will stay *pure*
And He'll guide our emotions and pull us **through.**

If you look at the **Fruit of the Holy Spirit** you'll *see*
That **Love, Peace, Joy, Faith** and the like **are emotional powers.**
The expression of these gifts seems plenty good to *me*
With **Love** and **Faith** *being the two tallest* **towers**

That we can set our lamps of God's light *atop*
To shine so the world can see His **light;**
And that the trial and tribulation or persecution or terrorism <u>*can't stop*</u>
God's Will *from shinning* into the **darkest** hour *of your* **night.**

Rich Kovatch
11-11-01

#55 My Christmas Poem

The Christian world celebrates Christmas Day on December 25th
But here's the thing that has me miffed;
Is *this* day really so special that we should exchange gifts
To show how much we love each other and or to mend rifts?

Should we not show this love daily and the willingness to forgive?
Is that not the message and the way Christ showed us to live?
Do we really love more when we're reminded of **Jesus'** birth?
Aren't we aware of how much **each** and **every day** is worth?

We should see that these opportunities come all the time,
Unexpectedly and often without reason or rhyme.
When we live our lives open to *what God wants* us to see
He'll show us how to spread the gift He gave us for free.

God gave the world the gift of his own son to pay the price
Because nothing we can do on our own will suffice.
The penalty for sin is death, and we're all born with that debt.
And all which haven't accepted God's gift, ***don't understand*** their
*Salvation **yet***.

But the followers of Christ have accepted God's way
Thus, we celebrate Jesus' birth each year on this day.
Even though He wasn't born that late in the year
This day has been chosen to spread goodwill and cheer.

Through these acts of love and kindness we hope to spread the news
How God *lives in us*, foretold in the written history of the Jews.
Israel was God's chosen nation **to show the world** His word.
Christians are those throughout the world who have **understood** and
Heard

God knocking on the door to our hearts of stone
When He told us He didn't desire us to go through this life alone.
He told us to read & study the *Holy Bible* **so we'll know** that when we die
We'll *ALL* be with Him forever in Heaven without ever doubting why!

Rich Kovatch
12-25-01

#56 The Intentional Will of God

Most Christians know that the Intentional Will of God is that every man
Should be saved;
But that won't happen, He's told us all, because His offer by most will be
Waived.
So does that mean that God is evil to let so many end up in Hell?
The answer is deep and multi-layered but I hope to explain it well.

God has a perfect plan laid out for all if we'll just heed His voice,
But all too often and most every day, we'll make a wrong choice.
And what this brings is pain and misery and sickness, death and sorrow
That makes too many lose their faith and wonder if God will be with
Them tomorrow.

And when one starts to walk the path that turns them from our Lord,
He allows things to happen, some not so pretty, that brings on great
Discord.
When mankind's pride comes before God's wisdom, things always go
Downhill.
He allows things to happen because, but <u>at some point</u>, **we'll all** have to
Stop and be still.

And at that point is when God allows our wills to make the call;
To cry out to God for guidance & help or to decide we'll continue our fall.
His word does say that we have a choice, and He will honor it truly.
***A Christian <u>will receive the power</u> to turn to Him* ...but the unrighteous
Will get more unruly.**

Thus; **God's ULTIMATE WILL** <u>*will coincide*</u> with **our own will**, that we'll
Finish the course we take.
The sad thing is that the lost don't see that forever in Hell might be at
Stake?
They've put their own will ahead of their own maker's so to state that
They're in control
They've been deceived by the great deceiver and the price was their
Very soul.

#56 The Intentional Will of God

Well that's enough; I've given the warning, now I should get back on track
To explain God's will and grace by exposing the Devil's subtle attack.
Satan uses our mistakes to confuse our minds so for an answer we're at
A loss.
But the one thing he cannot undo is Jesus' resurrection after the cross.

For His death on the cross paid the price for our sins so we can know for
Sure
That though we stumble and fall we know that in God's eyes we're still
Pure
Because we'll be led to confess our sins to Him and He's sure to give us
His best
And cast them into the **Sea of Forgetfulness**...which is as far as the east
Is from the west.

There's another will of God that's at work that I must try to explain;
His *new* and *better* covenant - with *GRACE - will* cover us until His
Understanding we gain.
He allows us to make many, many mistakes, as children often do.
I know that sounds a lot like me. Does it also sound like you?

The one thing that we must not forget is that **the law is still intact**
And when we go against God's perfect ways, **our bodies will still react**
Because it does not say that flesh and blood will inherit God's Kingdom
Of Heaven.
We all know that our bodies have sinned and are very full of leaven.

Thus they will corrode and decay and death is the penalty of sin;
But we all know that when the body dies is when our promised life will
Begin
In a resurrected body without spot or blemish; the bride of our messiah
Jesus
That will last forever in the new Heaven and on a new Earth that will
Most certainly please us!

#56 The Intentional Will of God

It is not **God's INTENTIONAL WILL** that we get sick, but it is His
CIRCUMSTANTIAL one
Because He has to stay true to His words of cause and effect of just what
Sin has done.
It has brought a curse upon generations of men from Adam right on
Down
To you and me and everyone that lives. The Law makes everyone frown.

Remember though, this curse can be broken when one turns from his
Wicked ways
And follows God's chosen path for us all of our live-long days.
If we follow the Spirit and not the world, we'll all be better off.
The Devil tries to pervert this truth and does cause many to scoff.

The health and wealth doctrines that many teach are not the truth we
Live.
It's so obvious for us to see that this bucket of false hopes leaks like a
Sieve.
Yes, if we'd live perfect lives as Jesus did, we'd probably have a good
Chance
To be healthy and wealthy and have all the gifts of the Holy Spirit, like
When the apostles took their stance.

But do you remember where their stances for Jesus took them all,
Without fail?
They were all martyred and killed; for the testimony of Jesus'
Resurrection they did hail!
For this is **God's ULTIMATE WILL** for all believers; that you give up your
Own life
Whatever it brings, be it sickness or poverty or agony and strife!

#56 The Intentional Will of God

Now, this reality that we live in today shows another will of Christ our
King;
And that's His **ULTIMATE WILL** that will not fail as we ran our race He'll
Bring
Us through our wondering ways, like he did for Israel in their desert
Years
We'll find God's true ways as we cry out in tears.

We shouldn't condemn someone who's lost and confused
Just because for now our good advice they've refused
And continue to walk down the path that looks likes destruction
For one day, if they're predestined, they'll follow **God's ULTIMATE WILL's
Instruction**

And find their way back into God's sheepfold and care.
**They'll discover God's grace and forgiveness and be amazed how He
Could bare**
The sins they committed in defiance to His lead
They'll see that they were full of their own pride, selfishness and greed.

Let us live by the Spirit of God **as Jesus did, no matter what it brings.**
Whether rich or poor, **or whatever condition he's in, the believer
Always sings
The praises of God and the eternal life in His son
And the victory over sin that Jesus' ministry has won!**

Rich Kovatch
3-29-02

#57 A Wonderful Ride

(Retirement Gift requested from my mom as helper for 25+ years

For Barbara Davis: "Special Education" Bus Driver – Mishawaka, In.)

There once was a woman who answered the call
Too be a bus driver for **"Special kids"** who couldn't stand tall
All by themselves without a little encouragement and help;
Which quite often was difficult and caused them to yelp!

She was there to take on the task at hand.
Oh, if there'd only be MORE like her in this blessed land.
There'd be such a spirit of giving with *unselfishness* and *unconditional*
Love
That the whole world would see that it must come from God above!

To be able to deal with their **"handicaps"**, as *some* people say,
As not such a nuisance, *but they just move in a special way.*
Kids that couldn't walk right, or talk right or even think straight;
She knew HOW to get them to strive and achieve using that **"special"**
Bait.

I'm SURE many of them could SEE the LOVE SHE HAD for them,
For when they struggled she would only OFFER HELP – NOT CONDEMN
Since it wasn't their faults they needed special care.
It was **in this woman's heart to make sure SHE WAS THERE!**

For **thirty years** this scenario **went on** and **on**;
She'd have to get up early, way before dawn
Whether it was warm out and dry or cold and snowy that morning
Not knowing what circumstances that day was forewarning.

#57 A Wonderful Ride

Like the day she rescued a woman from certain doom
Sitting in her car on the railroad tracks, dazed and confused with a
Child in her womb.
She quickly saw that it was UP TO HER
So out of the bus she moved like a blur!

This one incident might have gotten much publicity
But her **REAL PURPOSE** has much more simplicity;
Take the *"Special kids"* to and from school as their guide.
After thirty years all we can say is: **"What a Wonderful Ride"**!

P.s. **This poem** was **requested** by your **long-time equally dedicated** and
Loving assistant...I **KNOW** for sure first hand – she's *my mother*!
ANNE KOVATCH

Rich Kovatch
5-25-02

#58 ABSENCE MAKES THE HEART...

Absence makes the heart grow fonder...
Or would it make the flesh to wonder?
That's the question that was ahead to be answered;
Whether my heart had cells that would rebel and grow cancered.

The world has so many temptations that constantly pull
Our attention away from our loved ones so that love might fade dull.
The Devil knows exactly what **buttons in me to push;**
Pretty faces, revealing figures, and the occasional nice tush.

But that's really no different than every other day.
I thank God for the strength to ignore what his demons say.
He uses the same old tricks, with the distance his ace in the hole,
But I never fail to forget to which girl I've committed my soul.

The one thing the distance does is make me long dearly and strong
To be close to my wife and hold her near me all the night long;
Just to be near to my mate and hear her voice in my ear
So the last words I hear at night are " I LOVE YOU, MY DEAR! "

Rich Kovatch
11-24-2002

#59 VANITY: WOW!

Vanity: Wow! What a powerful word.
There's hardly another that's ever been heard.
It's the driving force on that wide road to Hell.
Such an intriguing allure it's not at all a hard sell.

Who's doing the selling and who's eating the pies?
Are you aware of who's telling you the lies?
Have you had good instruction and did you take it to heart?
I hope that this poem's not your start!

But even if it is, I'll thank God for that.
That may be why He told me to write it, so at this table I sat.
It's two o'clock in the morning. January first, 2003
After just watching on T.V. a disturbing movie.

"The Devil's Advocate" kept my attention at a peak,
The underlying question it asked was **"What do you seek?"**
Only a Hollywood movie, so it wasn't one hundred percent real
But it did show the danger of having a misguided zeal!

The Devil's so cleaver that you must learn to defend
Your thoughts and your mind and most surely you're rear end.
He wanders the Earth like a roaring lion seeking whomever he can to
Devour.
Sorry to say it's all of us humans who haven't connected to God's
power!

That's the power to save us from eternal damnation.
The first step is realizing that we each need salvation;
That we're not our own gods and we can't make our own rules.
All of you that don't look past your body's end are right now the Devil's
Fools.

God breathed His spirit into each one of us upon our birth.
Have you ever thought for one second how much that gift is worth?
The chance to live forever without worry or fear!
You know, the truth is the truth so you'd better get it in gear.

#59 **VANITY:** WOW!

If you don't believe in an afterlife you're just rolling the dice.
The stakes are enormous so you'd better think twice!
God's given us His creation, a conscience and the Bible in black and White.
And it plainly states that for *your soul* the Devil does fight!

Vanity: Watch out! It's the most dangerous trait
That only leads to destruction when the true way is straight!
It might do you good to look up its definition.
If you're too lazy or don't care to you're making the Devil grin!

That's vanity in itself...thinking that you know it all.
Tell me...do you know exactly what caused the Devil to fall?
It was vanity my dear person...thought he was #1.
He wanted to be worshipped; take the place of God's Son.

Vanity and pride, they go hand in hand.
Both make you look inward, makes you feel like a grand.
But both bring destruction, disunity and hate.
Causes one to desire what's on another one's plate.

I'll tell you the right way to look...and that's out.
See what's in need and make it come about.
A more powerful word than vanity is Love. For sure.
Because when all's said and done, **vanity will end but Love will endure!**

Rich Kovatch
1-1-2003

#60 Touched by Love

We're touched by love in many ways
But **sometimes we don't see it through the thick haze**
That the world and the devil put over our eyes.
Thank God it starts to clear up with our tears and our cries.

We feel the emotion and react as we do
In some ways that are old and some that are new.
Some give of themselves until it hurts.
And with these reactions our destiny flirts.

They mold us into the persons we desire to be
Which are as unique as the alphabet from A to Z.
Put together in ways that are one of a kinds
And we walk the paths that each one finds.

God is always there no matter which ones we choose;
Whether this love brings us happiness or gives us the blues.
And it doesn't really matter how each moment unwinds;
Of our true inner character they're the defining signs.

Do we have Gods' heart to feel love and joy?
Can we give what is needed, be it to a girl or a boy?
Are we hindered and made fun of if we well up with tears?
If you are you might consider finding a new set of peers.

There's nothing wrong with feeling your heart as it is.
It is what it is, your God given choice; not depending on your years.
To be young or old is not the issue at hand.
It's to look forward to see where your next step will land.

Is it closer to God with a heart of compassion?
What is the legacy you wish to fashion?
When He calls you to finish your time on earth,
You'll find out for eternity just what each moment was worth!

Rich Kovatch
2-13-05

#61 I Hate My LIfe
(**MATURE** READERS _ONLY_)

This is the last poem I shall ever write
'Cause with this rejection I just cannot fight.
I can't win for losin', and I can't handle boozing'.
So my question is...what path I'll be choosin'.

I've got _no one to love_...can't give _what_ I need.
My wife **doesn't give enough of a shit** that she'll **even care to read**
This **fucked up note** that won't even come close
Of telling _how broken my life is; it's so damned morose._

She _seduced_ me into caring about her weak, fucked up head
When she _used to be_ giving and **willing** to be _free_ in _bed._
Now she's _so lost in confusion_ I can't even come near
To the woman I've loved so long and so dear.

Well, it's too late now for her to make amends;
But if she really loved me she wouldn't have _made me_ dep_end_
On my **humanly ability** to withstand the _abuse_
Of her **stifling my spirit** and killing my drive..._it felt like a noose!_

Kept stalling my momentum...puttin' shit in my way.
Moved out here to Vegas...still got **worse** every day!
No sense of **teamwork** or what **a Godly wife** should do.
Tried telling her with poems numbering More than 52!

But it goes back to _her refusal_ to become "_one_" with me
Like how a _real_ God loving marriage should be!
So now maybe she'll go back and read my soul
Which I've _articulated_ so carefully; an open spirit would get full

#61 I Hate My LIfe

(**MATURE** READERS _ONLY_)

Of the sense that _I needed_ to have _a helper_ to live.
All she had to do _was allow me to give_
My Love which _I wanted to_ do all of the **time.**
She has _no idea_ of what God wanted me to give her of mine!

My time, and attention, and help, and support, and _direction_ . . .
All went down the shitter when she _neglected_ my _erection_
Night after _night_, and _year_ after _year_.
I had **no** release... drugs **didn't** do it; and I couldn't even cry out a
Good tear!
 (I **wonder** if she'll even **read this** after a year?)

I couldn't be perfect in how I dealt with my hand.
Unfortunately for Ronda I could no longer stand

That fact that I had _good_ things to say . . . _**but no one**_

**Would listen**.
I was too weak! So now, from this world...
I'm now Missin'.
                    (like anyone even gives a shit!)

Rich Kovatch
6-29-2007

#62 GOD IS Wise…Me..? Not So

I thank God for being so persistent
Giving me *His words* to which I'm *so* **resistant.**
As always when sin raises up its ugly head…
God's just showing me a part of me that's not yet dead.

Once again, I can see the effects of sin;
Self-pity, deflection and desperation from focusing within;
While my mouth speaks out as if somehow justified
That I'm above the place where I shouldn't be tried.

My place is to do what God's called me to do.
And that my dear is first and foremost to worship Him
By loving you!
He keeps telling me what a marriage love is to be.
I'm so sorry I'm not always the light you're supposed to see!

I'm asking you for forgiveness as I act out **my carnal nature.**
But the one thing I'm thankfully confident in for sure
Is that you know I'm trying to do what's right
And I'm not happy when we're in an unresolved fight.

Gods' Spirit impels me to surrender all to Him;
Quell the fires that tempt me to act upon a whim.
Love is to be directed outwardly to show Gods' will.
My life's not about me…I don't always remember that still!

Thank God for a new beginning…every morning and day.
I wake up each morning asking God to direct what I say.
I thank God for giving me the desire to know His leads;
To read and listen and ***watch His glory strip away*** my fleshly
Natures' deeds!

Rich Kovatch
1-17-2009

#63 REJECTED

I *finally understand why* I'm married to
Someone who makes me *so blue*,
Who year after year has rejected my **Love** and help and care;
To get a taste of what God feels **with an understanding** for me that
Had come *too rare*.

We're both constantly diss'd, and abused, and misunderstood.
She doesn't see we're always looking out for her good,
Having to implement a new twist daily
To communicate **Love** to one who sees thru the glass so palely.

She's selfish, short-sighted and shows little fear,
Not realizing that we long to walk with her so near
Where **God's heart** is reflected without a distorting motion,
Glowing pure **Love** and compassion and long-suffering, with the notion

That the day *will* arrive when I will *finally see*
The *real* Godly woman *He's been guiding her to be*,
Wanting to share the **Love He's giving her that she's been keeping hidden**,
After her heart is finally broken, seeing that in all my efforts - I also
Wasn't kiddin'.

We've given our lives as a sacrifice with the hope that one day
We'll hear the confession, face to face, in which she'll say
She's a "TRUE BELIEVER" who's "working out" her walk and longs for
The **Friendship**
And communion with the one who longs to satisfy her soul and walk
Hip To hip

Down the narrow path, next to and *along with me*, that leads to a life
That will *glorify the Father* of the husband, who's finally got the wife
God foreknew before the first time I had ever seen her,
Experiencing the Holy Marriage the Father ordained to occur.

An eternal kinship where us *two have become one*,
An example of the plan of *redemption* achieved by God's son.
Our marriage a working model of Jesus' union with the church;
A secure commitment with an unbreakable bond *of Love* on which it
Does perch.

Rich Kovatch
7-17-09 3:00 a.m.

#64 THE GIFT

'Tis the time of year, the most wonderful season
When hearts are touched by friends and families, and here's the reason;
Down deep inside *there's a longing to give*
A token of *Love for remembrance that there's a reason to live.*

Real Brotherhood happens when thoughts turn outward and *we think Of others*;
First towards our own families, our moms, dads, sisters and brothers.
But many think of friends and strangers too
And want to touch the downtrodden whose **hearts are blue.**

This *Love is kind* and the world needs much more.
This *g I v I n g o f h o p e* **comes from the very core**
Of a heart that feels it's *connected somehow* **to all**
By a **G**od who *is said to have* **destroyed the wall**

That **divides m**an against **m**an and **H**im from a world that's **blind.**
This **special** season is when **the lost** can **find**
The *ULTIMATE Love gift* that brings to life
The truth that **G**od's calling out to embrace **H**is wife.

This poem might seem to be changing its focus
But that last line was given on purpose to poke us
To realize there's a Love above all that can be shown *only in Marriage.*
If you *have it* there's *unquestionable* faith … if you don't … disparage!

The bond that's between a couple in **Love**
Has strength and **commitment** that will **always rise above**
Any trouble or strife that the world can produce;
Where the devil or the flesh will try to reduce

The relationship to the point where the ties get cut,
And bring pain and agony like a hard kick in the gut.
Seems like all hope is lost and no answers to be found;
Like their spirits will be separated forever and to hell they are bound!

#64 THE GIFT

But God's Love is so forgiving, so true and secure
That He's promised, *only to His virgin wife*, that *you* will endure,
And survive and be fruitful and even grow as it groans;
And even produce kind of like little baby clones!

Because **when children *are taught* and *experience its* ways**
They'll see and ***believe*** and ***will replicate that love*** during their days
In clone-like fashion, though not exactly the same,
Because only God created the rules, but at least be in the game.

The rules were given in the Old Testament days
When He gave promises, with conditions, of the ways
His bride, Israel, was to fulfill her chores…
Without idolatry or acting like whores!

Now, Israel became God's chosen race
So He could *show* the world *His grace.*
Israel means *"the prince that prevailed with God"*, you know.
Sorry, the nation of Israel did not follow the *right* way to go!

It became the *"harlot"* in God's own words written in His **"Good Book"**,
And worshipped idols and became ***"Babylon"***, if you take the time to
Look,
And study His truth with a heart that's not hardened
And discover the real "Israel" that He has pardoned.

The Israel that prevailed is **the *one with the Spirit***
That believes God provided the sacrifice that would endear it
Right next to His **heart,** forever without fail;
The perfect price paid for the demanded bail!

That requirement was performed without blemish or spot
And **the nation of Israel *in the flesh*** was not
The wife He demanded, with perfection being done,
But He said from the Tribe of Judah He'd provide *"The One".*

#64 THE GIFT

That *"One"* is **Jesus, The Lamb of God** in the flesh that came.
The only possible perfection, God himself, who's one in the same ! ! !
"One" **who cannot lie,** or **deceive** or removed
The conditions **He** set for **His** wife to be soothed

In **His** company in heaven, forever without sin
Because only in **Jesus He** gave her the power to win
The battle of deception in which the **D**evil wants us to ride
On a wide road to heaven thinking it takes just being **"*good*" enough...**
But that is just *pride*

By saying to God - I'll make my own rules
To get to the place of perfection **by using my own tools,**
And ignoring the fact that **God** gave us so many examples, like the story
Of **R**uth,
And of course JESUS - who's the *only* **Way, The Life** and **The Truth ! ! !**

Rich Kovatch
11-27-09

#65 Rose's 25th Birthday

Twenty five years ago, we remember the most glorious day.
When you were born **God** started showing us **"the way"**
To learn what life and love are all about...
That we were given **a most special gift** we'd cherish and tout

As a **rose blossom of love** being proof of how **God** does display
That love conquers all even when parents get in the way.
Our *perfect* and *personal example* of how *God holds us all in His hand*
While we were learning by falling and getting up again to stand.

Somehow by **God's grace** you've grown up exceeding what our hopes
Could even imaging could ever come out of such a pair of such dopes
Who were so selfish and unfocused on pleasing our Lord
It even led to our divorce because of the tongues two-edged sword.

But now resurrected & reconciled, **much good fruit of His Spirit is appearing.**
The **peace of mind** that occurs as maturity quickly is nearing.
And I'm speaking of our mindset that keeps faith in hard times...
Like now, when I used to bring home dollar bills, but now it's mostly **Dimes!**

That's change in my pocket just like our President did promise.
We're learning to trust only in **Jesus** & not verbalize the attitude of Thomas
Who doubted **Jesus'** return because his, and also our carnal mind, could
Not even conceive.
A new life awaits us all and **is here and now** if we'd only believe!

Because faith & belief don't need to be seen in this carnal, Earthly World
To be true.
That's why **Love is** a **Spirit**...separate from whatever my flesh may do.
Our flesh finds faults that are so *easy to see,*
Especially when it's usually with someone else...**AND NOT ME!**

But when **Love** truly is given to you by **God** himself which is HIMSELF.
The fruit of the Spirit will flow out with such abundant wealth.
Once again a **Jesus** lead family will grow up learning in life that truth
Never fails.
Jesus... "The Way, The Truth, and The Life" *paid* for ALL SINS...and *ALL*
The *small details!!!*

Rich Kovatch   6-7-11

#66 Happy Birthday Tammi

Happy birthday Tammi
You've hit the big 5-0!
I hope that you surely see
God has for you many more to go.

One thing He wants me to make clear
Is where His promise for that is written.
Right off the get-go He said to stay near
In His garden so you won't be smitten

With pain and suffering, if you choose to eat
From the one wrong tree of knowledge
That doesn't have everlasting life as its treat
But will put your butt smack in the fridge

So to make your heart cold for your mate Adam
And desire to take his place as the head
Of the union Jesus designed when you had' im
Right next to your side when you both were fed

From the rest of the trees in the Garden of Eden
Which He supplied to give health to your mind
If you trust in His words to have faith indeed in
His plan to fill the earth with only seed of His kind.

He said every tree gives only fruit that reproduces
Exactly what it was given to offer us.
And when it's squeezed it will squirt out its juices;
Words, either sweet or rotten, leading us to praise or cuss

Our situation we walk into of our own choice
Since He gave us our own will to walk where we see fit;
Either in the light where we can hear His voice
Or into darkness *where we're sure to fall into the pit*

#66 Happy Birthday Tammi

Of Hell which is separation from His guidance and we get on a roll
Because of pride or arrogance in our own deception
That we know what's best for us and we're in control
Of the path that leads to the wedding reception

In Heaven where the party will go on forever,
When we're His bride and enjoying health and companionship,
Where His promise is that He'll never sever
The bond He holds with our hand so that whenever we trip

He's promised to not let go if we stumble and fall.
We may get cut and bleed profusely
But He has His Band-Aids ready the moment we call
When we realize we're the ones who are hanging on too loosely!

The health and good life He offers will come from words of a friend
When they encourage this confession of total dependence
Because they see where our misguided path will end...
Right back to the place where we'll realize only faith in Him makes
Sense.

HE LOVES US ALL; **WE'RE ALL CHILDREN OF GOD!**
SOME WHO **WALK CLOSELY**, AND **SOME** WHO **RUN WILD!**
BUT EVENTUALLY HE'LL GIVE US ALL THAT SWEET NOD
OF **ACCEPTANCE** BACK INTO HIS GARDEN AS **HIS FORGIVEN CHILD ! ! !**

Rich Kovatch
7-8-11

#67 Depression

What a sad state that's holding me.
I'm in so deep it's hard to see
Where I'm to turn or where to run.
I often wish **my life** was done.

Because then I'd be free to show my love
To the only one who understands - God above;
Who'd accept the way I allow my love to show
Without always hearing the answer - **NO!**

The question I'd ask Him is "**While on Earth**, was I also **then** free
To share the love that was inside of me
By offering myself to someone I intimately know
Would _not_ return it back so we'd _both_ continue to grow?"

That's funny that this idea is on my mind
Because in His word is where I find
That His secrets He's hid on how love works   Prov. 25:2
Is at every turn in this life's endless quirks.   Matt. 5:7

No matter what I do or what I see
The trial or pressure that comes upon me
Always **has** **_hope_** of a brighter end.
The silver lining He never fails to send

Because that's how I grow. And so does my love for God
Perpetually covering my woes and sins of this bod,
Which for some reason just won't go away.   Rom. 7:14-25
I'm sure to step in more crap today!

That crap that always makes my next step slip
Is that I've failed to keep a really tight grip
On the law of reciprocity in which this world is set...   Gal. 6:6-10
And that is - what you sow...you'll surely get.

#67 D e p r e s s i o n

Jesus didn't come to destroy the law.   Matt. 5:17
It's just the way to overcome it, He always saw   Matt. 5:19
Because he listened to the Holy Spirit that was **within** him.
To always do right and never sin!   Matt. 7:24

Thus he reaped the fruits the Father knew.   Matt. 7:20
He ate only from the tree the garden grew   Gen.3:22-24
That gives eternal life inside the place called Eden
Where 12 trees that bear monthly fruit of which I'm to be feed'n. Rev. 22:2

The fruit of the Spirit is *__always good__*,   Gal. 5:22-23
Not to be burned up like hay, stubble and wood
Which is the rotten fruit of the word without His truth   2 Cor. 3:6
Like Israel of old and today's false church that's still in its youth

And hasn't matured to see God's plan...   1 John 2:1-**12**
That *His WILL* is to save *e-v-e-r-y* man ! ! !
Because **reproofs** of **instruction** *__a-r-e the way of life__*   **Prov. 6:23**
Our spiritual character *__only grows through this__* trouble and strife

Just as *my* understanding *__of God's__* does. The story's been told
In the lives that we've lived and Israel of old
That constantly roamed from the flock that God gave
To Jesus, to shepherd over, *because they wouldn't behave!*

Like dumb sheep lead to slaughter, **blindly lead in deception**
They followed their evil hearts, where these sins found conception.
Foolishly selfish and prideful we all want to be boss
Only to realize this only leads to great loss.   2 Peter 3:16

A new mindset we're told is what is to be framed
So **"a child of God"** is what we'll be named
After the old is burned out and the new one grows strong
When we realize He was right and us surely wrong!

#67 Depression

Depression I now see can be broken apart
If I keep His commandments tied close to my heart.
It's just de press **ion** - the **"age"**
Of this corruptible body that has my new spirit in a cage.

The world, my flesh and the Devil - this triune false god
Tries to keep me walking, like Cain, through the land of Nod
With the mark on my head that to die which I deserved.   Gen. 4:15
But *through Christ's blood* I now *know* *I'm reserved*

To be forgiven seven times seventy. To *God's promise* I do hold Matt. 18:22
Because in every book in the bible that's the story I'm told.
God's mercy is endless and shows me exceedingly **His GRACE**. Matt. 9:13
David wrote, to those who could hear, this is certainly the case.   Ps.100
(See **All** mercy verses. **Selah**)

God's judgments are **righteous**. *Their purpose is pure*.
He's promised His blood covers *all* sins of the world for sure   **1 John 2:2**
Including my doubts when His promises I find hard to trust   1 John 3:20
That He'll raise up my soul when my body returns to the dust.   Gen. 3:19

This is the "GOOD NEWS" that Jesus and the apostles *did teach:*
That *all* men *will* be saved *is* what we're to preach.
To love our enemies *until* they finally repent.   2 Peter 3:9
To draw *all* men to our Father is **the reason Jesus was sent** !!!
John 12:32

Rich Kovatch
7- 9 -11

#68 The Human Race

Dear Lord, my God! What have you done?   **T**
Put us in a world to make us run   **H**
A race that never seems to end   **E**
With trouble lurking around every bend.

No matter how fast I run the race   **H**
I always get the nasty taste   **U**
Of bitter defeat at every turn   **M**
When I discover there's a new lesson yet to learn.   **A**
        N

It seems just when I've passed the grade
I see another mistake that I just made.
It's like you change the next challenge I thought
I was ready to conquer, but your reigns just got taught

And turned my head for something different to seek.   **R**
It's only your way of keeping me meek   **A**
So I don't get too proud and haughty   **C**
And do or say something mean or naughty.   **E**

It's as though my race is through quick sand.
The harder I struggle, the deeper I land
In the muck and mire that makes me think
I'd better keep my eyes wide open and never blink.

That's a trick of the Devil to wear me out
So I'll get disgusted and start to pout,
Which only brings my thoughts inward
And makes me think I'm a big stinky turd!

It's here where you always bring me back in line
And tell me not to fuss and whine
And give me the power to deal and cope
Without having to turn to porn or dope!

#68 The Human Race

It breaks my heart because that's what I'd prefer   **T**
In my carnal nature to be the cure   **H**
Since I've used it so long to be the tool   **E**
To tell you you're not in charge...but I'm to rule!

I used it to bring me comfort from pain   **H**
But inside I really always wanted you to reign   **U**
Over my thought patterns that I knew led to death.   **M**
I thank God you kept me away from Meth.   **A**
        N

Or any harder drug that would have made
The price must costlier that would have had to been paid
By Jesus, of course, but by me in this skin.
And not only me but also my kin;

Which are my sister and brothers, child, father and mother.   **R**
Not only this bloodline, but there is another;   **A**
My neighbors and friends and strangers on the street.   **C**
I know it would have changed the way I would greet.   **E**

Because sin never stops with only one soul.
It always spreads to make much higher the toll.
Did God put me here to burden the world?
NO! He used them so this man's soul would be pearled.

Like an oyster whose irritation God turns into a precious stone;
No man was put here to run the race alone!
We are God's *HUMAN RACE* and He's promised not to forsake
The least of His children and the price it would take

To conquer over death, which is the picture He shows;
That a seed must be <u>buried</u> and <u>die</u> before it comes back and grows
As a brand new creation God foreknew with an eternal life
With Jesus as the bridegroom and *each human* His wife!

It's the Devil that seeks to stone the heart.
To make the blind cause division: to say some must part
And go to a hell forever because the victory Christ did not win.
Oh LORD, please let all know - that's the **MINDSET OF SIN ! ! !**

Rich Kovatch   7-11-11

#69 What the Hell!

Again, today crap hit the fan.
I just got up to seek your plan.
Got stabbed in the heart, it hurt like hell.
I felt like quitting, and then you tell

Me right on time by my radio.
Felt like showing vengeance...but you said **NO!**   Rom. 12:19
A different station than the normal one.
I thank you that I don't own a gun!

I might have used it on myself
Had you not brought my mind back to mental health.
It'd have been the easy way out to end this day
But again you chose to show me your way.

So many words that fill my head
That could never come out if I were dead.
But still it seems they fall on deaf ears
Since they've been coming out for over 13 years!

<u>I know they're really for my own good</u>
Because only I take them to heart...*maybe I should*
Just write them down in a diary
So only **you** and **I**'d be the ones who see

The violent struggle between light and dark.
But my character is like my Chihuahua's, I need to bark
At the things I see that I don't like.
Feel like I'm just putting my finger in the hole in the dike

Trying to hold back the flood I fear
That could destroy the ones I love so dear.
But here is where I've got it wrong...
It's you who's built the dam so strong

#69 What the Hell!

But allows some *cleansed* **water** to filter through
To *see* how I'd *react* and what I'd do.
Instead of letting this *pure* **water** wash my soul,
I misinterpret its purpose and it takes a great toll

On the energy you provide me new every morn.   Lam.3:21-22
I feel like your prophet that needs to warn
My wife and family and whatever friend
Will listen to the message that we're near the end

Of this evil age where mankind won't see   1 John 2:9
That in your sheepfold is the only safe place to be.
I see the signs you told me to look out for.   Matt.24
It's time to enter your ark before you close the door.   Gen.7:16

You promised never again to destroy the world with a flood.   Gen.9:11
Put a rainbow in the sky and promised to save all with your blood
                                                    Gen. 9:13
To those who believe in our Messiah - your Son
That pray for the **redemption of *all* souls** and ***teach others*** - it's been
Done!   John 3:16

Those who still walk in darkness - picture old testament Israel
Don't give hope to the lost world - they preach eternal fire of Hell.
                                        James 1:20, 3:6, 3:10
Like the threat of the *"new way"* Jesus taught, today's false church lives
In pride
And seeks to kill and destroy all who aren't on their side.   James 3:8-10

Their understanding is still waning,
That we're in the days of the latter raining.
Agape love in their hearts ***is still darkened***.   **1 John**
To our <u>command</u> to *<u>love</u> <u>all</u>* - they haven't harkened.   2 John: 6, 9

#69 What the Hell!

I've been told these poems go on way too long.
But people, listen! You've got to be strong
And not close your mind and ears because you're lazy and weak.
Remember, as your power fades - His is hitting its peak!   2 Cor. 12:9

So I pray today's the day God does in you His thing   1Cor. 2:10
So you along with me will be truly able to sing   1 John 2:2
The praises of Jesus' finished work on the cross   John 17:4 , 1Cor. 2:14
And the white sepulchre **over your true heart of gold** got cleansed of
More dross!

Rich Kovatch
7-12-11

#70 The Devil Redeemed

I started to write this poem the other morn
But it turned out the false church was who I did warn
Of how the lack of love and faith destroys,
And a few of the wiles the Devil employs.

Here's what God has shown this man.
The deep, deep truth of His well thought out plan.
The Devil - *which is only the spirit of unbelief*
Will be redeemed in the end too! What a relief!

The concept in all is not hard to follow,
But for the un - "born again" *impossible to swallow*.
Because to be **"born again"** means **"Truth and Spirit"** now reigns in One's mind
And the Kingdom of Heaven is now much easier to find!

Jesus came to forgive sinners...that's one and all!
He puts all *into darkness* until the moment we repent and to Him we call.
This *ultimate darkness* for most will be *when they die*
And realize the lives they lived were obviously a lie.

We'll all hit the place where we'll fall on our face
And cry out to God for **His MERCY** and **GRACE**.
The true church are the ones to whom God's "appointed time" was here
And with **AGAPE LOVE** for our enemies **destroy the gates** of their *sin of fear.*

Which is UNBELIEF that Jesus' blood will not cover their sin.
What? The **"ALL** KNOWING, **ALL** PRESENT, **ALL** POWERFUL creator is **not**
Strong enough to win
The battle with Satan - *victory for just only a few ? ? ?*
I just told you that from the beginning - the end... **God knew.**

Paul warned that the *darkened mind* will see
This truth as an excuse to let sin - just be.
But to those - to whom He's revealed to - knows why sin has its place...
It's to show God's character to how He responds with GREAT GRACE!

#70 The Devil Redeemed

Grace gives **_us_** power to give sinners what they don't deserve.
Jesus taught us not to condemn and keep judgment in reserve
Because daily we sin, Paul said he did too,
And it only takes one to get thrown into

The **"Fire of Hell"** if ones sins aren't confessed.
Trouble is - what this phrase means hasn't been put to the test
By those who want vengeance against all who aren't yet saved...
Like the publican who _prayed_ and **had pride** _but_ <u>Jesus</u> _said_ **misbehaved.**

This **"Fire of Hell"** is God dipping us in conviction to clean out some
Dross.
He's made us, each one, exactly how He planned. He's the potter and
The boss.
He knows just how to mold us, and how long it will take,
How many times to dip us, and how long we should bake

Till we become the _"new creation"_ He planned for from the start.
He's continually promised in the Old Testament He'd give us a _"new_
Heart".
Break the <u>old</u> **one of stone** that is **stuck in the old law.**
When Saul got knocked off his **"high horse",** the Jesus of Grace is who he
Saw.

God also had him write with words to be understood only by those
Who can now enter His Kingdom and explain why Jesus rose
From the dead - **as a picture,** _a First Fruit_ - of those previously lost
**Who now preach God's Mercy to ALL sinners** - His own life it did cost.

Jesus willingly put his faith and trust in the words he did hear.
Sacrificed his life, walked without sin, as we should too without fear
That we too will be raised up to a life without end.
This gospel of **"Good News"** with peace for all we're to send

To the ends of the world that has not been enlightened.
It's again - **the Devil - "UNBELEIF"** that has the lost sheep frightened.
We must remember - lost sheep must be brought back in with great care
With patience and gentleness - they're so easy to scare.

#70 **The Devil Redeemed**

God promised Jesus - **"King of Peace"** and **"King of the Jews"**
Who are not one outwardly but inwardly that preach **this** **"Good News"**
Who have been led to **bring in the harvest - converted**
And not spread some good news that the Devil perverted.

Remember, we'll all be judged on the works we did do.
It will be righteous - God knows our hearts through and through.
Did we forgive 7 X 70, **love our enemies as we should?**
Did we bend over backwards and give all that we could?

Of course not. If you say you did, you know you're a liar.
Do you want to be put back into the **"Lake of Fire"**
So you can confess this latest sin at your death and on your knees?
Like everyone else, you'll ask Jesus for MERCY - *PLEASE!*

"You are the LORD of lords and King of kings".
What sweet music in heaven this confession brings
When by all it will be sung, at once, *in true worship and praise*
That our Father drew us _ALL_ back by the Son He did raise.

Rich Kovatch
7-16-11

#71 JESUS' DOCTRINE

It's Sunday morning, peaceful and calm.
I'm still unemployed but your love is my balm.
A dream I had of how a crippled man still loved
His wife and the life given to them from above.

We went to inspect houses broken down and in ruin
For my wife and me to move into and fix up; **our own lives this is true** in
The sense that where we were looking was not where we should
But to move into our mansion in God's neighborhood   John 14:2

Which is the city of peace...the New Jerusalem
Built by God himself, not the false prophet Balaam,
Who only saw things of this world; built his doctrine on sand.
This is the house that will fall when winds come from God's hand.

This house is _man's_ doctrine where _pride_ in dead men rule.   Lu. 11:39-52
The law and the prophets. Jesus said don't _only_ use that tool
But see the _true picture_ of who was to come   Luke 24:38-50
So your mansion will still be standing when the winds are all done.

Of course - this is Jesus - the true giver of Grace.
If you'll wash the windows with **Mercy,** you'll soon see **Wisdom's** face
                                                          Rev. 22:4
And not only his backside; because with faith from a **TRUE** baptism
                                                          Ex. 33:17-23
You'll see that even in evil men, God is still in 'um.
                                          Rev. 21:3, 1 Cor. 13:11-13

You'll hear and understand what Jesus said in **John 8**
And **John 7** about the **last Great Feast** and eat from the right plate.
Then when you have filled your soul you'll see where God does now
Dwell...
In the Gospel of Salvation of _ALL_ MEN, _NOT_ MOST GO TO HELL ! ! !

#71 JESUS' DOCTRINE

Jesus' doctrine is that we're to speak and live only in love,
Which is Mercy and **Grace** given to *all* sinners with the gentleness of a Dove
(*Which sees through the flesh and into the heart.*)   1 John 3:14-24
Then the judgment and condemnation of the carnal nature will depart.

This is the Glory of God - **TO RESCUE THE LOST SHEEP.**
Today's false church message of eternal separation makes ME weep
Because LOVE **CONQUERS ALL** and **WINS IN THE END.**
Broken hearts are healed and confused minds start to mend.

It's not only the real, physical needs the **TRUE** church will meet,
But with compassion and forgiveness for the hurting is how we will greet
                                                         Good Samaritan parable
Each new opportunity appointed to us to serve the broken hearted
Because the *HOPE* in a God that **WILL STILL SAVE THEM has nearly Departed!**

What a shame it seems but was prophesized to be
That *the world will get darker so as few men will see.*
Jesus will come back asking if faith can be found.   Mark 13:31-37
Most of the **faith Jesus planted *IN ALL MEN*** they'll have **buried** in the **Ground**

And hid it, refused to water, and feed and warm it enough to sprout.
The parable of the sower and the seed is what this is all about.
                                                         Matt. 13: 3-30
The seed of faith, most people let die, don't understand the parables
Jesus told.   **Matt. 13:37-43**
But those that DO - will reap the harvest of 30, 60 and 100 fold.
                                                         Matt. 13:23

The harvest is people brought back into God's hand;
Who also will profess God's GREAT GRACE; join into His disciples' band
And sing the songs and play the right notes;
To believe the words they say in which the whole world hopes.

#71 JESUS' DOCTRINE

A God who *from the beginning* put the whole plan in motion   Prov. 8:23-26
With power to hold planets and stars and keep back the ocean   Prov. 8:27
To the exact place and timing of eclipses and tides;   Prov. 8:28-29
TO BRING ALL MEN BACK TO OUR FATHER'S FOLD, HIS HOLY SPIRIT
GUIDES.   *W a r n I n g : Matt. 12 : 30 - 37*

What **makes** men **disbelieve** this is just *comfort* and *fear*.
They don't *want to take the chances to tell lost sheep - He's still near*
And actually *lives in their hearts that's covered in stone.*   Jer. 31: 22-40
Each seed, every man from Adam to you, the *good tree* **does own.**

Can good fruit come from a bad tree that's rotten?   Matt. 7:18
Don't you see the ***Tree of Righteousness*** is where the ***first seed*** was
Gotten?
But the Devil did get the first seed to question God's Word; and *Adam*
Disbelieved.
It's all in God's plan - *till you're appointed time to confess it is*
Conceived.

I pray *that this time* for you *is not* at death's door.
The ***false* church** teaches **ETERNAL HELL**, but **IT** is **really** the **Great Whore**
Spoken of in the Book of the *Relavation of Jesus Christ's might.*
Only God & His Word are eternal - no beginning, no end - that's right!

Sin had a beginning - thus its end will come too.
Please* stop the Devil** = **unbelief, and believe what is true;*
That's *God's gift of salvation is irrevocable... His word won't return*
Void.
Don't follow the *FALSE CHURCH's* **doctrine without questioning – thus**
Just being its ignorant sucker *DROID* **! ! !**

Rich Kovatch
7-17-11

#72 Lost Sheep or Goat?

Oh Father, how hard it is to put on a face
With a big, happy smile in this evil, evil place.
Everywhere I look I see hatred and sin
Especially by <u>my</u> *friends* in *this* world's church. Where do I begin

To *gently* bring **YOUR lost sheep** back into the fold;
How to unloose the bindings of the false doctrines they've been told
Starting from the Garden of Eden where the first lie was believed
By **the "spirit of unbelief"** in your Word, **" the devil "**, and iniquity was
Conceived.

Even before *having* their first child Cain and the first family of man had
Started
The Holy Spirit of God in mankind had departed.
Thus the completeness that **was** in our body, mind and soul
Was lost, like the picture of us lost sheep, and sin takes its toll.

Now stay with me, we're now still in only Genesis 3
The total redemption of ALL is right here - God knew what was to be.
He put the *tree of knowledge* of good & evil in their midst **for them to**
eat.
He knew why they would, kicked them out, so now our only way back is
Thru a flaming sword with heat.

There's no way I can explain *every* picture in this short poem;
But I know the truth of God's MERCY, LOVE, and GRACE <u>if they'd only</u>
<u>Let me show 'um.</u>
Just saying these few words turns most lost sheep into a goat
Because of their pride that **they've** confessed in **a** Jesus - **they gloat.**

The trouble starts in these next words I'll write
Because **no matter** which ones I say, **they'll want to** start a **fight**;
Which is sadly a diversion tactic by a fool stuck in his way.
I'd love to study the book of Proverbs with them - one chapter for
Every day.

#72 Lost Sheep or Goat?

And focus on **KEY words**, **MERCY** and **WISDOM**, the **WISE** and the **FOOL**.
To the one who truly seeks the character of God, I'd take them to school
Which is what 2 Tim. 3:7, 3:16 + 3:5 try to convey - Jesus' power.
I wish, for whoever may hear this, that ***this*** **is** God's ***appointed day*** and ***Hour!***

That the light would come on and **destroy** the **mindset that's darkened**;
When the command to receive Agape love for their perceived enemies is Harkened
The **letter** of the law **kills - but the Spirit brings life**.
The second Adam **HAS COVERED** the sin of his unfaithful wife.

This **LIGHT** of the TRUE Jesus has the power to save
All of Israel - because ALL men misbehave.
You...because without faith you cannot please God...thus sin.
Another truth from Genesis 7 & 9 states the life and breath are in the
Body and blood within.

Jesus, who IS LIFE, shed **HIS BLOOD** for the sins of Adam on down.
In John 3:16 thru 21, Jesus' own words - THE TRUTH is found
That unbelieving men love darkness because their deeds are evil.
The darkness is only ***UNWILLINGNESS*** to confess the LORD'S retrieval

Of ALL men - remember Adam back at the start
& the curse that God put on him & what later would happen to his heart.
In Jeremiah 31:31 when A ***NEW*** COVANENT God would send
And their hearts of stone, he would - FOR ALL - MEND.

It's just that only - a few, the chosen, ***TRUE*** Israel *REALLY* PROCLAIM
The **TRUE SAVING POWER IN JESUS' NAME**.
Real saving love is hard and only **His HOLY SPIRIT** gives this power.
Are you a lost sheep now coming back - or a goat that's still sour?

#72 Lost Sheep or Goat?

I may have failed miserably in this poem by using improper legalistic
Words of encouragement to convey
Because the words, even to me, sound a bit condemning, but please
Listen to what the **Holy Spirit** did say,
PLEASE, "Come out of her" - *the religious system* where LOVE has been
Perverted
Accept the TRUE DOCTRINE of Jesus and the Apostle's words, *and get
Converted*...

Be willing to admit that you sin and lie way too often.
Proclaim that God will raise up **ALL** that live in their coffin
Of unbelief - especially when still walking around,
Because *only in dying* to one's own "PRIDE" and "LIFE" –
Is how "AGAPE LOVE" is found *!!!*

Rich Kovatch
7-21-11

#73 Though I . . . and *have not* Love

Though I have the gift of prophecy
And understand all mysteries of what's to be
And have all knowledge and faith enough to move a mountain
And have not Love, I am nothing of the eternal fountain   1Cor.13:2

Of love that overflows out of the heart of He
Who created the universe by calling it to be.
This Word sets in motion for this physical realm
The **LAW** and thus **GRACE**; to <u>again</u> **show us** he's still at the helm.
                                                        Eph. 1:3-14 (vs.7), 2:1-16

Mankind is His pride and joy, His very best creation.
He chose to reveal Himself to us all through one nation
And reveal to us that *we're all* **His precious lost sheep**   Eph.3:8-12
Set free by *HIS OWN* **BLOOD** <u>but still under the shepherd's keep</u>**!**

He won't lose one that our Father has given Him.
The deal's been paid for by Jesus to cover our sin,
And not for ours only but also for the sins of the <u>***WHOLE***</u> **WORLD,**
                                                        1 John 2:2
<u>**NOT**</u> **IMPUTING** their trespasses, the **Kingdom** of **reconciliation**
Unfurled.   2 Cor. 5:19

Which <u>*IS*</u> THE **"GOOD NEWS"** - **"The King of Peace"** lives **NOW** and
DWELLS <u>*among us all*</u> **!** **!** **!**
Christ is ALL *Love* and *Forgiveness* NOW, understood by those who've
Heard **HIS** CALL.
So get with the program. So many pictures from my Word I use to draw
Out.
Please My CHILD understand. Sometimes I talk softly, **sometimes I**
Shout !

#73 Though I . . . and *have not* Love

God spoke only good things...liked all that He saw
Till Adam discovered he had no mate; now here comes the flaw.
A body divided against itself cannot stand.   Mark3:24-29
That is why marriage was created...so a man and a woman would be
Blessed to walk hand in hand

And bond to each other in Spirit & Truthfulness with Love as their guide.
When one partner goofs up the other can take it in stride
Because LOVE IS ABLE TO *ABSORB GREAT PAIN*.
Love doesn't hold grudges ***but forgives*** and forgets all sins ***to gain***
                                                          Luke 6:27,35

A deeper relationship that grows and changes one into a vessel
In which **to question *the character of God to save all*** we do no longer
Wrestle   Rom.8:27
The Father's timing **to reveal** to each person is ***as He chooses***.
How much, how often and **how loudly** depends on the bruises   Gal.6:4-8

You've put into His Body...loved ones, friends or perceived enemies,
Unknown and everyone alike
When *YOUR* MESSAGE is UNRIGHTEOUS FEAR and ANGER, you
Misrepresent the power of the spike
That nailed to the cross, **The Spirit** of God Himself, the **REDEEMER** for
ALL SIN.
THE *SIN OF UNBELIEF* IN THIS IS THE *FIRST* PLACE TO BEGIN

To REPENT of the **Negative scare**, and NOW, *as Jesus did*, DRAW ALL
MEN with *Compassion*
That will never cease to partner with **MERCY** & **FORGIVENESS** - *always*
In *fashion.*
This relationship is our schoolmaster to bring us to **His Spirit of LOVE**
And **TRUTH**.
The perfect example He showed us of this is His Book of Ruth.

#73 Though I . . . and *have not* Love

The Kinsman Redeemer married a non-Jewish girl that knew Him not
Personally, but His character of Love to always draw her is what got
Her attention even in the midst of her miserable carnal life.
The timing to seek and serve with a hope of purpose cuts like a knife

Between the bone and the marrow, the soul and the spirit. The battle
Begins.   Heb. 4:12
Once again I must apparently remind all that the **Spirit** of **Love WINS!!!**
Its TRUTH is that to inherit the Kingdom of Heaven, He *WILL*
CIRCUMCISE   Deut. 30:6
The male's most sensitive, personal flesh - created for pleasure. *Now*!
When the spirits rise

Out of immense pleasure comes the gift of life and Fatherhood.
The Giver of life shares His Seed with the church that willingly would
Experience this spoken means through pain of separation, healing and
Regeneration
His **"True Israel"** in these last days, **reborn with power. The NEW
CREATION.**

"A People" that boldly declares God's love and promises to those who
Believe.
The carnal aspect of this is shown by His **"Few"** that Truly Receive.
People not scared to confess they are sinners, **but saved only by GRACE.**
                                                       James 5:16
JUST *AS* <u>YOU</u> ARE!!! I pray for your good, thus my hope is spoken into
God's face   James 5:15

That **radiates** with **every color** and **shade** - all emanating from **pure
White**
Which is our picture of diversity under one shepherd's eye that *changes
Our* sight.
Only Gentleness, Understanding, Faithfulness to Consistency draw can
Turn scared and hurt lost sheep's flight
From continuing into darkness where shadows are seen as the only
Thing that's right.

#73 Though I . . . and *have not* Love

Once again it comes down to... *and have not Love.*   1 Cor.13:2
Love never fails; Love always does good and is gentle as a dove.
Matt.5:44-48

Once again a picture of God's focused sight and awesome peace.
Matt.14:25

The peaceful dove has ***proper perspective*** of the bad tree's fruit, ignores
It enough **to cease**   Matt.8:23

Its influence and power of sin to indulge in things of this age.
The concept of time, **again a picture** of how **death is sins' wage.**
Rom.6:23

Time began and ends because **Jesus rose to defeat death** and **to
Proclaim His VICTORY.**   Isa.61:1

Life eternal that is only in Him, **freely given and paid for by Jesus - YOU
SEE ? ? ?**   1Cor. 2:12

Rich Kovatch
8-7-11

#74 Choose You This Day

Choose you this day whom you will serve   Joshua 24:15
But remember you'll get what you deserve.
God is not mocked; the price of sin is not cheap.
Whatsoever a man soweth, that shall he also reap.   Gal 6:7-8

The choice is constant throughout the day
To focus on pleasures of our flesh or seek *"The Way"*
Which is what **the movement of the Holy Spirit** through Christ's words
Was called
And the *religious system* devised by the proud Jewish priests *was stalled.*

Stalled, **like today's church system** because they had a misguided zeal.
                                                                    Rom. 10:2-3
The power and glory of God they were trying to steal
Putting themselves in the place of authority
Over exactly how my life is to be *for me*.

So close but yet so far.
It's your own witness before God you mar.
His word is **given to define good motives** and **authority**
Designed to be understood by only His "chosen", *not* the majority.
                                                                    Matt. 13:11-18
The two greatest commandments are really two in one   Matt. 22:37-40
That come together in the unity within His Son.
Love is the common denominator, so the difference is who
God shows you is your neighbor & who is yourself - **the clue**.   Luke 10:36

How big is the family of God *to you?*   Matt. 6: 9
Did **"our Father"** *design* to bless some and others screw?   Luke 10:23-24
It's a sad state of affairs that most are O.K. with an eternal hell.
Duh, Jesus foreknew His plan to reclaim mankind *before* Adam fell.

God hates those that bring discord among the brethren.   Prov. 6:19
God loves & saves some, but **loves and gives up** on us captured by our skin?
Our command is to **Love our enemies** into willing submission.
Putting up with exceeding sinfulness **and paying for it** was Jesus'
Commission.

#74 Choose You This Day

I was sent to only the Lost Sheep of Israel.   Matt. 15:24
ALL people ARE lost UNTIL God calls and their hearts feel   Matt. 18:11
The pain and longsuffering by our Father inflicted by all sin
And the mercy, forgiveness, gentleness and power of Love to win

Over to righteousness every precious brother you've been created along with
To show the world *the Greatest Glory of God...that there's no diff.*
Between the lost and found as Christ's whole body goes;   Rom. 10:12
Except some are made unto good works and through others iniquity
Flows.   Isa. 11:4

Choose you this day which god and /or idol you'll live and die for
Is it easier to do so for the rich and powerful than for the poor?
Different clay, purpose, timing and part of His body.   Acts 10:13
Don't call what I call clean, unclean. Especially the shoddy.   Lu. 12 5:12-13

Do not judge others by what you see on the outside.   John 7:23-24
God wants me to judge own my heart is what I'm to confide.   Isa. 11:3
When I see other brethren of humankind causing confusion and pain
God gave me authority as a king, priest and prophet to deal with the rain
     1 Peter 2:5-10

That surely falls on the good and the evil. Rain's not the issue.   Matt. 5:45
It's whether you perceive it as a curse or felt God kiss you.
Rain nourishes the weeds **and** the harvest, the chaff **and** the wheat.
They **look** *exactly* the same *until* harvest time is complete.   Matt. 13:30

The chaff is thrown into the fire - **the works** of the *carnal* nature -
Unbelief.   Heb. 3:12
Only the Spirit of God in me along with my soul will get relief.   Prov.23:14
The body was corrupt - thus cannot inherit everlasting life,
But my soul He does love. Proved it by dying for His wife

#74 Choose You This Day

To pay the price, have the dowry in hand.   Ex. 22:17
We've been bought and brought out of slavery to sin and into the land
                               1 Cor. 6:20, 7:23
Where Heaven will be possible to be seen as truly as "I AM"   Matt. 3:2
Born of the Spirit of God, living the life of the lamb.   Matt. 6:10

This Lamb of Peace will dwell with the wolf.   Isa. 11:6
Make his enemies his friends, even those that loaf.   Matt. 5:44
Gentleness and Goodness with purposeful judgment to bring all to him.
                                   John 12:32
If his fighter is still obstinate, it's back to the gym

To work out more of your salvation   Phil. 2:12
Through trial and error conforming into one nation   Ez. 37:22
Believers in Christ Jesus for the brotherhood of all man.   Rom. 12:1-4
The character of Love to redeem and heal is where I stand.

So choose you this day how you'll treat that one
Who makes your day *anything but fun.*
This **"one"** is inside of the hearts of you and me.   Matt. 12:35 Mark 7:21
Wisdom tells us that ***especially*** *in our **enemies*** *faces,* **it's Christ's face
We should see ! ! !**

Rich Kovatch
8-20-11

#75 Communication Breakdown

The problem with mankind and with me for sure
Is not the sins we all commit daily, but the cure.   John 3:17
Understanding of God's wisdom is waning.   Prov. 1:1-7
The favorite pastime of all mankind is complaining!

And that's the natural thing for a carnal mindset to do.   Mark 14:38
Thinking that the whole world revolves around you know who.
The paradox is that it does ...to the point
Our darkened minds the Holy Spirit does anoint

With clarity of thought **as to who we're to see**
As a neighbor to love **now** <u>and an enemy</u> - ***used-to-be***.   Matt. 27:40
We were all enemies of God until Christ did His thing.   Rom. 4:18
Paid the price ***demanded*** for all sin, thus harmony He did bring   1 John 2:2

Between all men - how we talk and walk - the MUSIC called "LIFE".
Which is diametrically different for His harlot and virgin wife.
We'll ALL sing a "New Song" when we follow the conductor,   Rev. 5:9
But in a carnal mindset we play solos, too often interrupter

Of **"The Way"** of ***"The Peace"*** that harmonizes the mix.
These words with wrong motivation will be burnt up as wood, hay and
Sticks.   1 Cor. 3:12
For the proper playing of the notes we're to speak
He says "no man can tame", so He continually has to tweak   James 3:8

What comes OUT of our mouths so not to defile   Matt. 15:11
The sacrifice God paid Himself and live in denial
That love conquers ALL and *was never shown as bright*
As the moment Jesus rose from the dead of night.   Matt. 28:5-8

Three days and three nights He lay buried in the earth.
Gave His life ***WILLINGLY*** so **ALL** CREATION will resound with mirth
For the faith Christ displayed in the word *He heard* our Father say.
                                                             John 5:19
He did walk perfect among and with us ***to SHOW US*** THE ***NEW*** DAY.
                                                             John 11:25

#75 Communication Breakdown

Jesus **_told us_** the Kingdom is near at hand, and **IS NOW!**

Mark 1:15 Rom. 14:17

Wisdom in choices is what Jesus taught and don't have a cow

Prov. 2:6-18

When trouble and strife come upon you. For this is God's plan;

Prov. 13:24

To purify "His church" through suffering - following that one man

1 Peter 2:21

Who went to His cross...**_willingly_**...in Love for God and us.   **2 Peter 3:9**

For God so loved the world...He destroyed it! So don't fuss.   Gen. 7:4

This world is symbolic of you and me who got corrupted by sin   Gen. 6:5

But washed and made clean with the water of heaven within   Rev. 1:5-7

Your heart which will now be burnt up in the fire of repentance

1 Cor. 3:13

Because like all men, except Jesus, we deserve the "Death Sentence".

Matt. 10:38-39

He calls us to die to self and to renew our minds.   Rom. 12:2

Knowledge is found after we pray at the **"Windows of Heaven"**

And He opens the blinds!   **Mal. 3:10**

The **"Communication Breakdown"** is all on our end.   James 4:3

His GRACE tells us a zillion plus ways this message He'll send: Rom. 15:4

No matter the time or the place, on Earth or in space   Rom.4:16

GRACE HAS **NO LIMITS** but sin will leave no trace.   Ps. 103:12

He's promised with His Word in writing and in skin

That for ALL He's created, death will occur but new life will begin

Rom. 11:24

In a state of purity where sin is forgotten.   Rom. 6:11

FOR EVERY SINGLE SOUL - JESUS' LIFE WAS BEGOTTEN.   2 Cor. 5:14

We're made from PERFECT LOVE where ALL LIFE IS KIN.   Rom. 11:26-27

The sword says you're going to hell because you have sin.   Rev. 13:10

The law was given because before - He overlooked iniquity.   John 1:17

To prove His RIGHTEOUSNESS He has to judge all He does see   Gal. 2:21

#75 Communication Breakdown

Some as vessels of mercy and others to wrath   Rom. 9:22-24
To get their walk straightened back on the path   Rom. 11:6
That leads to the view of ***the brotherhood of all man***   **Rom. 13:8 -10**
ACCEPTED in Christ, **FORGIVEN** & **LOVED as only God can**!!!   Rom. 12:14

His ways are above ours *but **His character** of involved correction we*
Do know.   Deut. 8:5
Again I tell you, through the life and works of Jesus, God did most
Certainly show
The false religious doctrines that men devised - especially His own!
          Luke 6:41
Note Jesus' responses to the scribes & pharisees *always cut to the bone:*
          John 5:18

To cut away the flesh *as to circumcise the heart.*   Matt. 5:30
Strip away the hate for the sinner for just doing his part   Luke 6:34-35
In the big musical called "Love Wins" where harmony incorporates the
Notes they miss.
We're **to overcome evil with good**...not with the sword, but a **K I S S !!!**
          Rom. 12:21

Rich Kovatch
9-3-11

#76 I Want to DIE

A scary title of truth but it shouldn't be
To those **to whom** it's been given to see.   2 Cor. 4:11-15
Like Paul desired to be with the Lord
But chose to serve Him and die by the sword.

By this I don't mean I'm to use mine to offend
It's just that the sword is used by the Lord to contend
With the first Adam's sin nature that I let allow
To influence and pervert my judgment of choice and go afoul.

There is no doubt God gave us this life/time as the place & chance to
Choose   Josh. 24:15
Adam and Eve heard God's promises **but understood not** what they
Would lose
Since sin had not entered creation until in their minds
They choose to seek knowledge of good and evil and ultimately how
LOVE BINDS.

The Devil that tempted her was the spirit sent by the Lord   Rev. 5:6
To test the willpower and longsuffering of the mother to cut the cord.
                                                                2 Peter 3:9
Faith is the picture of our umbilical cord supplying oxygen rich blood to
The fetus.   Rom. 3:30
It is God's neuma and blood that provide all that's needed so He can
Greet us

At the moment of our birth and cut us free.
The other picture scripture gives is what happened to my pee pee
                                                                Gen. 17:12
When my parents dedicated in trust to God - my provided skin
That He too will cut the spiritual excess called sin

#76 I Want to DIE

Which happens when we fail to conquer the pain and fear
And give it power and authority in areas not yet surrendered...but near
Luke 10:18-19

As He enlightens our eye to see how dark our own heart can be -
Ps. 139:23-24

Thus gives us **Mercy** and **Grace** enough to be the transponder of a **soul**
That's **FREE**

To discover AGAIN and AGAIN how God touches us at **_each "split atom"_**
Second.
Constantly speaking to *His* sheep *which hear* and *are beckoned*
Under the call to stop condemning everyone under the law   Prov. 12:8
Because the last time I looked in the mirror there was plenty wrong I
Saw.   2 Cor. 5:10

Our maturity *starts* with blood when the cord is cut
And life and love give us the constant reminder on our gut,   Rom. 8:35-39
And in our "gut" - the feeling of what really is true   2 Cor. 5:7
Combined with a *good hearted* mindset *of **what*** Love's to do.

Children make *IGNORANT* mistakes *until* they *learn*,
Especially that if you get too close to a fire - *you'll burn*.
That's the picture of God chastening His kids with WISDOM through
PAIN!   Prov. 24:3-4
So the next time that test and path comes up we'll choose the right lane
Matt. 7:14

That WILL cause me to **DIE TO SELF** and LIVE UNTO HIS WIL   Rom. 6:11
Which are pictures of the wineskin I desire to fill
To create a new vessel of which the potter WILL be proud   1 Cor. 15: 42-44
And will *thru gifts* - provided by God - *stand above the crowd*.
Rom. 11:29-32

#76 I Want to DIE

And proclaim with my mouth *how I see* Love at work.   *2 Cor. 5:14*
To confess __MY__ faults and __ask__ for forgiveness is the strange quirk
That **separates** the **spirit** and soul, the joint and the marrow.   Heb. 4:12
EVERY SOUL IS PRECIOUS TO OUR FATHER. Way more so than each
Sparrow   1Peter 2:4

Which He says He thinks good of & provides for it until it falls.   Matt. 10:31
And this too is the most prevalent way we hear His calls.
A righteous man **will** *fall* **seven** times **but rise up again renewed**
                                                            Prov. 24:16
Every morning with *Mercy __given__ him* because he's **constantly pursued**
                                                            2 Cor. 4:16

By LOVE to a new life where the old has passed away -   2 Cor. 5:17
After we've believed in His power through *His* **blood** *to pay*
For the sins of the world - especially mine most relevant to me **1 John 2:2**
Which gives me the light to obviously see

That God wants me to forgive myself - even *when I know I was bad*
                                                            1 John 3:20-21
Because I have someone walking with me thru the fire - MY DAD
                                                            Dan. 3:25
Who's protecting my soul from the flames of hell
As my body gets burnt and destroyed! And **ALL** is **WELL!**   Rom. 8:6

For this body is corruptible, but we will rise in perfection   1 Cor. 15:54
Cleansed by His blood after *our __set time__* of correction.   Heb. 9:27
Sin is thrown off **when I believe** God says "**NOW**... in the place
That this power __you've__ given your flesh...*I've given you grace*

And **Faith** to walk the path you really hope for".
Freedom to really live the good life **by opening the door**   Rev. 3:20
That He knocks on - without end - to bring about His Glory...   ***Rom.11:32***
SALVATION OF ***ALL*** SOULS - He DIED for ***UN***BELIEVERS - that's
HIS☐STORY.

Rich Kovatch
9-11-11

#77 **Creatures of Habit**

We're all creatures of habit... some good... lots bad.
The good ones give our Father joy, the bad makes Him sad.
But it's **_not_** that the bad habits are enough to make Him say...
I've taught you I FORGIVE WITH UNENDING MERCY...**_but not today_** ! ! !

I've had enough!!! You're sins are too great!!!
You worshipped a false idol **_and now it's too late_**
Because what you've done in your body has brought it to death's door
And this day I require your life. You can continue on like this no more.

YOUR blood is required for the payment of sin.
Your judgment is torment without end - **let hell begin**!
And I will give you forever to say, " I should of, I would of, I could of
Chosen Jesus and changed my eternal destiny **_myself_** from this hell to
Heaven above."

We're all creatures of habit and this spirit of wrath has been misdirected
To punish our souls without remedy from **a darkened mindset not yet
Resurrected**
Into the only thing there is without beginning or without end...
Life after the judgment, a consciousness of sin which we cannot defend

Without admitting it must lie deep within our own heart
And confessing to God that deeper down I pray it will depart. 1 Cor. 14:25
Now this is where the new habit is to begin;
That God **_created you_** and **_all_** men **for Jesus** not to lose **_but win_**

In His victory over the **_second_** death when by God's power He rose
And took the keys of hell and death to set free all God chose
From before time was when His plan was already set
Jesus will be the fisher of men **_and not one will fall out of the net!_**

Yet the net will appear to have found a bigger catch
Than one such gathering into the boat could match   Luke 5:7
So the lesson is that there are always more to be caught.
Love never ends when it comes to saving souls that are at aught

#77 Creatures of Habit

With the spirit of unselfishness, the willingness to suffer.   1 Peter 2:19, 20
The foolishness of fools, between a Holy God and evil men - love will
Buffer   2 Peter 3:15
The effect of the law would of, could of, and should have had on my
Spirit   Deut. 31:26, 27
Had not **Love's Spirit of FORGIVENESS** been given me and my mind able
To hear it.

For a father's love for his children can only be lived out   Matt. 23:23
After the child has been ***shown by mercy given*** upon himself ***what
Love's all about***.
Judgment is used **to bring the wayward back in line**
Until one figures out at which table one would rather dine.

At the table of the world and self and unbelief - which is sin
Set before us by God for us to daily choose which habits will win
And show their fruit through actions and wills to prove
If I'm in charge of what on earth and in heaven gets moved.

Or at the table set before us by the **Spirit of Grace and Love**
That knows the future but operates in time like a hand in a glove.
The glove actually touches the creation supplied by God for us to change
But time and love direct the action so that only God will ultimately
Arrange

All circumstances to eventually show God's glory.
He created all things for us to see this story.
Love for your fellow man goes way beyond what you can do
But with God all things are possible AND I KNOW THIS IS TRUE!

There's no greater proof of love that a man lay down his life   John 15:13
For another that is at that moment in time unable to use the knife
And cut away his own sin nature and so not be dragged down by it.
This is the picture of our unwise choices leading us into the pit

#77 **Creatures of Habit**

That has **no fulfillment** *__but__* *__to__* burn up sinful habits destroying life itself
And us **_ALL_** to be transformed like the smoke rising up forever with new Health
Set free from the sins that so easily beset us   Heb. 12:1
Like the prayers that enter God's throne room with thanksgiving and Praise for Jesus.

Prayers that will good unto all men so their sins may be forgiven
As Jesus did from the cross three days before He was risen
And ascended to sit at the right hand of the Father to judge all
And to make sure that *__all__* **eventually respond** to God's call   2Peter 3:9

Unto repentance of all sin through the revelation of the light   Rom.2:4
That you're going to lose out on God's best if you don't do what's right
And walk in all humbleness knowing you deserve God's wrath   James 4:6
And thank God & love Him for intimately correcting your path   Prov.3:12

That was headed for destruction - which is certainly an *__idiom__*.
A warning to prophesy that we should act like *Gideon*
A man of valor - in God's eye - who saw the end as it is.
To the blinded spirit, time is an enemy because he doesn't know the Promises of God are his

And has **no vision** to see the victory **_won by Jesus_** **_at_** **_every_** **_point_**.
He wins by showing wrath with the law such as so to faithfully anoint
EACH MAN with the oil of The Holy Spirit *IN ORDER TO* uncover his very Own sin.
To **impute** righteousness unto **_ALL_** SINNERS to show us **_GOD'S HABIT TO WIN_** ! ! !

Rich Kovatch
9-17-11

#78 Common Sense

As the light comes on in *my* eye
I see more of the **truth of love** and **why**
God created things the way they are.
To show me the significance of <u>each</u> tiny star.

As the light comes on brighter I realize
What the gift of God is and how to use the prize.
The gift is Himself...which will never be fully told.
Jesus said He had sheep that were not of this fold.

He was talking to *religious* people who have *its spirit*.
When Jesus told them the truth, *they just couldn't hear it*!
He explained it was in God's hand to choose the time
When that's to happen. To us it looks to be without reason or rhyme.

But as the light comes on brighter I see that **the little star** becomes a part
Of a bigger picture of the **Spirit of God that lives in my heart.**
The **darkness of the night sky** is the opposite of this light.
My carnal mindset is this darkness that fights with what's right

In the mind of God which has been unveiled to me
When Jesus *rose* the removal of religious traditions *set mankind free.*
God made a way for gentiles to speak directly at the alter.
Told me "Attitude determines the latitude I allow myself to falter".

As the **L**ight comes on it's a lamp unto my wandering feet.
The **L**aw of **R**eciprocity explains exactly only where I will meet
The blessings of good things He has in mind for me.
It comes at each split second I operate as a free

Spirit sent out into the darkness to be **a "Light"** in an *"age"*
That loves darkness because *its spirit* loves evilness and rage.
This world is my world. It exists only in my mind.
Specific to me and my choices *but <u>not</u> one of a kind.*

#78 Common Sense

This little star was set in place as a lesser light to stay.
It's to shine brightly during the night time as the sun rules the day.
Such a stark contrast between the total darkness and God's pure Light
But with billions together the Big Picture becomes quite a magnificent Sight.

As the light comes on brighter this scene changes like a magic picture art Scene
It takes on a hue of Peacefulness and Order and becomes totally serene.
Love exists even in darkness but is not part of it.
This is where most people in their search for truth...QUIT.

This light in dark hours comes down to **PURE HOPE**
Like I'm inside my **H**oly **S**pirit's oil drum pierced with rays of truth that Let me cope
With **HOW WHAT I SEE** depends on how focused my eye
Is on what the Light reveals! ...and it's because I sin I know I'll surely die

And pass on to Glory; **be set free from all sin;**
Made incorruptible so the future lines up with what's been.
When I have my eye on what Love has created
The whole image I physically see and process must be permeated

As the Light comes on brighter to put things in their place.
In the material world and of spiritual things I look for God's face.
God is the Spirit of the testimony of *the will* _of_ *Jesus Christ*
Who came to save all who believe *from fear* that the Devil will heist

My soul...or yours from the hand of God's gentle Grace.
That's IMPOSSIBLE in MY WORLD where **Love will plan my race.**
I'm secure in my dad's grip, though He allows me to find
My own steps *so **His** Glory* through me *is **ONE** of a **KIND**.*

#78 Common Sense

Because **it's a *personal* relationship** I have with my **dad**;
So personal **He** brings me His Wisdom to *LOVE SINNERS* which makes
Me glad.
It's only **"common sense"** ...and...the **"Golden Rule"**
**Our whole lifetimes are each one of God's kids going through Law
School.**

My school book is the Bible. God's Word written to all men
Who aren't slothful and ungrateful but probably were way back when
As I ASLO was willing to walk in the **DARKNESS** of **SELF-PRIDE** and **LIES**
Where spirits and principalities are set in place to sever my ties

If I operate in their power which counterfeits what's **G**ood.
All the glory of unworthy spoil will be burned as hay, stubble and wood.
Only things done with a pure heart will qualify as extra credit
To whom much is given much will be expected as a servant but a son will
Just "let it"

Flow out as from **"Living Springs"** from a source that won't end.
A Faith that won't break but with strength from the **Lord** ... bend
Over backwards to help someone lost or in great need.
Jesus said I'll be caring for Him when I give water and feed

His "lost sheep" that are in danger of the wandering lion
Who **loves to devour** those on **the wide road they *think*** leads back to
Zion.
It's not the destination that's my focus but my steps along the way.
But again, please stay focused. It's *His* **Glory** as *my* faults come on
Display.

Common sense tells me not only this sense is common among all
But there are *other* **senses** that may not be heard **unless with them** He
Should call.
The deepest sense of all is that my words and actions are seen
By **my creator** who I call **Jesus** with His power to change me being so
Keen.

#78 Common Sense

Now here again comes the fear factor of doubt
Of why the **"religious spirit"** says some go to Heaven and some are
"Locked out"!
Religion <u>only</u> **divides** because it courts <u>only</u> **PRIDE** and **FEAR.**
JESUS SAID **He**'d bring division between those who could and couldn't
Hear.

The division He brings is to bring to *my* dark side ***His*** <u>Light</u>.
This road I spoke of earlier is this surrender to **His Might.**
It's so strong even His corrections bring me great drive.
My life is about learning to respond to **His** Word and *" come alive "*

And surrender in submission with Humility, Mercy, Forgiveness & Grace.
These are some ways WISDOM shows me **God**'s beautiful face.
Jesus said " *If you've seen me, you've truly seen the Father* ".
The Father was **the Spirit of Forgiveness** with merciful compassion
Enough to bother

To visit the downtrodden, the lost, the sick and the weary
In order to save the lost world it was clear **He**
Chose to live as a man, walk sinless thus fulfill the law and die for <u>each</u>
Sinner.
He also **told us** to *<u>remember</u>* all this when we sit down for dinner

And we ***drink*** of **His** cup and ***eat*** **His** true heaven sent ***bread***.
We do this with understanding and gratitude only after we've been wed
To the **B**ridegroom of **P**eace and washed ourselves clean
And have been made spotless. **How much** in this poem did *your spirit*
Glean?

Rich Kovatch
9-18-11

#79 Godly Sorrow

There is a sorrow that makes us cry
Sometimes so badly you feel you might rather die
When we see ones we love hurt by our actions.
How deep it goes depends on our reactions.

To say "**I'm sorry**" *sounds like the giant step to most*
Then after that all you have to do is coast
On your laurels that you offered *your idea* of peace
Which is: just *forgive* and *forget* and all past troubles will cease.

That is SO true EXCEPT the main cog has been left out.
Godly sorrow leads to repentance and this life's course will turn about
2 Cor. 7:10
Concerning the exact issue He's bringing to the front of your mind.
Dan. 2:28
The SAME TEST AGAIN? The truth is you must *use* your faith and bind
Matt. 17:20

To a power and force we know basically nothing about!
It's called "AGAPE LOVE" which always means sacrifices that hurt
Enough to shout   Luke 6:27-38
Out loud over what misunderstanding and hardness of heart
Is causing **as** disharmony & turmoil. **Now, exactly again,** what was **your** part?

Denial of any wrong doing can be made **ONLY by Jesus.**   **Heb. 4:15**
His Light is meant **_to correct us_**, not just on the surface - please us
Prov. 3:11-12
But deep down inside *WE ALL KNOW* **WHEN GOD IS NEAR**   **HEB. 7:19**
BUT IT'S *THE PAIN and the UNKNOWN* **THAT WE REALLY FEAR.**

WE FEAR A GOD WHO WE'VE BEEN TAUGHT WILL PUT
MOST PEOPLE IN HELL because they wouldn't cut off their foot.
Mark 9:45
There are *SEVEN* **things that God hates**   **Prov. 6:16-19**
And **NONE OF THEM ARE YOUR SOUL** on which He encloses Hell's gates.

#79 Godly Sorrow

#1 a **PROUD** LOOK is not you but *the spirit of pride*   Prov. 6:16-19
#2 the **LYING** TONGUE just confesses what's on the inside.   Prov. 6:16-19
The **Devil**'s the father of _**ALL**_ **LIES and DECEPTION;**   John 8:44
God hates **HANDS** and **FEET** and **A HEART** that thinks up wicked into
Conception.   Prov. 6:16-19

#6 the false witness that speaks lies - again **IS SATAN.**   Prov. 6:16-19
Also, **he's #7** that **sows discord** among the brethren causing this **hate'n**
                                                   Prov. 6:16-19
Between the **PRODICAL** SON and the *PROUD* **SELF RIGHTEOUS** older
Brother.
*Story ends with the "*Born Again*" son and Father* REunited and *the
Complainer* someplace *other*!

Godly sorrow leads to repentance, *changing* ones course *towards* **the
LIGHT.**   Ja. 1:17
**LIKE A MOTH TO THE LIGHT...IT MUST DO WHAT THE MOTH KNOWS IS
RIGHT.**
It *represents* sin which gets *b u r n e d u p* by the great heat from the
Source.
Sin cannot exist when our spirit is one with our pure and Holy God, of
Course.   1 John 1:5

So as we get nearer to **the "LIGHT" ...the flames of Hell get hotter.**
It's **not** the threat of some *"ETERNAL Hell"* but *the design* of the potter
To let His searching sheep know what happens when we get closer to
"Him **given**" **TO** shepherd us.
IF YOUR AWARENESS OF SIN ISN'T **BURNING** YOUR **BUTT... you're still
Spiritually leprous**

Who's unwittingly unaware you're still flying around in the darkness...
Lost without sight   Prov. 29:18
Who can't see anything created by **God's "WORD"** and **POWER** and
MIGHT   Luke 12:15
Which is **RIGHTEOUSNESS** and **HOLINESS** which **converts ungodly
Resistance**   Book of Prov.
Into works only done and seen in the Spirit *demonstrated by our very
Existence*!   Prov. 16:25

#79 Godly Sorrow

It's necessary to make holy - separate what you are and what you do
Rom.3:20
With righteous judgment with **"WISDOM"** to understand the differences
Between the two. Prov. 13:12
His Spirit is with all things with breath, though the next one is not sure.
Eccl. 3:19
It doesn't matter in the sense you know **"IN Christ"** you're life's secure
Rom. 7:24-25 11:27-32

Which is an **ETERNAL SPIRIT** given *into* a *time awareness existence* to
Show *God's Glory*.
How **He** burns **the hell** *out* of you *as you understand* H I s t o r y.
Rom. 5:13
We condemn ourselves *when we think* others *deserve* an eternal fate
Different than "me".
Sorry...an eye for an eye and a tooth for a tooth. Only a *blind* **moth** can't
See Ex. 21:24 Ps. 11:5-6

It's a learning process to fear God which is the beginning of knowledge.
Prov. 1:7
The process gets more poignant as one gets wiser; and not from some
"Christian" college
But from **LIFE ITSELF** which is **WISDOM** *to find itself* in the **TRUTH of**
LOVE **Prov. 3:13 John 1:3-4**
Which is as wise as a serpent yet harmless as a dove.
Matt. 10:16

Another picture of fact that opposites don't attract...
Polarity in magnetism must be understood in the abstract.
EVIL and GOOD can't *co* **- exist in one place - our minds: LIGHT**
OVERCOMES the dark **Rom. 8:6**
But it's still seen to us as a matter of time...AS YOU HEAR **WISDOM'S**
BARK Eccl. 3:11, 17

#79 Godly Sorrow

That's why the "chosen" are the ones who will speak of God's GRACE.
Eph. 3:3-7, 4 :29
The OPPOSITE of what darkened spirits *give* to others *during their race*

Through this experience God's given us all opportunity to learn how to Love
2 Tim. 3:1-7
With AGAPE persistence - which is impossible by us - but to "a few"
Given to shove
Eph. 3:8, 4:7

Right out of our lives - SIN - which enslaves parts of our body.
James 1: 14-15
Our Spirit is to heal Christ's body of men's broken spirits that are so Naughty.
Prov. 17:4, 6:12-14
A body divided against itself can't stand.
Mark 3:24-26
The humbled and broken spirited *only* with Godly sorrow *will* land
Ps. 34:18

Back on his feet after turning to "The Way" of life
John 14:6
As the Holy Spirit's beloved and made clean wife
Rev. 19:7
Leaving behind the harlot's wife's *lifestyle* and not looking back
Luke 17:31-32
Except to remember the past to see how "LOVE" GOT YOU ON THE RIGHT TRACK

That was laid out by Jesus - submit to the SPIRIT of COMPASSION
2 C. 30:9
And profess the "Wisdom" of doing right by showing in the lives we Fashion
Luke 7:48
Under the guidance of our Father who'll never let go
Heb. 13:5
Of any soul He created, JUST IT'S SIN - don't you know ? ? ?
1 Sam. 18:2 Isa. 38:17-20   Rom. 6:22

Rich Kovatch
9-24-11

#80 Well...FoCUSS

Focus *is really what it's all about*
The ability given to one performed during a shout
Called a Chi-I which drowns out all interference
The secret of this so called trick is knowing what's your clearance.

To perform feats which to <u>unlearned</u> eyes are just unable
<u>To have even a clue</u> to which cards they could play on the table.
This physical stuff is all well and good
As long as it's glory doesn't get burnt up as wood.

So the gift God gave you to excel in your art
Like as in **karate**, it's as a white belt you'll start.
You first of all have to have been given a desire to learn.
In the Spirit this is felt as control starts to burn

This wood...your perceived control, will be **used as a fire**
To show yourself approved **by discovering** in *which ways* you're **a liar**.
I see as God shows me, focus, like beauty is in the eye of the beholder.
I live by faith, not by sight - I am a player not a consistent card folder.

I play my cards as I see them and sometimes I may pass.
But I don't play with fear like I'm walking on broken glass.
God gave me all...the cards, the table, the ability, and the prize.
I pray I may always give love to a down-trodden soul before its **Son-rise!**

As in karate - focus ability is a discipline with an end in mind.
Whether to break a board or ignore a demon, there's a power to bind
Together all distractions that seek to weaken God's move.
This is done then - in order - as God does all things - very smooth.

"Be quick but don't hurry" was John Wooden's proven M.O. as a coach
And life mentor
Of the most dominant run of NCAA victories using a team philosophy of
The inventor.
We're to **"wait upon the Lord"** for His strength to conquer in fight;
As foreknowledge generates power through confidence, waiting
Precludes speed **as darkness is overcome by light**.

#80 Well...FOcuss

The *second* and *harder* thing to do is *to desire to endure fire.*
This fire is longsuffering so when temptation calls I can say;
"You're preaching to the choir".
Enduring pain - including self-inflicted to condition and desensitize
This earth.
Pain is as this hell in the spirit **when Satan accuses me**, trying to
Diminish my worth

To the total picture of life that God has for us to discover.
Wisdom - which happens always in due time when we put nothing
Above her.
The teacher has given his students the patterns to be followed.
The Bible in the Spirit, in martial arts the Sensei is nearly hallowed.

They both teach to absorb pain and condition my focus
To issues that pertain to sharing life that always poke us.
Able to actually, physically change my own body to agree with my will.
The sky's the limit; I've been given dominion if my faith fits the bill.

My conditioning by choice is what makes my teacher proud.
The student's path is not above the teacher's which walked among the
Crowd
But did exploits never seen before after hearing the power of love
Speak.
He heard clearly from **"Our Father"** and He was able to tweak

Things in the physical realm under an even higher law
Than this one seen on Earth of death and sin. **Thank God** God saw
The end from the beginning ... **in control of all the whole way.**
I had conditioned my wrists and shins to deaden pain reception so the
Other guy'd pay

If I had to make contact with a block or a blow
The enemy would find out - decisively - such aggression must slow.
If it *continues* a harder lesson *is soon to follow*.
But His **"letting go"** *so you'll choose* to reject Him forever *makes His*
Promises ring hollow.

#80 Well...FoCUSS

The whole picture of life is a father, mother and kids with their
Combined face
That will eventually leave, to cleave to and mate with - to extend the
Race -
Someone else's kid...so of the circle of life keeps happening, and
Elimination
Of the human race won't happen - **only if** over 2.2 kids **are born** per
Generation.

Euthanasia, homosexuality, a one -child policy and abortion-on-demand
Are *anti* - life
Perverting the very reason God brought Adam his wife
His command was to **"Go fill the Earth"** with the **living images of love**.
I'd prefer a world where **FORGIVENESS** and **MERCY is the way** - rules
From above.

Because a loving teacher and /or parent **will** **not** **lose focus**
On correcting the student and child from influences that choke us
From the life - giving blood and breath and love He offers us all,
We'll use WISDOM and **RIGHTEOUS JUDGMENT** when we hear His call.

And as we progress in rank He gives us much more...
With a tougher competitor to keep testing me right to the core
Of my very being - do I really want to fight or make peace?
Do I demand **"The Law"** being implemented **or** through **Christ's GRACE**
Have hatred cease**?**

We're to teach our children in the way they should go.
Only an instructor who's earned the child's respect will know
How hard to drive and which gift has been given
To the student of love who now knows **"Who's"** life he's now live'n.

This awareness of what life has to offer
Balances out the fear and disrespect of scoffers
Who'll with mad verbosity try to influence your choices
To those made as a white belt following unwise voices.

#80 Well...FOcuss

Staying in the **"School of Hard Knocks"** will eventually shape
Your character to one that's **either solid as "The Rock"** or held together
By duct tape.
We all choose how fast we'll progress to Black Belt.
The color progression of which is ironic was given me understanding
While in prayer I knelt.

White, yellow, green, purple, brown <u>then</u> **black**
With the tougher tests just now beginning because experience I no
Longer lack.
From innocent white to unknowable darkness our self-righteousness
Succumbs.
Seems the better we know how to fight, the worse the fight becomes.

That's what God has to say..."Are you my Gideon...
A man of valor" that lights up in today's world like **neon**
That really catches the eyes and minds of a world that's lost
Not understanding your willingness to stay in school is what life costs.

The more one endures the greater one can teach.
The higher you've ascended, the lower you can reach.
My teacher *has risen to sit* at **G**od's **R**ight **H**and of **P**ower
And has <u>already</u> reached into "Hell" <u>to</u> <u>rescue</u> <u>each</u> faded flower

Which was clothed with more glory that King Solomon himself.
Wisest man ever born but God's handiwork is the shelf
That displays His creation - *time and material for us to see*
The GIFT of SALVATION to <u>*unbelieving*</u> men - ALL ! - God's Greatest
GLORY ! ! !

Rich Kovatch
10-1-11

#81 Only *2* Kinds

There are **only *two* kinds** of people. An open-ended, hypothetical
Statement.
It depends on exactly what message this debate was sent
To unveil in each ones heart where one now stands;
To reveal if Grace lives there **or if the "Law" demands**   Rom. 6:4

Retribution for a wrong made against your spirit.
"Vengeance is mine" says the LORD. **Wisdom is speaking.**
Can you hear it?   Rom. 12:19
The two kinds I'm talking about are **the "Wise"** and **the "Fool".**   Prov. 1:7
"Reproof are the way of life". *Love* **is our teacher, God's "Law"**
The school.   Prov. 6:23 Gal. 3:24

Adam and Eve ate from the **" Tree of Knowledge of good and evil "**
                                                                          Gen. 3:6
Which deceives us all to sin...thus die. ***God's means of retrieval***
                                                                    1 Cor. 15:52
Of our spirit - **God's "Free GIFT of HIMSELF"** - His ***"breath"*** and ***"blood".***
                                                                Gen.2:7 / Gen.9:4
For there is where life dwells; a second wind designed after ***"The Flood"***
                                                                          John 3:8

Where God destroyed all mankind **except** for **"His EIGHT" in Noah'sark**
                                                                         1 Pet. 3:10
Because evil was constantly on their minds **lost in the dark.**   Gen. 6:5
The Earth was null and void, without form until **"The WORD"** was given
That **"LIGHT"**   Gen. 1:2-3
Would now rule. The Sun **(SON)** over the day...Moon and Stars
(TRUE CHOSEN ONES) at night   Gen. 1:14-18

#81 Only *2* Kinds

Given as His sign to all mankind that He's forever present.   Gen. 1:14
To discern the times and the seasons and God's redemptive story in the
Zodiac - which most do resent   Ps. 145:14
That **He is in charge** and shows mercy on whosoever **He chooses.**
                                                    Ex. 33:19, ⬚ see entire Bible
**Love's overriding theme shows MERCY to ALL ! Jesus SAVES ALL He's
Given *and none* He loses.**   John 18:9

God **"Our Father"**, the **"Holy Spirit of LOVE",** has given unto Jesus
                                                              1 John 4:8; 16
All power and glory to judge and redeem all that He pleases.
                                                              John 3:35; 5:27
So the difference between the "Wise" and the "Fool"   Prov. 26:7,9
Is knowing what Jesus came for - **to SAVE SINNERS –**
And God's Law is the tool!   Gal. 2:21

So here we go again...there are **two kinds of "Law".**   Rom. 3:19-31
One that brings sin and death **but the other** "will draw"   John 12:32
"ALL MEN" unto Himself. His "Longsuffering" is "Salvation by GRACE"
                                                              2 Pet. 3:15
As He raises **"His children" to proclaim** *His power* during each
Human's race;   Phil. 3:21

To see **the character of God** to **hold** *all* things in *His hand*;   Heb. 1:3;
                                                              1 Pet. 2:15-17
That the **"Seed of Abraham"** will be like all the combined oceans sand.
                                                    Gen. 22:17, 18; Heb. 11:12
"Uncountable" is the number, the "Outer court" cannot be measured.
                                                              Rev. 11:2
The life/death/"Born Again" pattern is "the gift" to be treasured.
                                                              John 12: 21-24

#81 Only *2* Kinds

God said that a tree will give off seeds of its own kind.

Gen. 1:11-12

Two trees in "The Garden" for Adam...and he made up his mind.

He didn't know what "Death" meant and he loved his wife "Eve"
Even after she "ate" to know God better, he chose his own flesh and
Bone on which to cleave.

Gen. 3:5-7

But the **"Second Adam" - the Spirit man" - Jesus** inside this shell

Cor. 15:45-47

Lives in our **D.N.A. - D**ivine **N**ature of **A**donai- but the body goes to hell

Gen. 4:19

And returns to the dust of the Earth, because **"Hell"** is never satisfied

Prov. 27:20

And that's good if "This World" goes on forever - then His Glory is
Forever gratified

After the process of the seed being buried in dirt.
6´under is standard procedure. **This "Death" - NO MAN will SKIRT ! ! !**

Heb. 9:27

But the **"corruptible body"** is buried and the one of **"incorruption"** rises

1 Cor. 15:53, 54

Free of the **"Law of sin and death".** The **"Law of GRACE"** compromises

Gal. 5:22-23; Rom. 2:12-16

And bewilders the carnal mindset of natural law of death.
A "Fool" cannot see in his darken mind the "width and breadth"

Eph. 3:8-19

Of "Love's patience" - because he sees himself as a rat in the race
Instead of a **"Child of God"** being molded into **Christ's** image thru
"GRACE".

Gen. 1:27-31

#81 Only *2* Kinds

This image of the *"Living* God" will be **seen at nighttime** as light   Gen. 9:5-6
Being reflected like the moon with a gravitational pull with great might
To lift the waters off the Earth's shell as the tide lifts us.
He's our *"Living* **water of life** *"* being drawn out of our body's
Corruptible "bus" .   John 4:10

"If we drink of this water we'll never thirst again".   John 4:14
The **"Wise"** see this as **profound as anything else Jesus said** He'd send
To **"His sheep"** *"that hear"* & follow this power of GRACE.   John 10:2-5
Agape Love _is_ what Jesus' will _is_ for the whole Human Race! *1 John 5:11*

LOVE fights for life and <u>never gives up</u>.   Eph. 2:13-19
A "Hell" FOREVER for our conscious mind to endure is pure corrupt.
                                                                              1 Cor.13:4-8
"FORGIVENESS" is "The GIFT of God"- which NO MAN can earn!
                                                                              Rom. 5:15
The **"Hell"** this body feels is **_NOW_** when sin's effects **start to burn**!

When your awareness of your evil act is brought to light   Rom. 3:19,20
Jesus delivers **"Righteous judgment" - He does ALL THAT'S RIGHT.**
                                                                        REV. 16:7, 19:2
TO THIS KIND OF PERSON - **WISE AND FAITHFUL - HE'LL LIVE AND LEARN**
AND GLORIFY GOD - *RIGHT HERE AND NOW* - WHEN OTHERS SEE **_OUR PATTERN_ TO RETURN**

Back onto **the "Narrow Path"** when we've wandered out too far.
                                                                              Matt. 7:14
When we're out that far - our reflected light is not like the moons - but
Like a tiny star!
And **_what a_** gravity pull **_difference_** - nearly like night and day!
But still that **"little star's"** twinkle of "HOPE" is seen when someone
Does say

#81 Only *2* Kinds

A word of encouragement to one with **"poor spirits"** and "in the Dumps". Matt. 5:3

As Gehenna was - and if your "works" are "unworthy", you'll take you're Lumps

Because "God is not mocked" - we'll reap what we sow. Gal. 6:7

I choose to learn and live more abundantly as this **"second wind"** starts To blow

And spread "The GOOD NEWS" that Jesus saves _ALL_ ISRAEL
Rom. 11:26-32

Which <u>includes</u> "UNBELIEVERS" in the spirit to which today's church Does tell Ps. 78:38

WILL NOT BE REDEEMED AS A SINNER...**BUT <u>WAS</u> MADE <u>FOR WRATH</u>**
BY THE CREATOR OF THE WORLD WHO DIRECTS EACH MAN'S PATH.
Prov. 4:18

He's in control - not you - to decide **"Who"** He loves enough
To invite and enjoy the **"Wedding Feast of the Bride and Groom"**...
No bluff. Matt. 22:1-14

It's hidden in His "WORD" - He hides secrets from "Fools".
Gal. 3:2, 3:23; Prov. 3:32

Satan, Sin and Death are the **"gods"** of this world - **void** of any "Light" -
But of ALL CREATION - JESUS RULES !!!

Rich Kovatch
10-8-11

#82 The Character of God

I know the Character of God so well.
I know the **Power** of **LOVE** and the **TRUE** UNDERSTANDING of **HELL**.
Prov. 27:5
A really bold statement - most will say.
A PERSONAL relationship with our Father and creator? No way!

Of course that's what an unschooled mind will think.
And there's nothing wrong with that until one comes to the brink
Of the edge of reality of walking without God's Spirit.
God continually has His Word speaking to all, but most don't hear it.

It's described as a still small voice so quiet   1 Kings 19:12
One's soul has to be at peace and ignore the riot
That's going on around us, full tilt, with evil in charge.
TRUE PEACE is through UNDERSTANDING and WISDOM means livin'
Large.   Prov. 1:1-7

That's what God created us for...
To answer our shepherd's gentle call and open the door
To my heart - to desire Him to bring the light that burns
Sinful ways out of my heart of stone and into one of flesh it turns!
2 Cor. 3:3

Every day more of His character I find out as I live out His GIFT
Of the CONSCIENCENESS of the Spirit of LOVE that will eventually lift
ALL **SOULS** out of darkness while only those enlightened while living -
His TRUE CHURCH
Which won't hide His LIGHT under a bushel but set it high on a perch
John 3:14

That the dark world (designed by God) might see   `   Gen. 1:1-2
His righteous motivation for the Fruit of the Spirit to be
Shown - as His apostles learned...Disciples seek after...but Jesus DID
As He heals ALL who come to Him in FAITH and have gotten rid

#82 The Character of God

Of the controlling nature of carnality into which we're all born. **Gal. 4:29**
WE understand the significance of when Jesus died - the veil was torn
That separated the High Priest from entering the Holy of Holies.
He's now our advocate to proclaim our guiltlessness against the
Accusations of Satan and his bullies.

It's through FAITH - GIVEN US by God - to understand that spiritual
Event.
His **"called out"** ones will hear WISDOM soon enough to prevent
A choice we will make to cause harm to God's character of ALWAYS
Being GOOD.
So even thinking like that becomes an **"old nature"** surrendered and
Burned up like hay, stubble and wood.

The **"GOOD NEWS"** is so simple a child can understand it.
God is GOOD, created us to enjoy Him in a world He sees fit
For us to be **"pilgrims"** in - **a place** of TIME and SPACE
Of **ONE BODY**, ONE **SPIRIT**, ONE **BAPTISM**, ONE **FAITH**, ONE **LORD of
GRACE** !

God **loves** the little children. **ALL** the children of the world.
Kids sing and believe this song knowing that God first created it, then
Twirled
To blend it together as one HUMAN RACE. Red, Yellow, Black & White.
It ends with - WE ARE *ALL* PRECIOUS IN HIS SIGHT!!!

So what are the pictures and patterns God's given us to see His glory?
Creation itself, Family and relationships with **ALL** mankind. And it grows
The more He
Proves Himself through His written WORD - none to come back void.
And those whose spirit believe God *DOESN'T* SAVE ALL MEN really get
Annoyed.

#82 The Character of God

Children **understand** that a family has **good** kids and **bad** kids in it,
A mom and a dad to keep order even when one throws a hissy fit!
A child acts as a child. So true in the Spirit as well.
But even the child knows he's still loved and there's a good reason for
Punishment or **"hell"**.

A beginner is going to make mistakes and the guardian will correct
According to the needed action to get the child to inspect
His own closet to discover there's still stuff in there not right.
This **G**od given GIFT to desire to be loved draws us to dwell in **H**is might.

Which *is* the **POWER TO FORGIVE** balanced w/ RIGHTEOUS JUDGMENT.
"Train up a child in the way he should go"...is the message **G**od sent
In the **B**ook of **P**roverbs and *EVERY* **BOOK** in the **B**ible states
He **loves all us sinners...but it's the sin He hates!!!**

Because sin makes it impossible to be in step with Jesus.
Only people aware of **G**od's character are aware of the power of sin to
Seize us   Heb. 12:1
When we succumb to an ungodly desire and just go with the flow.
But *God is CREATED THRU US* when our "new man" walks in
Righteousness and true holiness. Don't you know?

This **G**od being **"created"** is not **"The Father"** but **H**is **"WAYS"**.
Moses asked to know them - the **L**aw was the **W**ord for those days
Which promised blessings and curses if followed or not.
His judgments are true so you'll deserve what you've got.

Do you have **H**is **AGAPE Spirit *to give* Grace** to fallen man?
Don't you know you were one too, **(or still are)** lost unless you can
Have the patience to withstand the abuse that will come upon you.
When they see **H**is **S**pirit working THRU you in the things you do.

#82 The Character of God

As a teacher, beware. You'll have to answer for what you taught.
What will you say *if* He says, "Depart, I never knew you" because you
Sought
To be lifted up before men because of your confession with your tongue.
Even if persecuted, it will be unrighteous and your cloak covered with
Dung.

The problem with knowledge when it comes to the carnal mind
Is it's impossible to relate to His Spirit of Mercy to find
Forgiveness of **ALL SINS** through Jesus' life and blood freely offered and
Accepted
To be the **"FIRST FRUIT"** of all who through faith will be resurrected

Because their name will be written in the **"Book of Life"** the very minute
You make it to the planet Earth - so your name's definitely IN IT !
But this **true "Book of Life"** is the **ETERNAL LIFE IN CHRIST** given to
Only His church folks with **AGAPE LOVE** *RIGHT NOW* which will do

"Greater things than these", Jesus said because the Holy Spirit will be
Poured out
To the entire world at **Pentecost** when the true gospel gained clout.
The 7 feasts which *are* the **appointed times** of the Lord are the best
Picture
Of the salvation for all that would agree to be a family with **G**od being
The focused fixture.

It **isn't** through their **own obedience** that **ALL ISRAEL WILL BE SAVED**
BUT **G**od making covenants with them and promises to be craved
Not for one owns comfort or glory , but mostly to be shared.
When lost souls are <u>won</u> back <u>into</u> the Kingdom by the way we <u>cared</u>!

#82 The Character of God

The Devil wants to divide mankind to accuse **others** to hell
& say God lets them choose some **eternal place** in which they CAN'T tell
God that they now know they're DEFINITLY GUILTY and sorry and finally
Will repent.
When Jesus went into Hell ***and set the captives free*** because ***EVEN
THERE*** the redemptive power is sent !!!

Now what exactly HELL **IS** a teacher would be **WISE** to learn
It definitely is a place where **ones conscious will burn**
With the knowledge of their sin - what was learned in the GARDEN.
When one walks in a sin - in this area - one's heart will harden

Because sin has pleasure - but only to the CARNAL **MIND.**
Real pleasure is loving God and **ALL MEN - ESPECIALLY** enemies who'll
Try to **grind**
Into dust our insistence that **ALL** will be restored as ORIGINALLY
DESIGNED
BY JESUS' FAITH and **PRAYER** *on the cross* that God *will* forgive **ALL**
IGNORANT **MANKIND!!!**

Rich Kovatch
8-23-11

#83 The Saddest Thing

The saddest thing that God has to endure
Is that so many people don't believe Jesus' blood is the cure
To **the UNIVERSE'S biggest problem. The sin** of **dis**belief
Which keeps the carnal mind in the torture of **Hell**'s grief.

Our Father cries as Jesus did when compassion overflowed
When He was walking among His unbelieving creation; especially when
He showed   Luke 10:36-37
Those near enough to Him to see that only in Him is true life.   1Cor. 2:7-16
All who came were healed of their specific ills because of the knife
                                                             Luke 6:17-19

Edge of the Sword of the Spirit of Truth that it is one's own choice
Of words that make it out of our mouths so to which spirit we give voice
                                                   Job 33:1-4   Deut. 30:14-20
From our heart at that moment. Proof of if we're experiencing the flesh
Or Spirit.   Prov. 10:6, 11-13
The humbling part is that whoever's near enough to us will be effected if
They hear it.   Isa. 2:11&17

Now, if I see this situation dishonors God somehow and it makes me
Break down and cry
It's like God's crying picture in nature when rain falls from the darkened
Sky.
He speaks of the former rain and a latter rain that will pour
                                               Jer. 5:24   Joel 2:23, 3:2
Out *His* **Spirit** and flood His entire garden with Love...this time with
Grace the door

To faithful eyes which see thru His creative ways how He shows His
Character to His flock.   1 Cor. 2:7-16
It's God's Glory to hide things; but the honor of kings is to search it out
And not mock   Prov. 25:2
The way He's working His plan out in everyone else...and especially in
My own talk   Jer. 29:11
Because my brief time in this testing body is to show God and **ALL** if it
Matches my walk   2 Cor. 4:17-18

#83 The Saddest Thing

This glorious Garden of Eden is my soul in which He's planted
The **_Seed_** of **_Faith_** - a measure given to **_ALL_** MEN - granted.

2 Cor. 10:13

But the seed falling from the tree; getting buried in earth; being watered
And lifted up
As a brand new tree is His **_Picture of Life_** to **_any_** who **drink** of His cup.

Adam - made from the Earth was destroyed in Noah's day
Except for the family of 8 in Faith who spent 120 years keeping disbelief
At bay
1 Peter 3:16-20
As they were mocked and ridiculed for building such a thing
As an Ark - which symbolizes our relationship with Jesus during our
"Spring,
1 Peter 3:21-22

Summer, fall and winter" with our carnal nature buried in snow.

1 Peter 4:1-2

But the pattern is Spring returns and seeds looking dead to the world
Rise to show
God always has a way - a **"First Fruit"** of new life which always blooms
When we understand it's His joy to be patient with sinners while He
Grooms

US **_ALL_** into His Glory which is why He loves and created us for.

1 Cor. 6:19-20

He keeps knocking and knocks even right up to one's own death door
To humble **each** soul - even at that moment rightly justified to be
Forgiven by Jesus' shed blood
Which is **the _new_ picture** of God covering **_ALL_** SINS during the flood.

Those eight in the Ark chose early to walk in belief and were saved
From the **whole** process of this qu**ick** destruction of **ALL** who misbehaved.

1 Cor. 5:5

Our Apostle Paul said the whole body may be delivered for destruction
So the soul may be kept.
2 Cor. 4:16
THIS is the saddest thing that filled Jesus' heart so with compassion that
He wept.
John 11:35

#83 The Saddest Thing

His Spirit grieved because they understood not that He **IS**
The **R**esurrection and The **Life** standing right in front of us but only vis-
Able to whosoever He's chosen ***at that moment*** to enlighten
That He'll guide ***All*** *LOST* men back to the Truth...even if He has to
Frighten

Them back! With **Hell's** threat??? ONLY BY one who doesn't understand
The <u>purpose</u> **of judgment is** *to* <u>*correct*</u> *the wild child* so he'll surely land
1 Cor. 2:10-16

Back in God's hand...safe and secure again - **BECAUSE LOVE - LOVES ! ! !**
Heb.10:6

And ***DOESN'T*** **GIVE UP** because the child's rebellion constantly shoves
See O.T. Israel and Judah

His corrective hand away...only to take the SAME TEST again**!**
His desire is to spread His wings and protect us like a mother hen
Matt. 23:27 Luke 13:34

But we run around the barnyard like chickens with their heads cut off
And sometimes into the street
Where we're in imminent danger of our sure sudden destruction to
Meet. Col. 3:25

So many pictures & patterns God shows His kids of His way   Heb.9:22-23
To be the hero who rescues the distressed maiden and saves the day.
New life always returns because the life is secure in its seeds   Gen. 1:11-12
Which are always kept by God Himself to glorify Himself providing our
Needs

His tool - the church of Truth and Spirit that provides itself as servant
John 4:23-24

Only this group will wash the feet of the dusty road's entrant   Luke 9:5-6
Into the house of the Lord of the brotherhood of Forgiveness and Mercy
That understand that God's still working on them so they'll eventually be
ALL of 1 Cor.

#83 The Saddest Thing

The finished product of God's effort to expand His Glorious Kingdom.

Rom.8:1-8

This Kingdom means a king rules and has followers to which He's
Bringed 'um
Other lost sheep like **ALL** **MEN ARE** _until_ He also saves them **by** **_Grace_**.

Heb. 10:1-22

That's the ONLY WAY because the Law makes nothing perfect in this
Human Race. **Heb. 7:16, 19**

And the saddest thing to choose to endure
Is to stay bound to a married partner who looks to any other cure
That's personal to each person - we have IDOLS we cherish more
Than Christ's Way and it's His pleasure to show us the door

To Hell - where only fools walk into because the prouder and taller they
Stand
The harder they'll fall - another lesson we've been taught - that we'll
Land John 3:27
Flat on our butts where pride will take the biggest hit.
The cushioned areas on our physical body designed to absorb judgment
As a loving Father sees fit.

Another picture of His brilliant design to bring my life good
As a child I felt it from my school principal and his paddle of wood
Right on this soft spot to sting but in no way harms.
The pain we cause ourselves when we try to pull out of God's arms.

My father in the flesh was like the picture of my Father above.
He spanked me with a whip when necessary to discipline with the iron
Glove.
Again... the picture of Power of He who rules
Who's **NOT** WILLING that **ANY** PERISH BUT **_ALL_** **COME** TO REPENTANCE
And be the jewels **2 Pet.3:9**

#83 The Saddest Thing

ON Jesus' crown of Righteousness God's Spirit has provided.   2 Tim. 2:4-5
His inheritance - **ALL** ISRAEL - **ALL** UNBELIEVERS in **SOME** aspect
Highlighted   Rom. 11:26-**32**
As Jesus said would happen - we'd sees twigs as logs in other eyes but
Think the log was but a twig in our own!
Come on now! Does your spiritual eye *finally* see after that last bone
                                                                    Luke 6:42

I've thrown you - that **ALL** MEN ARE CREATED EQUAL IN ***GOD***'S MIND.
The thing to always remember as a disciple is that *it's a personal time*
For each to find
That what the false church preaches - that what's available for "
Christians" to cherish
Is *never* taken away *from anyone* so in their conclusion - they *won't*
Perish

But be transformed in the twinkling of an eye.   1 Cor. 15:52
Quicker than lightning flashing across the night sky.   Matt. 24:27 Luke 17:24
Yet another picture of God lighting up dark souls
With flashes of insight that there's an end to the night when the bell
Tolls,

And at that time "old" ears **will now hear** the call to repent and now live
In as many gifts as you believe **He's given you to now give**
Back to the broken hearted and widows and those in prison.
Another picture word story to spread the gospel that He's Risen

And **has** the "keys" to "Hell" and "death". No longer Satan in total
Charge.   Rev. 1:18
This ***personal revelation*** of the ***Power*** and **Life of Jesus is so large**
That knowledge is easy to those who understand these pictures.
                    See ***"Understanding"*** in Book of Prov. & (14:6)
Wisdom and Love and Righteous Judgment means ***ALL*** SOULS ***will*** be
VICTORS ! ! !

                                                        Rich Kovatch
                                                        10-30-11

#84 I Demand My Rights

I demand my **"rights"**. What an ignorant saying.
What **"rights"** do you think you own and what game are you playing?
Who made **YOU God** over how others should act towards you?
I'll tell you exactly - it's the **god** of this world - Satan. That's who.

The problem with writing anything down on paper or on stone
Is there has to be an authority that talks and someone who's already Grown
From a child into a man and has matured in mind and spirit
So when the **Holy Spirit** communicates - this **"One New Man"** will hear it.

So the problem is that no matter what gets written down;
If the reader isn't in tune with the ONLY FREQUENCY on which the Message can be found
It'll go in one ear and out the other without an effect at all.
So only when one understands **WISDOM** will one answer the **shepherd's** Call.

And it's so easy that a child will accept and believe it to be so
Because the young mind is like a sponge designed to assimilate water And grow.
But the child must be taught that there is also a **counterfeit** voice
That constantly drives the immature mind to question **God's** choice

Of how each moment in time should be arranged and played
And especially **WHO'S** conducting...**God**...or some **god** which has swayed
You away and formed a musical band **(religion)** of his own to sing out **(False doctrines)** his **"rights"**.
The written word has recorded that this **god** is **Satan** - the causer of Carnal based fights

When the **god (self)** demands **God (JESUS)** to make things so;
So **self** will be comforted and if anyone doesn't like it they can go
Right to **Hell** because of the spirit that voices *"I'm* the boss and what *I* Say goes".
It's *my* **"right"** to choose & *my* life is most important to *me*...& it shows

#84 I Demand My Rights

In actions and words that kills a friendly spirit in others in order to lift
Oneself up.
Always is done by degrading others with the condemnation cup
And fills it a with carnal generated wrath thinking one is doing **God's**
Will.
The *spirit* of pride...the same god that <u>Saul</u> of Tarsus <u>had</u> (a legalistic
Jew of the Jews) is alive and **kic*king st*ill**.

A child must learn he has **NO** "RIGHTS" except those graciously given
By the parents who share in the direction he should be driven.
Now this is deep here, so I hope you won't be drowned.
The <u>**Father is Spirit**</u>; the <u>**Mother**</u> is <u>the **body**</u> through which **TRUTH** is
Found.

God our Father is the giver of life who breathed into the clay
He formed from the **dirt** - Adam - the **1st** man - the body of today.
But the **2nd** Adam - **JESUS** - dwells in a place *not made* by hands.
God is Spirit and **to put off** this old carnal nature is the <u>*first*</u> *one heard*
Of God's constant commands.

What He commands is that you love **Him** and **Agape** <u>*ALL*</u> others
Which can't come from the carnal spirit that **desires to <u>*stone*</u>** your
Brothers
As punishment **deserved** from the *written* law purposed to cause **ALL to
Die.**
EXCEPT JESUS of course; God Himself come to save ALL MEN. NO LIE !!

ONLY *JESUS* walked perfect according to the law - thus won
The legal ownership back after the **1st** Adam's purpose was done.
God's chosen vessel and way to breathe life into the earth - **YOU.**
Now here's the **"rights"** you now will be taught to teach others & to do.

#84 I Demand My Rights

Now these **"rights"** can only be done with **A**gape Love as its **power.**
The **1ˢᵗ "right"** is that of choosing now *to forgive* so our disposition will
Be **sweet** not *sour.*
This is what Jesus did for ALL men by FREELY OFFERING HIMSELF for
Sinners
And RIGHTEOUSNESS ACCEPTING it and according to His PROMISE
Transforming us losers into winners!

So the opposite of this right would be the wrong thing to do.
That would be refusing to forgive - making the prisoner - **YOU!**
Holding the opposite mindset of **G**od puts *YOU* in **HELL** - the **KEY** is to
KNOW your dad.
He always forgives but uses punishment to bring about an ending
Making everyone glad

That He's the Conductor of the "Love **U**nlimited **O**rchestra" - **His**
Preachers
That sing out the **"Good News"** that men are more than just **G**od's
Creatures
That He's **NOT** given *MORE* POWER **to choose death** over life than their
Loving maker
Who's **S**pirit has **conquered ALL** - including death - *although many are a*
Partaker

Of the path in which no light will be seen if you think you are "The
Man".
Like **S**aul, you'll get knocked off your high horse and land flat on your
Can
And **G**od **WILL** SHOW HIMSELF to you *after* you've been *totally*
Humbled.
This happens only after hours and hours in which you yelled at **G**od and
Grumbled

#84 I Demand My Rights

That your **"rights"** were violated - child remember **WISDOM** is our guide
That will bring you back down to earth after you've seen you're pride
Has died.
God has given us power to become **"S**ons of God" if we so choose.
He also gives us the power to choose death *but it doesn't mean God
Will lose*

Your eternal soul - dear sweet child and my brother in Christ *be secure
In the fact*
In Ephesians God gave us **17** things over which His *redemptive Will* has
Never lacked
The **POWER** to have victory - **17** - it's biblical # - another sign revealed in
The spirit only.
**Does your perceived "rights" bring you closer to ignorant lost lambs in
Order to witness light or just more lonely?**

Watch out for what you wish for because you just might get it.
It is true, you will reap what you sow, and **G**od won't let you to forget it
So He constantly has to punish our wrong moves but graciously *__blesses__*
The *__good__*.
THIS IS WHAT LOVE DOES - *correct the foolish lost sheep __like He said He
Would__*.

It's not our place to bitch at **G**od but to enter the **K**ingdom through
Worship and praise.
And this happens not when an immature Israelite grumbles but when
Enlightened voices raise
The **cover of darkness - false doctrines of eternal death -** *off* the glory
Of Light
*That God is Good and Love Forgives sin and __ALL__ get saved from the
Darkness of night*

Which is God's picture of the awareness of his Spirit working in our life.
He doesn't want to be married to a *Carnal* Israel - His judgment
Provoking harlot - wife
But desires to experience life through His virgin bride and conceive His
Bountiful offspring...
New souls **with minds transformed** *by God* when one sees the cross and
It's wholly **H**oly **L**ove offering.

Rich Kovatch   11-12-11

One   is the Loneliest Number ?

Three Dog Night sang; "One is the loneliest number that you'll ever do.
But two can be as bad as one"...or worse, more than a few.
The three dogs picture comfort on a real cold, lonely desert night.
Though alone, his three "best friend" companions took away any fright

That he might not survive the loneliness and die alone.
Like Daniel chose to walk into a fire with his invisible chaperone
And his two buddies in the flesh but all three united to the Spirit
Which revealed the **4**th to the enemies that couldn't get near it.

7 times **hotter** than normal temperature used to try to kill the three
Because they wouldn't conform to the world's wicked king's plea
To consume the unhealthy diet and adapt the customs of their captor.
They were slaves in the flesh but knew their spirits would soon find their
Rapture

If that's what **G**od would choose their humbled fate to be
They were pictures for us to help set our world infested souls free.
3 men of faith willfully chose to follow their heart.
They heard the still small voice - that they've been **"set apart"**

To walk where the faithless fear to go!
The **"Spirit man"** will lead the **carnal** into God's *purifying fire* so
The **7 Spirits** *of* **God** will remove **the** <u>dross</u> that <u>must</u> be burned
On the altar enjoyed as sweet incense to God. That's <u>*sin*</u> being **burned**
<u>*Not*</u> <u>people</u>...*<u>the</u>* lesson to be <u>learned</u> !!!

1,3,4 and **7** are numbers associated with this story.
1 is the Spirit that **Truth WILL PROVIDE Jesus' redemptive glory.**
3 is the number for resurrection and might picture our body, soul and
Spirit being willing to die.
So **4** enters the picture as the number of the world during this fry.

One　　　is the Loneliest Number ? #85

God's Word speaks of a mingling of the wine and oxen messing up the Place.
This is the Holy Spirit giving His disciples clues on how to see His face.
7 - the number for completeness and spiritual perfection is how hot **"Hell"** will feel
Which will draw out sin in one's life and cause him to squeal

Which is a Good and Holy design so that every soul will kneel
To bow and confess in worshipful thankfulness that Jesus will finally Reveal
That the death sentence sin legally demands to justify the law
Was - **like He said -** *paid for* by **His blood** for 1 and **ALL** - **without a flaw.**

This group of two or more I mentioned at the start
Pictures what God said would happen when men don't share the **AGAPE** LOVE that flows from God's heart.
2 - united against God - started with **Adam** and **Eve**
When the 2 got together and decided not to believe

God's Word that in that day they'd surely die.
Adam desired *his* **mate** - **like** *every other creature had* - **is why**
He chose to be complete with his wife - no matter what **"to die"** meant.
He had **NO CLUE** because death **hadn't yet entered** God's creation as
The vent

To release sin and the Devil and his charges to a place called **Tartarus**
So evil can be the companion of evil and stay far from the rest of us.
As far as the east is from the west - God remembers it NO MORE!
All religious systems including **false Christianity** are pictured as the **Great whore**

In the Book of the Revelation of Jesus Christ - **WHO IS SALVATION**
To His people of faith who've been shown Abraham's great nation
That will bless the entire world with the Gospel of **"Good News"**
That **God revealed His plan to save** *ALL* men through the favored Jews.

One   is the Loneliest Number ? #85

They were favored as a nation because **God** spoke to them in **WORD, ACTION,** and **WRITING**
The picture is that when more than **1** person have an issue...it usually
Leads to fighting
Unless this **"ONE"** is the **Spirit of Truth** that *ALL* MEN ARE BROTHERS.
God has revealed in His **"Good** Samaritan" picture that **AGAPE** LOVE is
Like that of desperate mothers

Who'll pay *any* price and *do anything* to *ensure* the battered soul's
Survival
Including sacrificing her own life to defeat her rival
For the life of her child - that's mankind and Jesus the **LOVER.**
The INNKEEPER is the **AGAPE** CHURCH that deals with the cover

Of how this FORGIVING *LOVE WILL* TRANSFORM this wild olive tree
By trimming off the unfruitful twigs that hinder a pure growth set free.
This process causes sharp pain but from it will come great gains
When this downtrodden soul is redeemed from his woes and Love now
Reigns

In his heart - fully made new with a joyful spirit
That *REMEMBERS* the **Love given** to him when he cried out and
"Religious" ears didn't hear it.
Imposters for Christ who didn't think it right to touch their perceived
Enemy.
God told Peter - **SALVATION** IS FOR **ALL** NATIONS and **PEOPLES** that put
Nothing ahead of Me.

His story is told through *history* of the *entire* human race...
That *all men fail* to completely override the *need* for **GRACE.**
Even Jesus had this Grace and he took it to the limit.
It gave Him power over every **evil** thought so of **G**od's **LIGHT** the world
Failed to dim it.

One   is the Loneliest Number ? #85

This is why most men can't stand the **LIGHT**.
They Love the darkness of evil and live to fight
Really against spirits and principalities and things held in high places.
The **carnal** **nature** of condemnation **prevents** most from *seeing* Christ in
ALL human FACES!

GOD'S Spirit judges the heart and His "Peters" do understand the truth
Of God's way.
To be a fisher of men is to be patient and return Good for evil in order to
Say
By **ACTIONS** *not* words how TRUE LOVE ENDURES ALL
No matter how many times my brother repents... **then** I see *again* fall!

7 X 70 times **IS HOW JESUS SAID LOVE WORKS !!!**
Is **a** punishment of **"Hell"** *without* *redemption* one of God's **plan's "little
Quirks"**
Where **His PROMISE TO SAVE** the 100th **LOST SHEEP might** *not* **RING
TRUE ???**
Is THIS the **ALL K**nowing and **ALL P**owerful **G**od you preach to save
Others from **ALL SINS ...and** *you* ???

Rich Kovatch
11-13-11

#86 TONE

Out of the mouth comes the issues of the heart.
The question is: Right now and every moment do you desire to start
To hear the **TONE** of **LOVE** and **GUIDENCE** in Jesus' words _to all_
To draw His lost sheep back to Himself with reassurance in His call.

OR... do you hear our **"Good Shepherd's"** voice in a **TONE**
That **DESIRES** to _punish_ forever _ALL_ the Father doesn't now own?
That's great ! And true ! And I believe that too.
Now here's what **LOVE** has shown this rebellious lamb to be **TRUE**.

There is a vibration that runs through each **atom (Adam also)** and past
Into a realm where **ONLY GOD'S WORDS, TRUTH** and **PEACE** will last
Even in the perceived vacuum of space where the atoms are missing.
This darkness is part of the **bigger picture** for us to see how He's kissing

ALL of mankind with His story of **Redemption** for _ALL_ in the skies.
Of course this only happens when **TRUE LOVE** has opened ones' eyes
To the Spirit that can **FORGIVE** to the uttermost. **Yes...EVEN SINNERS.**
So God's most glorious pleasure is turning **"losers"** into **"winners"**!!!

Now..._my TONE_ when I say **"losers"** ... _to all it will be clear._
The religious Jews rejected the message..._but it drew sinners near!!!_
The "loser" is the mind that has not been renewed.
Like the older prodigal "_**brother**_" _who refused to join the celebration but_
Rather stewed

Over the fact that his **"brother"** who wasted _his_ time and material
Was again welcomed back to all the Father still owned - _**ALL**_ **ISRAEL.**
All Israel is not all Israel. Again...what **TONE** do you hear?
Do the joyful tones of a party sound like love celebrating victory and
That draws **you** near?

All of Heaven rejoices when ONE lost lamb is returned.
Where is the older brother at this time - was his heart not burned
With feelings of envy, or hate, or anger for such a display?
For he thought his legalistic walk should have _earned_ him his day

#86 TONE

When *he* could kill the fatted calf and party with *his* friends.
The Father said he was welcome to *every day* because the party never
Ends.
The party is about how God's GRACE COVERS _ALL_ SINS
Except the "unpardonable" one which is **TO DISBELIEVE** LOVE WINS ! ! !

So did the **TONE** you just heard again support the **"death"** penalty
For all that don't repent, or confess...but die in their sins only to see
ETERNAL TORTURE with a clear conscious of their Creator turning His
Back _ON_ _THEM_
BUT HE CHOOSE "TO SAVE HIS CHURCH" - some religious sect **who _DID_**
S.O.M.E.T.H.I.N.G? Ahem.

To **"EARN"** their way into this Kingdom where **PEACE** and **TRUTH** rule.
God chooses on WHO and WHEN and HOW He'll have MERCY shown,
And the **"Law"** is not the tool
For a PERSONAL Salvation gaining walk; but for us to fear and tremble
And **_UNDERSTAND_ the purpose of punishment and judgment** is to
Resemble

Christ in His effort to bring God's **LIGHT** to the lost.
The sins **_of the world_** were **IMPUTED** to Jesus who **WILLINGLY _PAID_**
THE COST
That has **ENDURED** with **LONGSUFFERING** the disrespect **"Old**
Testament" Israel shows.
This is the picture of your walk as your **_hate_** for people **_dies_** and the
"NEW ISRAEL" grows

To fill your heart with God's compassion and forgiveness for lost souls
And believe in your heart - Right Now - YOU'RE PRAYER TO SAVE ALL
Rolls
Out of your mouth with the **TONE** of confidence to tell all
That **EVENTUALLY** every person WILL PRAISE God for **His GRACE** to even
Call

#86 TONE

Such a **wretched soul** with a righteousness covered with stains
PERSONALLY up to His chair
Of JUDGMENT where only those who are given entrance will be His
HEIR.
I thank God that His **WORD that *vibrates* forever said Christ is "All in
All"**.
And **"ALL"** things **include *people,*** death and confusion and are subject to
His gavel's great fall.

And He's said He's already condemned the world - here's the picture -
Your carnal nature **is doomed** but there is a Spirit nature in the mixture.
This battle of which one dominates each moment comes out in your
Song
Of what God will do with people who __you__ __believe__ are doing wrong.

His command is to judge righteously as He does like a good father does.
He sees what this scared, ignorant lamb for what it IS — not what it WAS.
Forgiving 7 X 70 times and **totally forgetting the past. Prideful in His
Work**
To change the darkness by filling the void earth with **LIGHT** His biggest
Quirk

That those not "**B**orn **A**gain" with the **S**pirit of Love and Truth *__that__ __saves__*
Just can't grasp because they don't **know H**is heart -just how he behaves
Which takes the discernment of Spirits and time to build a relationship
So each can honestly tell the other their deepest hopes and fears that
Might tip

The scales of justice towards a judgment seemingly in fear and not to be
Enjoyed
If not understood that the big picture **G**od has MERCIFULLY employed
Is **H**e judges **EVIL** and **SAVES HIS CHILDREN** from its deathly grip.
Once again...MY **TONE** is to praise His **WILL *TO SAVE*** - not strip

#86 TONE

Any last ounce of **HOPE** a lost soul may still have that SOMEHOW, SOMEWAY, SOMETHING, SOME**ONE** actually **STILL LOVES** them - **RIGHT NOW!**
Even <u>while</u> trapped in sin and without even the ability to control its Limit.
This last ounce may be my words to him or her that **Jesus** - deep down - IS STILL IN IT ! ! !

And THAT is what I do pray - that all mankind would hope that all R.I.P.
Only an EVIL SPIRIT with death as its pleasure would WANT so that none Would see
This **LIGHT** which is **Jesus** - everlasting life consumed by **LOVE**
Which has always been - but death came after Adam chose to shove

God's Spiritual world out for **H**is created world - **MAINLY EVE,**
And worshipped his own flesh of his own flesh rather than believe
This **"death"** would come upon him "that day" should he eat of the Wrong tree.
What it exactly was and we know now **IS *THE LOSS* OF THE LIFE *FOR YOU* ONLY GOD CAN SEE !**

Rich Kovatch
11-27-11

#87 The Carnal Mind / Blessed Hope

Right from this title God *shows us* the line
Between those that choose death and those who's **LOVE IS DEVINE.**
The **Carnal Nature** has **death** as its **permanent end.**
The **"Born Again" Spirit Nature** understands **JESUS IS** our friend.

Division is the Devil's agenda to keep our minds diverted.
Right from **Adam** and **Eve** he *persuaded their minds* to process the truth
Perverted.
They walked with the **S**pirit of **L**ove in the **G**arden of **E**den which means
Paradise
And came upon this tree **L**ove put there *so they could choose* if they
Each wanted to roll their pair of dice

Which they did *knowing* the results *are ordered* and *guided* by their
Loving **F**ather in **T**ruth.
And chose the adventure *to reveal* how **G**od will glorify **H**imself -
Explained in the **B**ook of **R**uth.
A **gentile** (non-**believer**) who *somehow had a desire* to serve
And *was given* the true riches that each man born does deserve.

To clarify this let's go back to the first stanza where our friend is
Mentioned.
"Our" is the word in which the **D**evil causes the greatest contention.
Does **"OUR"** mean **"the Church"** which WILL be saved from some end
Which would divide men from each other by trying to prove **J**esus is
ONLY *THEIR* friend

Because **they** "believe" and have "repented" and now preach the power
To save...
But *this* **G**od they preach will only save you *if you* don't misbehave;
Because **punishment is promised** and it's a thing to **FEAR...**
SOME *eternal* **consciousness** of your *separation* from **LOVE** *somehow*
Makes CARNAL MINDS CHEER!??

#87 The Carnal Mind / Blessed Hope

As if the **B**lessed **H**ope doesn't apply to **ALL** men - **His offspring**
And **JUDGMENT** and **PUNISHMENT** aren't **designed to ring**
As *warning* **bells** that this path will demand total *justice* and *retribution*.
But **evil** men who ***don't*** <u>**understand**</u> judgment and **allow** <u>**love**</u> to rule -
P*refer* *<u>electrocution</u>*

That will **shock** the life **out** of their enemy but somehow also
Continuously get worse forever.
There's only **Fear** and **PRIDE and Witchcraft** connected to that **Carnal Mind** that could *never*
See the **light of forgiveness** and the **TRUE POWER of Jesus' blood to Redeem.**
Only when Love has encompassed ones **heart** will this *perceived* enemy Seem

Like the **100th "Lost Lamb"** that has wandered out of the sheepfold
Like the ***picture*** of mankind being **H**is sheep and **H**e's our **S**hepherd is
Why **H**is **S**tory through the **B**ible is ***told***
To reveal how **G**od ***always leaves a way to escape***
To a nation or mind that gets stuck in the Law's **RED TAPE.**

Jesus didn't come to destroy His Law ***BUT SHOW US*** HOW TO JOYFULLY ***FULFILL***
The **p**ower of Love **to redeem lost Israel - - -** ***WHICH IS*** **GOD'S WILL.**
This **"Born Again"** moment happens when the **p**ower to **o**vercome sin Rules
And one starts to ***understand*** that ***enlightened minds*** are Jesus' **crown Jewels**

And ***do actually bring*** heaven's <u>***ways***</u> down to Earth <u>***this***</u> **day.**
This is Jesus' ***answer*** to how **H**is followers should **j**oyfully pray -
That we forgive those trespasses *willfully* done by others **and** our self.
This is ***how*** Grace **to All** ***is shown*** and the Blessed Hope our **wealth**

#87 The Carnal Mind / Blessed Hope

And **health** that can be given to prisoners of the great whore
Which is the **religious spirit** - *see* Jesus' *answers to how* He does abhor
This division between the clean and unclean in the "Good Samaritan"
Story
Or the scrolls in Peter's *vision* that gentiles are **ARE INCLUDED** in God's
Glory.

This "Blessed Hope" is another dividing concept to look forward to,
And / or be.
Does it mean some future (after my death) so my spirit will be free
From **sin** - and *even* the *ability* **TO** - WHAT A GREAT VICTORY - God
WINS!!!
OR IS IT <u>REALLY</u> *LIVING BY FAITH* THAT God <u>*WILL*</u> **COVER** the World's
Sins.

This means when I **LOVE** someone - **even if they hurt me,**
The Carnal Nature gets affected but the Spirit Nature *will see*
They hurt me because *they* hurt and the Spirit of Love *has built* a
RELATIONSHIP *with* this sinner;
And my words of this "Blessed Hope" *WILL TURN* THEM from a loser
Into a winner.

So do I offer *a picture* of somewhere - *not* here and now
Where his pains and worries will disappear and somehow
Be able to agree that ALL EVIL PEOPLE *deserve* to be **tortured**
But his ability to love and forgive and absorb pain will forever be
Nurtured

As we live with God - WHO *IS* LOVE - WHOSE PATIENCE *IS* PURE
But in some way *because* of justice - Jesus *REFUSES* **TO ENDURE**
And wait until each soul willfully decides to come back to Him;
But to permanently put them with the Devil and his angels in Taturus to
Begin

#87 The Carnal Mind / Blessed Hope

A sentence pronounced with Righteousness and *each* soul's *own good*
In God's mind.
THIS <u>ATTITUDE</u> BY GOD'S SPIRIT OF LOVE - <u>NOWHERE</u> IN THE BIBLE
<u>WILL</u> <u>YOU</u> <u>FIND</u>.
It is **the sin of disbelief** that Christ has ALL SOULS in His hands.
THE DEVIL **DIVIDES** and SAYS YOUR GOOD **IS** *NOT* IN GOD'S PLANS.

This is where the power of Love *really shows* its face.
CAN YOU <u>LOVE</u> YOUR ENEMY **ENOUGH TO** *<u>FORGIVE</u>* FROM GOD'S
GRACE
And not demand a quick change of direction - RIGHT NOW
To a new child in the faith you've just proclaimed the "Blessed Hope" *IS*
HERE somehow.

It's the Spirit of "The Comforter" who'll **NEVER** let **YOU** go
Who *gently guides* the wild, rebellious, terrified and hurt 100th lost
little Lamb to grow
In the knowledge of the LORD - Who **IS WISDOM** for abundant life.
He's precise enough to cut off the sin from your spirit with His Holy, **fiery
Knife.**

It's the **sword** of the **S**pirit of Truth that He wants **ALL to see**
The law doesn't justify but is the **bare minimum to guide you so now
You'll be**
Made available *when* *<u>you</u>* *realize* **you** were *<u>made</u>* to go *<u>above it</u>* to a
Place more righteous
Than that of the scribes and Pharisees. So Christian - to take flight just

Be lifted by the **S**pirit to become absent from the body and present with
The Lord.
The real battle is in our mind as thoughts come and persuade us to
Think we'll be board
Without the pleasures and carnal things of this world of flesh and
Bones.
That's the Devil's deception that everything created HE now owns

#87 The Carnal Mind / Blessed Hope

Including your soul which **A**dam supposedly gave away to **S**atan
So we're **ALL** born into this body with a **sin nature** and destined to exist
In **Hell hatin'**
God more than we did here, and specifically for not giving _**our**_ soul
THE GIFT He chose to give others.
NOW HERE'S **THE LIGHT** THAT **HOPE**FULLY **OPENS YOUR EYES TO SEE**
YOUR BROTHERS

Like **Esau** and **Jacob** - _**BOTH**_ FROM the _**SAME**_ DAD.
But God **does NOT hate** _as_ the **Carnal Mind** _does - so be glad_.
The _picture_ of a **G**ood Father **IS He** _corrects_ the harmful _nature_
So the child will learn **R**ighteousness **is** to Love - not _hate your_

Neighbor and enemy just because **G**od hasn't yet _revealed_
Himself to the **dark**ness in an **evil, prodigal son mind** that hasn't yet
Squealed
And cried and confessed to **G**od he **NOW** KNOWS he's been **d**eceived.
And when I tell him God _NEVER LETS GO_, _GRACE is received_ and he's
Totally relieved

Of the _**responsibility**_ to be perfect, thus earn **H**is love, but _given the_
Desire to obey _according to_ Love's LAW.
Because you _NOW SEE_ the **C**ity of Jerusalem not built with hands which
Abraham _saw_
Is the _PICTURE_ of LOVE dwelling in your heart with **W**isdom at its gates
And _you_ _understand_ HOW **sin** and **Love** _relates_.

LOVE _COVERS_ ALL SIN **except** the one of **DISBELIEF**
Sadly - while realizing this time on Earth they wasted, but then
Mercifully and thankfully a BIG RELIEF
When Jesus **FORGIVES** them TOO - JUST LIKE _HE_ _**WILL**_ **FOR YOU**
Because he Loves sinners **SO MUCH** He DIED and **SHED** _**HIS**_ **BLOOD to do**

What the Law **NEVER** COULD - **justify their acceptance**
Into a place of perfection _only_ _**washed**_ _clean_ by repentance -
Even if this confession should come at the time HIS knees bow
ON HIS JUDGMENT DAY with praise for Jesus **W**HO EVEN THEN

#87 The Carnal Mind / Blessed Hope

IS WILLING TO SAVE because they THEN *WILL* SEE
The **scars** on His hands and feet and the sword wound which all will be
This **EVERLASTING REMEMBERANCE** of the *PRICE* JESUS PAID
For EVERY MAN to whom God gave life 1ˢᵗ on this planet He made

With the Tree of Temptation to answer the question of exactly *WHAT* is
REAL JOY;
IT IS being able to provide the needs for each girl and boy
That has EVER BEEN BORN - *THIS NEED IS HIMSELF*.
The **ULTIMATE** pleasure for God IS *WHEN* YOU *SEE* YOUR BROTHER AS
HIS WEALTH.

As the three stories Jesus *told* of **lost items** being found,
The TOTAL FOCUS was **TO RECOVER** THE LOST ITEM, then rejoice with all
Around.
And of course if YOU'RE **not** around because of some **selfish, pride**
Based reason
This shows that to God's **Law** of **Love** you're committing Spiritual
Treason.

God has a continuous **wedding banquet** party going on where every
Angel rejoices
And the New Song of Moses is sung verbally by **ALL** of creation's voices.
It's the song glorifying the power of **Love** *to save* EVEN THE WORST
SOUL.
So ONLY WHEN God RE-ENTERS it - IT AGAIN BECOMES WHOLE.

Rich Kovatch
12-3-11

Picture the Body   in Motion

#88

The **body** *in motion* is a **beautiful t**hing.
The voice box can bring out sweet loving **words** that sing
Of the **G**lory of God ***THAT SAVES*** ALL MEN THAT **B**ELIEVE.
Now, there's *another part* of **The B**ody that's *designed to relieve*

The vast majority of the ***ingested materials*** that had no lasting **value.**
It's like the fruit of the **T**ree of **K**nowledge of **G**ood and **E**vil is the pal **you**
Have to discard because it was only ALONG *FOR THE R*IDE
AND IN **NO WAY** CAN MAKE IT TO THE *SPIRITUAL SIDE*

Of ***"The BODY"*** you're a member of that needs no **C**arnal **f**ood,
But the **"Living Water"** & the **"Bread of Life"** that come from above. **D**ude.
Picture: **"Water"** from **"The Rock"** and the **Manna** and **Ravens** that fell
From the **s**ky.
Without this ***MIRACULOUS*** provision – the children of Israel would
Surely **d**ie.

This is ***REDEMPTION'S PICTURE*** of Jesus' **RESCUING HIS** LOST SHEEP.
MOSES – AS **The "Law"** that legally proves there **IS** a **WAY** to **K**EEP
Your foot from wandering away from The **"Good Shepherd's"** watchful **e**ye.
So this **IS** the *Spiritual PICTURE* of a soul without the **"Law"** will also die.

THIS WORD is for **Christ's BODY in motion** – IT'S TIME TO REST
And **WAIT** UPON the **LORD** to do HIS very **b**est.
The *Spiritual PICTURE* of *LONGSUFFERING* and *PATIENCE* come **ONLY**
From **L**ove.
So we can **NOW WALK** in the **"New Jerusalem"** Abraham saw come
Down from **a**bove.

What has to be *excreted* is the mindset the **"Law"** brings us **o**ut
Of this world **G**od created ***TO SHOW*** **HIS GLORY** and **s**hout
That this is the way – as it has always been – some Jews did try to **s**way
A **"religious"** community designed, named Israel **that exists still** to this **d**ay.

Picture *the Body* in Motion

Judaism was man's **2nd** attempt to walk in communion with **God.**
The **1st** was by Adam and Eve – who also failed and ended up in Nod
Which is the ***PICTURE*** of the **wilderness** *outside* the "Garden of Eden"
Where **ALL lost souls STAY** – as long as it's from the wrong **Tree** they're
Feedin'.

"Feed my sheep" – Jesus told **3 times** to the Apostle called **Peter.**
The **"*Rock*"** He referred to was not a man but the revelation that's
MUCH SWEETER.
JESUS SAID THE **"*Gift*"** **OF T**he Father came upon him when he answered
Jesus' question right.
"*Who* do YOU say *I am*"? The answer IS pure dynamite!

Jesus **IS** mankind's **REDEEMER** AND God's only begotten *Son*
Who **O**UR Father preordained as our High Priest, Prophet and King who
Battled and *WON*
Against *principal*s and *powers* in high places that demand that you again
Build a larger barn on your farm.
Jesus said **"sell it all"!** His Ways and Words – God's TRUE ANSWERS -
*********************** This **3rd** time the charm! *******************

The barn is the ***PICTURE*** of all this world's desires that **b**lind
Our **Spiritual EYES** so the Carnal Mindset – the "Blessed Hope"-
Can never find.
The Kingdom Jesus brought down with **Him** to a world ruled by FEAR.
The epiphany Peter received opened his **EYES** that EVERLASTING LIFE
Was **N**OW HERE!

Not in the **physical** body Jesus possessed for **33 ½ years**
Which was conceived **1st** in God's Mind, then Mary's womb & delivered
Through **PAIN** and **t**ears.
The *Spiritual PICTURE* is the BIGGEST one believers like Peter and Paul
UNDERSTOOD.
Only thoughts MOTIVATED by a Holy and Pure Love will last...Selfish
Things burnt as hay, stubble and **w**ood.

Picture *the Body* in Motion

It is the compassion for sinners and His WILL to ENDURE rejection from
His OWN
And *willingly* offer HIS BODY and SPIRIT from the CROSS to be lifted up
To HIS throne
Where He NOW RULES over HIS Kingdom with Power and Might.
The "church" is His "Priests" and "Kings" and "Prophets" that proclaim
Exactly WHAT were to fight.

It's not against FLESH and BLOOD but principalities and powers in high
Places.
The *PICTURE is Spiritual* – Paul said. We're to SEE God in *ALL* human
Faces
And NOT JUDGE someone's MOTIVES, but certainly show them their
Current direction
With Love and Gentleness and Kindness and Compassion so we might
Be a reflection

Of the "Light of the World" – Jesus'Spirit – which awakens the sleeping
Soul.
Another *PICTURE* of how Love COVERS tragedy – if your neighbor's ox
Falls in your hole –
You're to give retribution – make up for even giving access to the pit you
Made.
If you *NEVER ENDINGLY* do this – *your character will be proven*
TRUSTWORTHY *and able* to persuade

Even the HARDEST HEART of STONE to melt from the CONSTANT
Warmth of LOVE.
PICTURE an egg being warmed by the hen UNTIL THE DAY arrives when
The chick WILL shove
Off the shell that once protected did crack after being hardened by time.
This SHELL is the flesh BODY and NATURE being *removed* and PAID FOR
On Jesus' dime.

Picture *the Body* in Motion

The *PICTURE* is the "Good Samaritan" who did **NOT** unrighteously just
Walk right by
As the 2 other "**religious**" minded men **did** because in their *doctrinal eye*
This broken down soul was not one of his own nationality...thus dirty
And unworthy of his time or attention.
But the "**Law**" has ways to cover sin, but effort is required by sacrificing,
So many ways I could mention

Which in itself is a *PICTURE* of the one being sacrificed.
Gentle and Peaceful with a singular vision of purpose *that sufficed*
As the *propitiation* for the sins of the world... God's plan from the start.
The "**New**" covenant PROMISES to soften EVERY **stone-hard** heart

And He WILL ENTER and LIVE in and TEACH of Himself to the lost.
This IS Jesus' **promised "Comforter"** after they **WAITED** during the
Feast of Pentecost.
Spiritual PICTURES – the **7** anointed times of Feasts for Israel and the
Zodiac of the coming Messiah in the stars
Coming TO SAVE *ALL* of LOST ISRAEL when they FINALLY **SEE H**is scars.

All these *PICTURES* have **motion** and actions vibrate on forever.
Energy can't be destroyed, just refused and quenched but never sever
Completely that last strand of Hope that ONLY God keeps TURNED ON.
So even the physical body's death is not the end and our souls won't be
Burned on

Forever like the *PICTURE* of **Gehenna** Jesus spoke of *to warn*
NOT of a *never ending* situation that *can't* be *reversed* – but *HOW* a
New Spirit is born.
It's *WHEN* the trash from the world *STOPS* getting thrown into the pit
The **FIRE** *WILL* BE **PUT OUT** ONCE *YOU DECIDE* THIS FEEDING *NEEDS*
TO QUIT.

Again back to the *PICTURE* of feeding our Spirit from the Tree of Life
That we DESIRE to continue – NOT the 1st Tree of strife.
Remember God set **FIREY ANGEL MESSENGERS** to guard The "Pearly
Gate".
THIS IS THE **JUDGMENT that burns up ALL EVIL** & **PURIFIES** on that date

Picture   *the Body*   in Motion

And anointed time that **ALL** must die and then be judged for the world
Of YOUR creation
And on their **"good works"** offered and joyfully completed with
RIGHTEOUS MOTIVATION.
These **"good works"** – *only* derived from intentions *to heal* a hurting
Soul.
Did following the **"Law"** fix the real problem or just keep you from
Falling into *that* hole?

The only way to stay out is to stay on the right path.
Teaching that the **"Law"** will allow you to pass those flames is not good Math.
NO MAN – NO NOT ONE – is justified by the **"Law"**, Paul wrote.
This is so Jesus gets **_ALL_** the Glory and **_NO_ MAN** WILL GLOAT

About the **"good works"** he did **on his own** while alive.
This is the deception of the harlot wife on which she tries to survive;
But WILL *NEVER* FIND **_REAL LIFE PICTURE_** you're a fish trying to fly.
It's not even possible with a Carnal weight so heavy you won't even try.

But when released – the **_PICTURE_** of Jesus' **BLOOD** washing away **ALL**
STAINS.
The **"FINAL"** you – God SAW from the beginning – **Purified** – **IS ALL THAT**
REMAINS.
So you're gladly welcomed into the Kingdom – flying right past those
Gates.
The Grace of God **LOVING YOU** and   FINALLY *OPENING YOUR EYES*   is to
What that relates.

You see – we can't look upon Pure Light until **_ALL the CELLS of our_**
Spiritual Body *agree*
And **_EVERY_ OUNCE** of our being is eating from the right Tree
That also was set – but right in the middle – of the "Garden" for Adam
And Eve to consume.
So only ways that bring lost minds **_back to Peace_** will continue to bloom;

Picture   *the Body*   in Motion

Thus **MOVE** the **BODY** of **C**HRIST to continue **o**n
To give HOPE to the widowed, sick and those in prison that we *HAVE*
ARRIVED at a **"new"** day's **d**awn.
That _looks past_ and over the sins of others _because_ we know we're also
Not **f**ar
If we **TOO** decide TO DO **OUR** OWN THING and apply onto Jesus another
Selfish **s**car**!**

The **"Law of Moses"** doesn't enable us to fly into **H**eaven.
It was ONLY GIVEN *TO SHOW* mankind that SIN IS LEAVEN
That **W**ILL eventually *__affect__* the ENTIRE **BODY** and KEEP flight from
Happening.
But **G**RACE **IS A**BOVE the **"Law"** and **"ALL THINGS"** are now possible – so
Stop **d**ampening

The **HOPE** in the darkest soul that **G**od *STILL HASN'T* let **g**o.
But the only way out of any prison is to know how to **s**how
God and your fellow man that **"The Key"** _ONLY_ JESUS **h**olds
And it's only *DISBELIEF of this FORGIVENESS* that a *darkened* mind
Molds

Into this shell that the embryo – turned into a young chick must **c**rack.
When you realize the *__TRUE WILL__* of God *IS TO SAVE ALL* – NOW you
Won't **L**ack
ANY POWER **NEEDED** TO BREAK OUT and **LIVE** – **H**ERE and **N**OW – **FREE!**
NOT to grow up *to be a chicken;* but be a *bold lion* for all **e**ternity.

This *__BODY in motion__* will never end if it's the **S**piritual one you're
Speaking **o**f.
The Predarism belief explains how this might be **H**is plan to continually
Shove
Evil __out__ of **H**is newest souls born into this world – totally different but
Yet the **s**ame
As in any time of **H**is **S**tory – it's all in the plan of **G**od's life **g**ame.

Picture   *the Body* in Motion

Now **_PICTURE_** how **this game ends** with a Carnal **BODY** buried **6 ft.** Under.
Never to rise again so the Earth's elements will continue to plunder
This "shell of the man he once was", as the saying spoken in compassion
Goes
When you understand the time he spent trying to please God has come
To its close.

So again, the TRUTH of **HOW** and **WHY** he tried to please God is what
Will be judged.
Only someone *totally intimate* with the man *can relate* to how many
Times God nudged
His heart and read the response correctly - always ready *TO CORRECT*
If in <u>any</u> way, shape or form - the <u>other</u> person's <u>best</u> interests he did Neglect.

This is the **_PICTURE_** of **HOW** God is <u>**GOOD**</u> - **_ALL_** **OF THE** TIME.
He's like the gentle father who always washes off the **road's dirty g**rime
From the FEET of **H**is children - not their entire **_BODY_** - Jesus' perfect
Walk *legally* did this for **YOU.**
It was TRUE when **H**e did it for **H**is Apostles and its *Spiritual message* **IS**
STILL UNDERSTOOD by few.

1st you must rest your **BODY** and **STOP** *the MOTION* so your feet can be
Washed clean.
The servant of **God** and man - Jesus - washed sin away with **H**is **blood**
Covering <u>the screen</u>
That **God** <u>*looks through to see you and me*</u>; & **OUR ADVOCATE** at our Trial
On that day when <u>*all*</u> men <u>**WILL**</u> **CONFESS** Jesus as **LORD** and **KING**...with
NONE still in denial !!!

So, <u>**_Spiritually,_**</u> a child <u>*is to be taught how to become a wise*</u> young man,
Possibly a parent, deacon and elder.
The walk becomes **MORE LIFE - GIVING** *after* he's found **his mate** & *Held her*
Through thick and thin, in sickness and in health to make strong his
Children's mother.
"Her" is **WISDOM** - **WHO *IS*** JESUS-and nurturer of the <u>TRUTH</u> that *<u>EACH</u>*
<u>MAN IS YOUR BROTHER</u> ! ! !

Rich Kovatch   12-4-11

#89 The *Happiest* Thing

The **_happiest_** thing that a man could ever dream **of**
Is on a <u>lower level</u> than the **_JOY_** each person is _offered by_ the same **D**ove
That came down from Heaven into **Jesus** and those who **God** chooses be
His **W**itness
And be changed like a Saul into a Paul - the Apostle who spoke of a
Spiritual **f**itness

Using the physical Olympic Games as a picture of there being only 1
Winner.
But miraculously and on **God's** time table DOES HE **_TRANSFORM_** EACH
SINNER
Into a _more perfect image_ of the Son of God by molding,
In _this_ age, with the **Fire** of **The Holy Spirit** in which men hear **God**
Scolding

Evil people with warnings of what future they will **f**ace
If they continue being continuously controlled by the **Law** - **NOT G**race.
The Law NEVER brings one into a Righteous relationship with the **S**pirit.
Only living in total Grace - which is **HIGHER** and not even the same
Realm - brings anyone anywhere **n**ear it.

<u>**His** Glory</u> is this **_Joy_** He's given **His** **"Called out"** nation of believers
Who know **His "Ways"** and prophesiers against messengers of world
Based peace who are really **d**eceivers.
His voice becomes so much clearer when you correctly start loathing
And discerning the spirit of the ravening wolves dressed in sheep's
Clothing.

Everything about anything in the physical realm that doesn't shine **God's**
Light
On how YOU do radiate this **AGAPE Spirit** to reveal wrong from right
It is NOT in condemning words as a means to a fatal **e**nd,
But **to burn off** the **"religious"** nature that if I'm to **"get to"** some
"Heaven" it will **d**epend

#89 The *Happiest* Thing

On whether I confessed, or witnessed for, or even spoke of **Jesus' n**ame;
And rejected - especially - **all** carnal **"works"** - the BIGGEST part of the
Devil's tempting game.
It is not what you do **but** *the* **why** God does constantly <u>test</u>;
Although what you do shows **His "seal"** in you and you enter **"His <u>Rest</u>"**

Which is the **Joy** of an *"intimate"* relationship to THE **Father** and **His
Attitude.**
This transforms the MOTIVATION to serve "fallen man" - from obedience
To gratitude.
Obedience is better than sacrifice - that's to be sure;
But obedience to a Righteous Law only opens the door to live your life in
God's cure.

Jesus is the **picture** of **what** a **fully** *obedient* **"fisher of men"** may do...
And much more - **Jesus** promised **His disciples** when we follow **His c**ue
When **He** speaks to our hearts - which always melt and **d**eflect
Whatever this evil system dishes out, and bounces back to **r**eject

Some bump in the highway that took you off course for a **w**hile.
But after each fall **a Righteous man** will rise and again **s**mile
When you **realize** at this point in time **how** God worked **y**esterday
To show **Himself** to you - *usually in Great Mercy* - so **you** <u>didn't have</u>
<u>To pay</u>

The price for a sin you committed yesterday - **"Death in that d**ay".
But sins are **forgiven 1**st from the **desire** to...and **2**nd the **Grace** to say
That I did wrong - some**thing** the <u>carnal</u> nature can **NEVER a**dmit.
When we finally learn how sin has affected this part of us we'll then **q**uit

The destructive habits we once embraced as just "living it **up**".
But simply will not happen anymore because it's drinking from the **c**up
Of the **"Wrath of God" who cannot ignore or accept s**in.
But **He** demonstrates it on your **carnal body** to Redeem the *real* **y**ou
Within.

#89 The *Happiest* Thing

And when this tough outer shell has been burnt off and discarded,
We won't throw stones to kill each other like Old Testament day Jews.
That's retarded.
Grace has fallen on us like **The Dove** upon Jesus
Because we **now** see what we once **perceived** as bad now does **please us**

If today I'm a more compassionate person to friends and enemies alike.
An enemy as **God** sees him is just a "lost sheep" on the **D**evil's skewer
Spike
Doing whatsoever he will with him - **rotating him in the f**ire.
This **Hell** is the picture **Jesus** tells us is **ALL UNHOLY D**ESIRE

Which will have **Pride** or **Arrogance** or a **Controlling Nature** to it.
With power and position to **"sit in God's temple"** - **OUR HEART** - THE
Anti-**C**hrist **doesn't f**it.
So when **God's "New Covenant"** goes into effect in you, you
PERSONALLY will **see**
The **SCARS YOU'VE PUT** on **Him** when **He** entered you and set you free !

When **He** tells you they *DID* hurt - you'll relate to how you hated -
(**Murdered**) men
And walked right past them and *ignored their great need* and retired to
Your comfy **den**
To possibly even study "some" Bible that is not giving life to others - but
Your own **p**ride
Having confessed Jesus has SAVED <u>YOU</u> - *but perfectly content* that all
Sinners' end will be that they **died**

And end up being *tortured* without end. Is this what **Jesus s**aw
In His "Good Samaritan" story about the man beaten down by Jewish
Law ?
Not the **Law of Moses** that has provisions to **recover**
The descendents of Esau - Jacob's brother by the same **m**other.

#89 The *Happiest* Thing

Actually his twin ! - a great picture of **God's** way.
He didn't hate Esau in the way hate is used today.
God hates evil - see Proverbs 6 for His list.
This is to show the things Esau's nature couldn't resist.

And even Jacob had his issues but after wrestling all through the night,
He finally submitted to let **God** do whatever **He** sees as right.
He gave Jacob a new name - **Israel - but had him walk in *great* pain.**
The picture of how **Jesus** suffered and died but ROSE AGAIN TO GAIN

HIS HARVEST - the **1st Fruits** - people who tend to the husbandman's Vine;
Pruning unfruitful branches that **will *die*** as the sign
That God's Spirit DOES DWELL IN them - these are sins done only against **His S**pirit.
But the **carnal mind STOPS** at its Israel Olympic wrestling match and Gentiles won't come near it.

If **God** is powerful enough to graft in unnatural branches - **unbelievers in Jesus...**
Did **He** write down all these PROMISES TO REDEEM *ALL* just ***to tease us,
And really mean* He's** planning on saving only an elite narrow group that Think...
But have their heads so far up their **butt**s, that their own **poop** doesn't Stink?

This shows **God's** power to overcome the unnatural system on Earth
Which is **D**eath to **ALL** FLESH - but **Jesus promised** each soul REBIRTH.
THIS IS WHAT LOVE DOES - OVERCOMES ALL TO WIN IN THE END.
God sent **His O**nly Begotten Son **Jesus** to be the MEDIATOR with the Power to mend

#89 The *Happiest* Thing

This division that sin brings between a **Holy God** and **sinful man**.
This is what **Love** and **Grace** do that even God's Law never can...
Bring back all men - ALL **SINNERS** - to a Righteous standing before the Judge
Who is **Jesus** over ALL things - the **LAST FOE** - **DEATH** - **His** biggest Grudge.

Jesus came *to tell* the religious nation of Israel they've *heard* Him *wrong*
And **He** *came to REDEEM THE WORLD* - this is a Spiritual ding-dong
From the warning bell that carnal thinking is certain death & pointless.
Spiritual intuition from Love expels life in words & actions not anointless

From the oil of the **Holy Spirit** which **WILL HEAL** each broken spirit and Heart.
God's plan for **His** "Church" - like **Jesus** did - is to do their part.
Jesus' was to create, redeem and teach, and now to dwell
In the heart of those that understand the meaning of Hell.

God only does things that please **Him** - punishment included !
This is not done because He chooses some to forever live with **Him** but Others - excluded
This world **He** created to show how Love can save even the worst soul Polluted
With the hate for SINNERS upon whom they say **God's** justice demands **Eternal Death** and are still deluded

By the _sin_ nature - how many times is this brought up?
Jesus said He drank the entire wrath of **God** upon men but would not Sup
With men again until the price had been paid.
And the real **"Gospel" of Jesus** is that you too will rise after you've been Laid

#89 The *Happiest* Thing

6' under - the carnal / physical body's existence - the shell removed.
It's **Dead** - no control - and the **Best News** is this *can happen now* in
Your spirit now improved
To the point **Christ** lives through your actions and words of life
That encourage others to see that the cause of their strife

Is somehow their own choice - yet God in control
Like the **Father** of **ALL** He **IS**, He has *compassion* on *every* soul
And **Mercy** that's *never endless* because HIS **Love** leads to Life.
Like the prophet Hosea who WAS *TOLD* TO MARRY A **HARLOT WIFE**,

What better picture can God provide of His UNENDING devotion
To continue on until your darkened attitude receives the notion
From the **LORD** - not these words - that will crack that hardened shell
Of HATE that wants even 1 soul to be tormented FOREVER in Hell ! ! !

All through the verses **He** goes back and forth, nearly every other verse
Anew
Saying what UNFAITHFUL people will do, and also **God t**oo.
Continuously - because **He** has not man's spirit - **His** Mercy Gracefully
DRAWS
The HUMBLED SINNER **- not the proud religious zealot** *who focuses*
MOSTLY on **YOUR** FLAWS ! ! !

Rich Kovatch
12-10-11

#90 Your Last Second's COMFORT

Have you ever pondered about what you'll desire
To be *the last thing you hope for* just before you're called up to a higher
Plane of existence - some call **Heaven**...others **FEAR** of **HELL**.
No man can tell you the Truth; **but** you comprehend it enough **to tell**

Rom. 1:22

Yourself and others **what to do and how to t**hink?   Rom. 2:21
That's the way *God* designed it - to bring each man to HIS OWN **brink**
Of the edge of existence as he understands the Truth - THIS LIFE BITES.
And finally submits that there is a spirit of the world that fights

To cover your mind with darkness as Genesis 1: 2 states   Rom. 3:18
And the Earth was without form and void and covered in darkness -
Which *God* HATES.
The Holy Spirit hovered above this creation until the Word came out
That **when the *time* was right** - "The *Light* " came to turn about Rom. 2:11

Men's evil thoughts that constantly fill their hearts and minds.
So at **YOUR LAST SECOND'S moment** of life here on Earth one truly finds

Micah 7:18-19

What will bring COMFORT and a *GOOD* END to this TEST ?   Prov. 24:14
Is it you think you'll be allowed INTO **G**od's Eden Garden just because
You TRIED YOUR **B**EST ?

Or is there STILL A HOPE IN A SPIRIT OF LOVE that will *forgive*   Joel 2:28,

Hosea 13:14

Because you'll surely know your own row boat leaked like a sieve,
And you truly trusted in your ABBA - daddy - Father of all souls to keep

Mal. 2:10

You from some eternal end where you know you'd constantly weep

IN REGRET that you **somehow chose to reject** something you couldn't
Even see.   Rom. 1:24, 28, Rom. 3:3
His Word says EACH MAN'S TIME and PLACE to be
Judged will be alongside the **"great and the s**mall".   Rom. 3:3-6
ALL MANKIND HAS ALREADY BEEN JUDGED and PERSONALLY
EXPERIENCED THIS **F**ALL

#90 Your Last Second's COMFORT

Into the **Pit** where the Holy Spirit's **fire BURNS THE *HELL OUT* OF US.**
Like King David - we'll plead with God not to leave us there to cuss...
But **DRAW US OUT** - brothers and sisters, friends and foes.
There is Truth shown when Light reveals on to WHAT God delivers His
End-time **W**OES.   Prov. 25:11

You see - this end-time woe will be when you say, **"Woe! My time has
Ended"**.
Then Christ is revealed in YOU that the Loving Comforter has indeed
Befriended
YOU - **AS WELL AS ALL SINNERS** because it's IMPOSSIBLE to please God
IN the FLESH.   Matt. 14:26
BUT His Mercy IS *NEVER*-ENDING and NEW EVERY MORNING so we can
Now mesh

With the Spirit of Health to give **NEW** LIFE to seemingly dead seeds.
This **NEW** LIFE occurs when a man's heart meets another's needs.
The **Good Samaritan** is the **Spirit** that is in all to do good.
**The problem is the Religious spirit perverts us from doing what we
Should**

Which Jesus has told us - is to Love your *enemies* and show God's Light
And eventually this hard cover will crack; you're Religious doctrines take
Flight
**BACK INTO THE DARKNESS FROM WHERE THEY ORIGINATED -
DISBELIEF...**
And you'll have GREAT JOY when you ***UNDERSTAND HIS JUDGMENT*** -
WHAT A RELIEF **! ! !**

He'll judge you - GUILTY - as *ALL men* EXCEPT JESUS *are*.
You'll be judged on your "works"... **and rewarded for all - up to p**ar
With perfection in action and thoughts because **GRACE** motivated **Love**
To act
To show through **"good works"** you're will to *overcome* the carnal
Nature that lacked

#90 Your Last Second's COMFORT

Even the caring cord of brotherhood, *but chose* to think of his good,
Pick him up off the ground, take him to an innkeeper who could
Assist in the **transition time of healing** that **Jesus says DOES HAPPEN**
And we'll thank **Jesus - He's** that **"Good Samaritan"** and your pants
You'll stop crappin'.

Because **you know that happens** when the *body* and *Spirit* separate.
The false church's doctrine somehow teaches that **DURING** the moment
Of death - it's too late!
They can't tell you exactly how this happens - but speak fear - not Comfort
Prov. 28:5
If you don't speak out loud before you're last breath because the angels
Will sort

Out the chaff from the wheat - **but forget *God is good* - especially at**
That time!
You and I and all are guilty - but God gave us Jesus to pay the fine.
This has to be the *mind of Christ* to give comfort to those about to die...
They *will* soon *be confessing* on their knees *with adoration* that His
PROMISES TO SAVE ALL IS NOT A LIE.

THIS IS THE UNITY OF THE BODY OF CHRIST - THAT HE DID IT ALL
And we all definitely missed out every time we dropped the ball;
But our **Spirit Brother, Friend, Father** and **Creator** has our back
And **GRACE** allows Him to bring **ALL MEN** back **because *Love* doesn't**
Lack

The **Power, Desire, Wisdom** or **Compassion** needed **to REDEEM lost**
Man.
What weak, carnally influenced minds deem impossible - God certainly
Can
And surely DOES SUCEED in finishing because *EACH* SOUL is as precious
As ALL His creation
And God's picture He gives His children tell this dying soul of *HOPE'S*
Elation.

#90 Your Last Second's COMFORT

Truth *that saves* gives *peace to each* troubled soul.
LOVE is God's PROMISE TO ALL that on the highway to Heaven - **He's PAID** the toll.
The wide path to destruction we tend to walk on is made so we'll ALL be HUMBLED...
ESPECIALLY ones who *denied* Jesus' power to REDEEM *ALL LOST ISRAEL* - The Truth they totally bumbled.

It was 1st given to His Israel - but since **DISBELIEF** set its fate -
Total destruction for the nation happened because it realized too late
It was walking as His **harlot** wife and thus does not dwell well in His Company.   **Book of Hosea**
Darkness can't co-exist with **the Light** - the significance isn't some funny

Euphemism, but serious as life and death from words our tongues speak
- Each one accounted for
To show you when you die if you were His Virgin wife or His whore.
Thank God He gave us the prophet *Hosea* and his persistence to believe
That at the end of the day - right before dark time - his hope is relieved

And comes true and his wife returns back to a proper marriage
                                                                Hos.13:9-14
Because **God WILL RANSOM** them from the **power** of the **grave** - no
Longer in **d**isparage   **1Tim.2:6**
For the **long-suffering, patient, trusting** preacher who still did his thing
                                                                2 peter 3:9
Which always has a message that Love *will* **endure...and TO THAT
WE'LL** *ALL* **S**ING **! ! !**

BELIEVE *BELIEVE* BELIEVE BELIEVE BELIEVE *BELIEVE* BELIEVE

(strange word now that **I've** printed it like this, **no?** Ha. **)**

(way **mo**re *just funn*y to me *****Just moti**va**tes contemplation & **JOY)**
*** My whole purpose of this MAGICAL BOOK ***

Rich Kovatch
12-24-11

#91 God's Hide-n-Seek Game

God **has a game** He says that **He** does certainly **play**.   Prov. 25:2,
See hide, seek in concordance

It's not really a game as we perceive it, but it is **His way**.   See understanding
& wisdom in concordance

I know this sounds perverted because of its disastrous **end**
For those that don't find **Him** - the **religious spirit** says **He** does **send**
Prov. 28:5

Straight to Hell...you...don't pass GO or get another **c**hance   Prov. 11:9
And that really sounded to me as the way it is at first **g**lance
Because that's what I was taught in this end-time **age**   Prov. 11:20
That makes proud, haughty, evil-hearted men hate their perceived
Enemies with **rage**   Prov. 6:34

Any and all men that don't get it right before they **die**.   Prov. 11:12
But **AGAPE LOVE** has revealed to me that it's **the Devil's favorite** lie
Prov. 10:32

Which *divides* mankind into winners and losers at the end of this **life**.
Prov. 6:9

The Gospel says this way of thinking only brings on our spirit pain & **strife**.
Prov. 10:12

The Gospel is the **"Good News"** delivered by **Jesus** Himself while **here**.
How the **"religious church"** *SEES* an **eternal Hell** *as love* is woefully
Queer   Prov. 11:23
And **sick** and **perverted** and *way off the mark*.   Heb. 6:2
The mind that wants their brothers to suffer forever is ***still in the dark***.
Prov. 10:6

I ask all the time for them to explain how this could **be**.   **STUDY LOVE**
They usually say it's up to you - stay a slave to sin or choose to be **free**.
Rom. 1:28

Come on now, **the scriptures clearly state** we cannot even **choose**
John6:44

To make this choice unless **G**od opens our **eyes, heart & mind** about **who's**
Rom. 2:4

#91 God's Hide-n-Seek Game

Really in charge of each man's soul - it's **Jesus Christ** - not us.   Gen. 1:1
And the **confusion** at THIS POINT is really **why** they love to throw lost
Souls UNDER THE BUS.   **Prov. 15:28**
IT COMES DOWN to **PRIDE** or **DESIRE** & **IF** YOU **REALLY** *WANT* TO KNOW
   Rom. 3:10-11
The **God** of Heaven & what words of **WHO'S** faith & **HOPE** you're to sow.
   Gen. 1:31

Is this faith you proclaim of your OWN DOING and **power**...   Rom. 3:10
Or is it **Jesus'** faith and perseverance to save the lost that is *revealed* to
You in **THIS HOUR?**   **Rev. 18:10**
TRUE UNDERSTANDING OF **THE WAYS OF Love** cannot be understood
   John 21:23
When the perversion of God's **RIGHTEOUS** JUDGMENT *fails* to seek out
The **good**   Prov. 14:21-22

That *is in* every man's heart but *enslaved* by **pride** and or fear.   Heb. 12:1
Does scripture say **He's** a **G**od that hides things or does He steer
   Refer back to line 1
The **humble heart** to live and learn what it REALLY MEANS to care
   Pray for **God's** LOVE
For the downtrodden souls & give you a bold voice to proclaim & **d**are

To prove what you say - **in actions that save** men from their sins ?
   1 Peter 2:24
This is when we stop fishing for carnal food, and the reeling in of lost
Souls **begins.**   Matt. 4:19
We're to be like the **carpenter Jesus** and put up a sign saying **"Under
Construction"**   James 5:20
And turn around (**repent**) of our evil, self-serving ways - that's the **road
To d**estruction.   **2 Cor. 7:10**

#91 God's Hide-n-Seek Game

And when **Jesus** spoke of this destruction of the soul leading one into
Hell
He was speaking of **the grave** - from which *ALL* **WILL RISE AGAIN** like
Jesus - pray **tell** !
In **Matt. 25:41-46** when **He** spoke of those on **His** left hand, **He** spoke of
The curse and fire
Prepared for the **DEVIL** and **his ANGELS, not men**, it's <u>**NOT**</u> an **eternal**
Hell in which lost souls will **retire** !

The word translated as punishment is **KOLASIS,** meaning **remedial** and
Proper in its **purpose to c**orrect.
The word translated as eternal is **AIONION,** meaning a period of time
Until the debt is paid, **so h**eck,
This passage that's most often used to support an eternal hell is, in
Fact, one that most strongly opposes it !
So I was reminded by **G**od that **H**is **nature** is always to **lead** us to **repent**
And that old understanding no longer **fit** !

It's similar to **John 15:2** where **Jesus** spoke of pruning the vine where
The word is **Kathairo** in **G**reek
Which means - the pruning of bad branches **(evil ways)** so it will
Strengthen the **m**eek.
And **G**od is able to and will graft the natural and unnatural branches
Back onto the **vine** - which is **H**im.   **Rom.11:23**
This can and does only happen when each man learns and has repented
Of the evilness of his own **s**in.

The **parable** of the **"Good Samaritan"** and the lessons taught by **Jesus**
Are don't have a **love** that's so **s**hallow.
I **understand** who that nearly dead guy is and how we're to see what
Was once thought as unclean we're to **h**allow.
As in **Peter's** vision in **Acts 10:15,** I **understand** that it is in **G**od's
Appointed time when the lost soul will **repent.**
To heal the brokenhearted and save the LOST SHEEP of ISRAEL is why
Jesus was **sent** !   **Luke 4:18, Matt. 15:24**

#91 God's Hide-n-Seek Game

God speaks of taming our tongues like rudders on a ship which are able
To turn souls from the **fires** of Hell   James 3
But out of the same mouth proceeds blessings and curses, which
Happens if we speak of **Grace** or tell   James 3:10
A lost soul he'll burn forever if he doesn't confess out loud his sins he
May not be able to confess to you right now
Because YOU haven't built a relationship with him, and he doesn't trust
YOU as God's representative somehow.

But when **you** finally **UNDERSTAND** the **GRACE** of God and His
MERCIFUL CHARACTER TO DRAW
Even the **DARKEST** mind back into His **Light** of **PEACE** and **FORGIVENESS**
Because **He** is **LOVE** and Law.
Show how **Jesus** has come into your life and cleaned up your act and
Given you a **heart** that shows compassion
For people like him that have been **scared stiff** and **fear** the God they
Had heard must continue lashin'

Out at lost souls in a **Hell** because of their *perverted* hearing of justice
And think they can no longer be redeemed.
It's no wonder why the organized **"church"** of today has lost its power
To convert and is no longer esteemed
And given tithes to or even support by the unity of the brotherhood of
All men which are good and bad.
The **transparency** of *hypocrisy* does not bring in *souls trapped* in
Addictions and *the fearful - and that's so* sad.

You will be able through your own testimony show him how God's **LOVE**
Is true and pure.
Then the lost sheep will gladly and thankfully and confidently confess of
His sinful nature.
You will tell him the God of **PEACE** is still knocking on his **heart's** door
And he will end up with God for sure.
But TODAY is the day we want you to get saved, start living for others,
And turning from selfish ways as his cure.

#91 God's Hide-n-Seek Game

He'll be *directed* by **Christ,** and *the Law* **the driver** with leashes that will **Mercifully** get taught
And turn the **humbled** soul back on the road to life and off the one That's **wrought**
With anger towards a **man of sin** - *himself* - **instead** of the *things* and *Reasons* we *all* stray.
This **"man of sin" attitude** is and always has been the **walk in darkness** Before the **new d**ay

When God's **Light** shines forth and the true **Sabbath Day** rest begins
Gen. 2:1-3
When you realize that *ALL SIN will be* destroyed & *in the end* **LOVE W**INS !
We've been given the ministry of reconciling **the lost** world back to God.
Matt. 9:12-13
This "lost world" is our **sons** & **daughters** that continually ignorantly **t**rod

On **the road to *destruction*** and *death* without seeing the **Holy love** that **S**aves.
And on that *"last day" ALL* SOULS *WILL* AGAIN RISE, like **Jesus** did, from Our very own **g**raves
And we'll all be **judged** by **Jesus Christ** on our works **100% true** and **R**ighteous
Carnal (selfish) works **burnt up, Holy** works rewarded when we **m**ight just

Finally understand that *"last day"* **IS HERE AND NOW** when **His secret is** *Revealed*
John 14:6-7
And **the mediator** between a **Holy G**od and **sinful man** is **the Love no Longer** concealed
1 Tim. 2:5
That is willing and able to stand in the gap and pay the full **p**rice
1 John 2:2
That means longsuffering and wisdom to *keep teaching* our *enemies*
Who are not **n**ice
2 Peter 3:9

#91 God's Hide-n-Seek Game

To us or our message that **Jesus *SAVES ALL*** and **proves H**is **Love** for our
Souls   1 John 2:2
And what the last book means when its secrets are revealed about ***the 7***
Bowls   Lev. 26:44-46
7 vials, 7 trumpets, 7 plagues, 7 seals, 7 thunders, 7 candlesticks, 7
Angels, 7 spirits and 7 eyes;
AGAPE LOVE *7 stars, 7 churches, 7 crowns, 7 heads, 7 mountains, 7*
Kings, and 7 Lamps **of fire** that *reveal* ALL lies.

7 is the number of completeness - it's *revealed* that **Jesus** is **ALL - IN -**
ALL !   1 Cor. 15:28, Eph. 4:2-10
This plan was conceived and put into motion *before* Adam and Eve's fall.
His **AGAPE LOVE** *reveals* this **secret** that <u>even</u> <u>though</u> *we're a sinful*
Human race
The **"GOOD NEWS"** is that we've **NEVER** *TOTALLY* **FALLEN** FROM **GOD'S**
GLORIOUS GRACE **! ! !**

GRACE is when one and all *are given* what we don't deserve.
That's what **Jesus** did - left **His** perfect world **to come in the flesh** *to*
Serve
AND **REDEEM HIS** MOST PRECIOUS CREATION - THAT'S ME AND YOU **! ! !**
THE LAST SECRET *REVEALED* is that from **G**od's viewpoint - space - this
Planet (like our **F**ather's **Love**)
Is no longer **void** and **without form** - but like **His water** of **Spiritual**
Second-birth **baptism...TRUE B**LUE **!**

Rich Kovatch
1-11-12

#92 Our 3D 4G God

Today's world is so far from what
The Apostles could have ever imagined, but
The specifics and details don't matter one iota.
Like whether **you** drive a Porsche or a Toyota.

Technology, innovations and imaginations gone amuck.
It's impossible to keep up with it. A quagmire in which the flesh is stuck;
That will not and can not find the peace that surpasses
Anything any **pastor** can learn in a lifetime of **religion c**lasses.

Head knowledge does not save **your** butt from the fire.
That's what the Greek mindset does in order to conspire
Against the truth that **Paul** delivered - of trusting ONLY in the Lord
Because a lifetime of driving the wrong road does not bring the **"one Accord"**

That the scriptures say of you being your brother's keeper
And are all through the Bible and conveyed if the understanding is Deeper
Than the *carnal* level *that condemns* the failure of a brother to **pay**
For the wrongs done against what is right, **you** better look out for
Judgment **D**ay.

There are **three different ways** peoples' minds supposedly **w**ork.
Two of the ways are not **"in the Way"** so **you'll** look like a hypocrite or a Jerk
To others watching **you** in your daily walk
And the message **you** speak and the tone **you t**alk.

The **1**st **way** I've already mentioned is that **G**od must prove that **He IS.**
Greeks forever seek knowledge of things, and what the *religious* spirit
Brings - like carbonation - will finally fizz
Out to discover that their search was totally **IN THE DARK**
Because **you** constantly need more proof - **you're** response to **The Light**
Is always a loud **bark**

#92 Our 3D 4G God

Which signifies *FEAR* mostly, but also tries to manipulate and control
Because *when* your *Love for sinners* really turns on - **you'll** get on a **Holy Spirit** lead roll
That will be what that **Spirit** was waiting for all along to **do**;
And finally it all **GETS THROUGH** that **thick skull - enough already about Differences. Today** - history is new

To do *moment to moment* what a kind, forgiving and merciful heart will **Desire**
Give *ALL* THAT IT HAS...and then some...before going on to retire
To the place in **your** home (heart) where **you'll** rest and recoup.
Christ often did this and intensively prayed that the **Father's heart**
Would give **Him** the scoop

Of *even* *this* 3D generation which has 4G capabilities.
Where this is all headed is only for **carnal** pleasures and tranquilities;
The Devil's deceptions of diversions to spend and thus waste valuable **Time**
On the fruit of the vine after it has fermented when words come out **Without rhyme**

Or reason, or logic, or **Wisdom**, or **Truth of Peace**...and basically of life.
When **one** gets drunk on wine (**fruit of the flesh** and **false religion**)...*it Causes* the reaping of strife
Which **OUR LORD** *foreknew*, *foresaw* & has *fore planned* what He *will* do
After **we've** chosen our last step, word, and action from which grew

Like Levin into a bad loaf on which **we'll** feed daily from.
And certainly the further down the road **we** walk to the beat of our **OWN d**rum,
The *sicker* and *more perverted* **we'll get as** the **darkness** gets **darker**.
Then **JUDGMENT** occurs *exactly when* God knew the contrast **NEEDED**
To be much starker;

#92 Our 3D 4G God

Which is God's timing, positioning and DOING - so don't get in a tizzy.
Just profess **the Love** of God and His willingness to forgive an over-busy,
Distracted, deceived, confused and most assuredly hurting **soul** - even at
Death's door.
God has **His** Perfect 3-D and 4-G capabilities **so far beyond** what **we**
Could even imagine *we'll all* hit the floor

In **total** *AWE* of His Greatness and how He shows Himself in *EVERY*
DIRECTION.
We look out with telescopes and marvel at patterns never seen before
But have discovered through inspection
Which **He** desires **us** also to do with microscopes in the other direction
To also find exquisite function and detail
And order never ever even dreamed possible or needed. His ways are
Exposed not at wholesale but only retail

And available for only **those He's** led to **"sell all"** to buy the **"pearl"**...the
Great find.   Matt. 13:46
Because when **each soul** finds it - his **S**piritual **eyes** are no longer **b**lind
And **G**od has opened the doors of **His Wisdom** and heart to **H**is **d**isciples
Who **H**e has study **H**is written word and hear **Love's Spirit** and **r**ecycles

This willingness to suffer whatever is demanded and prove **through**
ACTIONS with righteous PRINCIPLES.
We shall come before kings and rulers and be God's army of Gideon
Invincibles
Following the **W**ord given and heard to **us common men** of valor with
Urgency and willingness of heart
By our **G**od who reads it & has **His soldiers** positioned & ready to **s**tart
xxxxxxxxxxxxxxxxxxxxxxxxxxxxxxxxxxxxxxxxxxxxxxxxxxxxxxxxxxxxxxxxxxxxxxxxxx
Coming up against the **G**ates of Hell - so **we're** to RAZE them.
They have no power to hold - **Jesus** does - *so we too have been given,*
Like Peter, *the keys* to **sin** and **death** to **t**ell
The whole world this **"Good News"**. **Jesus** commands **us** to use them to
Start **our S**piritual motors.
We'll then be noticed as **people** joyously thankful for everything in
Life...but not profiteers or **g**loaters   Matt. 7:23

#92 Our 3D 4G God

Of certain **"gifts"** which are the **"talents"** God says He gives a measure
To all of.   Luke 6:38
Some 1, some 2, some 5 - the amount is not the issue but our duty, so
Shove   Matt. 25:16-28, Rom. 12:1
That **carnal** mindset of **"more is better"** out - but as His **Spirit** unveils –
The opposite is **true.**
Give - to give - from **Love's desire** and He'll out-give **you** back 100 fold –
Old ways turned new.

The **2ⁿᵈ way people** think is like the way the **"people of God"**
          interpreted
God's voice to His flock.
They certainly provoked God's wrath - and His **Word you** can not mock
                                        1ˢᵗ & 2ⁿᵈ Kings, Psalms, etc.
And get away with it in the end - He'll righteously judge and deal with
Each **man.**   Gal. 6:7
But His **"Way"** is to REDEEM the **Lost** - not throw **them** down the can

And into the emptiness of forgetfulness made *blind* by *pride.*
On the coattails of their **forefathers** *they* just think *they* can ride
Right past the gates of Hell - which are the Holy Spirit's fire.
The deeper the denial of God's purpose and **mercy** gets, the flames of
Conviction only get **higher**

To now bring out the **3ʳᵈ way,** which is to bring out this starkness
Between right and **wrong**
And become the **prodigal son** who realizes who is **strong**
And who is weak. It's God's holding grip of **Love** that saves the **day**
When this **prodigal son** sees he's really been all along going **his** own
Way;

And **Jesus** finally opens **our** eyes that man's ways **can't s**atisfy,
And that's why **we** crumble in despair and **confess our** faults and **cry**
Out for mercy when **we** all will see **His** scars.   John 20:27
Then **ALL** of **Israel** *will be* **redeemed** & **He** breaks the bars Rom. 11: 26-29

#92 Our 3D 4G God

Of **unbelief** which separates willful **sinners** from the perfect SPIRIT
That **Jesus** showed while on Earth...but the **RELIGIOUS Jews** wouldn't
Hear it
Because **their** position **under the Law** was to be the **people's** guide to God.
But without **GRACE** and **UNDERSTANDING**, in the Old Testament
Blindness they still trod;

Which was a **PICTURE** of the **dead end** street that **unto salvation the
Law** can't and wasn't made to provide.
But **we** see this **GRACE and God's longsuffering** that's always been when
On the narrow path **we r**ide
Which leads to an abundant life - here and now - so **we'll** share **God's
Agape Love** - the *REAL* **"Good** News"
That only through a **PERSONAL RELATIONSHIP WITH JESUS** will bring **joy**
And conversely **the b**lues

When **Love** and **the Law** shows **us** our sinful heart and thoughts so **we**
May then take action.
Christians are given the *ministry of reconciliation* - the strongest
Attraction
That a **H**oly **G**od of compassion and patience can soften a hardened
Mind so it may melt with its **h**eat.
We'll understand that with other **men** of different nations and religions
We're not to **c**ompete;

But in *ONE* **SPIRIT** be the ultimate *teacher* shown by **our** words,
Reactions and **w**alk
By being *MORE LIKE* **JESUS** when **H**e dwelt among **us**...so please don't
Balk
At the message of this **"Good News"** that it is **Jesus' WILL** and *promise*
To SAVE !
Now - if *you'd* like - or AFTER **your** selfish live has ended and **you're** in
The grave.

#92 **Our 3D 4G God**

This **Holy Spirit's** _UNCONDITIONAL_ **LOVE** won't build an unscriptural
Doctrine on such shifting sand
Demanding a **man** _MUST_ CHOOSE _before_ his body is destroyed _or else_ in
UNENDING _torture_ **he'll** land
According to the _Devil's_ **Doctrine** _of fear_ from this ONE verse, Heb. 9:27
WHICH DOES **NOT** SAY THIS.
It **ONLY** STATES that _all_ will be judged after this appointed time and
Here's where **their** doctrine goes amiss.

The truth is that at this moment - ALL our **WORKS** will be judged and
Dealt with accordingly.
Evil works will be **burnt up** and _righteous_ ones rewarded and **Jesus** _will_
_Be_ there _mediating_ for thee
As He always has - He's the **potter** and **molder** of **all**; and this age of
Mixed iron and clay
Described through Daniel's explanation of the King of Babylon's dream
Of THIS **DAY**.

The King of Babel - which means **confusion** - is what has happened as
Religion has built up _this_ man - **YOU religious** sages!
The head is **gold (CHRIST)** and gets mixed with **men's** _doctrines_ which
Get weaker down through the ages
As **the body** gets revealed it shows the ages of understanding of the
Unity **God** has with fallen mankind.
And eventually gets to the point to where **it** _can't_ **stand** firm and then
The **ROCK we** rejected we'll find

Will come down and destroy _this_ **man of sin** and start **(in you)** the new
And everlasting **age**   Dan. 2:44
Where **Jesus** _WILL_ **REIGN** and **true Love** _will_ set **(YOU)** free from the
Gates and **cage**
Of **Hell** - **disbelief** of the holiness and favor of **God's** directives to eat
Only from the **TREE of** LIFE
And eat not of **the tree** _of knowledge_ **of good and evil** that can only
Bring the reaping of strife.

#92 Our 3D 4G God

This is the **PICTURE** of the circle of life that God's plan has **for each s**oul.
The first **A**dam of dirt which is made to return to the dust when it finally
Releases its perceived **c**ontrol.
The second Adam - **JESUS** - **is that of SPIRIT** - incorruptible - turning the
Heart of **stone** into **f**lesh
As *promised* in Jeremiah **31:31**...a New Covenant put in **our** inward
        parts
So the whole *world* will eventually **m**esh

Into **a kingdom ruled by Love** for **one another** but still correcting the
Wayward ways of **children** of the **D**evil.
Having the first Adam's nature **doesn't mean we're** not God's **child**, but
Israel's rebellion showed in it **we** do revel.
Jesus explained this to **Nicodemus** - a **teacher** of the Jews, and was
Astonished that **he** had not **p**erceived
The **TRUTH** and **SPIRIT** of **G**od's teachings throughout the ages that it is
He which was revealed to **His people,**
The **Jews,** but never **r**eceived.

This is the **PICTURE** of **YOU** and **ME** before **we've** been **"Born Again"** of
This **repentant n**ature.
We'll never be perfect in the sense of not falling now and then, but
Quickly **you'll** *learn* to hate **y**our
Carnal nature that is stuck to **us** - the **PICTURE** Paul describes as *the*
Burden we carry on **our b**ack.
This is **our** *thorn* in the flesh, **the cross we'll** *understand* that's **ours** to
Bear, but **the power** *to do so* **we will not** lack.

Because when **Jesus** sends **us** the **"Comforter"** AND **WE** RECEIVE
HIM...these days **we** will truly **c**herish
Because **we'll** *no longer lack the* **"knowledge"** *of The Way, The Truth*
And The Life that once caused **His people** *to perish.*
The Book of Hosea explains this mystery of how **our loving** Father *will*
Never let *completely* **g**o
Of His **children** - *me* and *you* - and *the truth* that **He** **_will_** reap what He
Did sow.

#92 Our 3D 4G God

This reaping is the harvesting of ALL SOULS made clean and pure *by* His Blood.
Again, a PICTURE of His Love was recorded for us in the story of Noah's Flood.
He got rid of all mankind that had evil constantly on its mind and in Their hearts.
Here's where the AGAPE LOVE *overcomes* the "world, flesh and Devil"
And His everlasting Kingdom starts.

Only Noah's family, those that "rest" were "saved" from this QUICK Destruction of flesh, which He *has* to judge.
Disciples of Jesus understand this correlation between the flesh nature And the Spirit and give HOPE to nudge
With the gentle spirit of compassion and mercy to those *still* lost in the Dark and bring God's light
To this world that loves its own way (this world is people) not literally The Earth and soil - that's right!

The "land", the "Earth", the "nations", the "waters", the "lost sheep", And "Egypt" are all PICTURES of us
That He's promised to "REDEEM" because Love *never* fails or gets Corrupted like wetted iron only to rust
And lose *its* strength and power *to* save His 100th lost sheep.
Jesus promised not to lose a single one, but *ALL* MEN the Father has Given Him...He WILL KEEP

Under His watchful eye as the Shepard of the flock and to the whole World He has told
That He has sheep that are wondering aimlessly in the dark and are not Of "this fold".
This "fold" are the "believers" that are willing to suffer and die
For those that die in unbelief of God's word and never really found His Abundant Life,
But lived their entire life in the Devil's lie.

Rich Kovatch
1-20-12

#93 Love At First Sight

Love at 1st sight is a glorious thing
When the Love Bird that lives **in both** hearts **starts** to sing
And makes a most beautiful song that sounds so sweet
Both know it was ordained by God that they should **meet**

Sometimes His voice will be heard inside one's **head**
That the other child of God is to whom you'll be **wed.**
And the relationship starts off with a shock and a **bang**
Like you've just started your love life's race & the starter's gun just **rang.**

The **surge** of **energy just manifested shoots** you **instantly** *up to* **cloud** **n**ine
And you realize your life is now **"OURS"** and no longer just **"MINE".**
You become anxious to be joined in Holy matrimony before God & **friends,**
And are blessed & comforted by God's promises that **"true Love never e**nds"**!

All that may happen with such total amazement and quick **s**uccession
But will not be the real thing unless both give a TRUE **C**ONFESSION
Of how your Spiritual relationship with God and Jesus are expressed in
Your daily **w**alk.
Because without this foundation of **HONESTY** - the future won't jive
With your present *talk.*

One has to be careful that the "One New Man" is **"True Love"** and **NOT
LUST**
Because if PATIENCE isn't proven and your FRIENDSHIP built first **- it will
Surely** rust.
LOVE is not in a hurry, but our flesh natures say…Let's *do it* ! *NOW* !
LOVE comes with a cost, and it's paid by both partners by their
WILLINGNESS to **b**ow

Before our Loving creator and agree together to build upon **"The ROCK".**
You'll prove to one another that you're both in God's **f**lock
That is guided by the **"GOOD SHEPHERD"** & listen closely to His **i**nstructions
And understand that **HIS LOVE** account has **UNLIMITED VALUE** that can
Absorb countless **d**eductions;

#93 Love At First Sight

Which will be the submitting to one another and the **Voice of R**eason
So you're marriage will get stronger and stronger as it goes through each
"Season**"**
Which are as different as Winter, Spring, Summer, and **F**all
And have their own hardships and blessings that make **"TRUE LOVE"**
Stand **t**all

And be an example for your children and the world to see how **g**reat
It is to become **"one flesh"** and you're willingness to **s**tate
That the **LOVE you each perceived** right at *1ˢᵗ sight*
Was truly **NOT f**leshly **l**ust, but delivered by God with ever-expanding
MIGHT!

Rich Kovatch
2-10-12

inspired by: The Holy Spirit
given to: Rich Kovatch
for: **ALL**
         seeking God's union
         of flesh and **Spirit**
         Into the
         "One New Man"

#94 Love... *BEFORE* First Sight

My last poem was about human's **Love at First Sight**.
But it only led me to write about **God's** might
That was able to **Love** us *ALL* BEFORE **He** even saw
The Human Race that only makes it more the necessary for **His Love** to *DRAW*

Us sinful souls that live in this world that has been corrupted by sin.
When the 1ˢᵗ Adam chose to disobey **God's** word spreading this nature
To all his kin;
Which is you & me who live with the dichotomy of obedience & self - will
Which now is called the **Fire of Hell** when we jump onto *correction's grill*.

This *grill* is where *the change* of our sinful mindset to *sanctification*
Occurs.
But the *FALSE* **CHURCH** since **Jesus** has perverted and its purpose blurs
Into a fear that IF you should FALL through the grid - which is **His written**
Law,
You're FOREVER LOST and CAST AWAY from **His Mercy** and **Grace**. And
THIS IS THE FLAW !

His word is **full** of **more than 160 verses** that **promise** of the
"**Blessed Hope**"
That are given to resurrect even those that HAVE FALLEN THROUGH
Because they can't cope
With the things WE DO that separate our walk from the best **He** offers.
When we confess our shortcomings we are "**Born Again**". But it doesn't
Happen to scoffers

Which teach if you should die in your sins without a confession, or full
Belief,
Then **God's promises** weren't for you and you'll be TORMENTED
FOREVER - **w/o** the **possibility** of *any* relief.
This is SO FAR FROM THE TRUTH because even the body's life and death
Are NOT BEYOND
The POWER of OUR **FATHER** TO **REDEEM His** lost children, because of
Even THOSE **He's** fond

#94 Love… *BEFORE* First Sight

Of *way beyond* what sinful men **can imagine** - that's **His AGAPE LOVE**
That **HAS** saved
Not ONLY **His** so "self thinking" obedient children, but **ESPECIALLY** those
That hadn't behaved.
It seems way too unfair to the **False Religious mind** that this can be
JUSTIFIED.
But **Jesus** lived and died and rose again to show us "Real Believers" who
Aren't mystified

Or prideful in our own "works" - which we're told DON'T MEAN A THING
About **True Love's** ability to **conquer ALL** THINGS *INCULDING* the **LAST**
ENEMY - **DEATH**. So let's sing
The praises of the **Power** of **Christ's Blood to Redeem** the "Lost Sheep"
That has wandered away from the protection of the **"Good" Shepard's**
Safe keep

And into the world's ways and fleshly desires and the **Devil** - which is
UNBELIEF,
Which doesn't glorify the **Father**, but sadly brings **His Holy Spirit** grief.
Because like the Hebrew nation brought out of the slavery of Egypt
(the world)… *ALL DIED* in the wilderness
Except Joshua and Caleb and all under 20 years of age who were given
The **Grace** by **God's** tenderness

Of **Love** and bestowed the blessings of crossing the Jordan River so **His**
Nation would continue on.
So TO THIS DAY…*WE'RE* given the same chance *to see* the new dawn
Of the **"Age"** *inside* **each soul**…which continually dies, but repents of
our Silly ways
That cause **"spiritual"** death, and even **"bodily"** death if we can't apply
This truth to *these* days

#94 Love... *BEFORE* First Sight

Which is the whole reason the **"Law"** and the **"Prophets"** were given...
To be a schoolmaster that will lead
To our **Merciful, Forgiving** - 7x70 times **Father**. Does this Hell
Condemning spirit concede
That **He** doesn't tell us to do anything **He** doesn't do **Himself** - especially
For **His** enemies !
Which we ALL ARE - every day - because we're still in this flesh body that
Too easily conceives

From lustful thoughts born in our hearts, then spoken with the tongue
That **refuses Mercy** to the sick and poor
But **puts fear in these "lost sheep"** that **one day God will *REFUSE*** to
Open the door.
As if death is the obstacle that CAN'T be overcome and we won't still
Have that chance
To truly see our **Saviour** - who we all put to death - FACE TO FACE...AND
NOT JUST AT A GLANCE.

Because we now only see palely through the glass at the Power **He** does
Spread
To those who are bold enough to believe this - that *ALL* **WILL RISE TO BE
WITH HIM from the dead**
And only our "works" that were carnal will be burnt as hay, stubble and
Wood,
And be brought back Spirit and Soul with an incorruptible body *because
He only does what's "good"* !

This **"good"** is to **"save"** and return the "lost sheep" back to the **Father**.
Because **Jesus** and the bold **"ecclesia"** souls refused to let persecution
Bother
Their testimony of **Jesus Christ**, **His** salvation through **His blood**, and
Were willing to die.
This may actually be physically and end this mist of an "age", but truly
Means *while* living...and this is why.

#94 Love... *BEFORE* First Sight

Paul said he **"died daily"** - which meant he constantly forgot the past,
Confessed present failures, and looked forward
To bring unbelieving souls onto Noah's Ark of **"rest"** and be looking
Toward
The only way that brings life to a dead mind - **RESTING IN *HIS* FINISHED
WORK...**
Not on what we see we ourselves and others do - but **His** children won't
Shirk

The responsibility which really is only what they were **"called"** to do...
Turn from evil, encourage the wayward, and be **Christ's** light to the few
He's brought into your circle of friends and enemies...so you'll be a
Beacon
To hurting people who aren't aware of the **God** who's ALWAYS seekin'

The children of the **Devil - DISBELIEF -** to bring a new life
That will then also be given the blessings of **His** Spiritual wife.
A **Love** that's the opposite of the chastening **Love of *correction*.**
His bride has cleaned up herself using **God's** Power and walk the right
Direction

Following the **2nd Adam** that **DID** DO *ALL* the **Father** did tell **Him** so he
Could begin
Legally and justifiably the right to pay the price to be the ***propitiation*** for
EVERY SIN
Ever committed by *ALL* humans...your brothers and sisters in the family
Created by **His WORD.**
ONLY **DISBELIEF** - THE **DEVIL** - PUTS in the *SINFUL* MAN'S MIND the
THOUGHT of **PUTTING**
Fellow men into an ETERNAL "HELL" *TO SUFFER* the **PUNISHMENT HE'S**
ALREADY **PAID FOR . . .**
**HOW SAD, SICK, DISTURBING, PERVERTED, UNFORGIVING,
UNMERCIFUL, UNGRACEFUL, UNBIBLICAL, UNHOLY,** AND **OBSURD ! ! !**
P.S. (just to name **a few** adjectives)   **HA.**

Rich Kovatch
2- 15-12

#95 The Candlestick of the Lord

The candlestick of the Lord is the **picture g**iven
To all of mankind to show us light as we are livin'.
It can burn brightly and be a light unto the darkness to **g**uide
Or get blown out prematurely to end this Earthly **r**ide.

The difference is in which spirit gets **m**anifested
And *which food we eat* and *gets d*i*gested*.
There's **the manna diet** from **Heaven** which supplies *all* out need,
And the carnal and earthly diet which is only lustful **greed**.

The **picture given** is when the Hebrews gained **freed**om
From Egypt - which is worldliness from which the Lord did **l**ead **um'**
Away from and *into* the wilderness, but with Canaan in **m**ind.
A nine day journey which took the nation 40 years to **f**ind.

The manna was given each morning except on the Sabbath **D**ay.
Twice the normal was given the day before because God did **s**ay
The **Sabbath** means *"to rest"* and *no works* to be **done**.
The Spirit given His disciples *understand* that our efforts are covered by
God's **s**on

Jesus who came down in the flesh **to show us God's f**ace.
He brought **Peace** & **Mercy** *to teach us how to forgive* with **Agape G**race,
And to withstand the wiles and lies of the Devil - who's only UNB**E**LIEF,
So if we stay in His sheepfold we'll be SUPERNATURALLY
Protected...**GOOD G**REIF **!**

They were **led by the Cloud by day** and **protected by the Fire at n**ight.
The Cloud, for His followers today, are His witnesses that walk by
Faith...not sight.
The Fire is the **awareness of sin** in the **mind** that **feels like Hell**
Whenever we do wrong, and not **r**ight.
So we'll confess **our shortcomings** knowing full well that though WE
MAY LET GO, **He holds on t**ight.

#95 The Candlestick of the Lord

But the person that does not care about anything but pleasing his selfish
Wants
**Manifests the spirit of disobedience, rejects wisdom, and becomes a
Fool** and a dunce.
And the candlestick's flame will burn out like a flash in a pan.
Bright for a moment...*then that's the end of this life* for that man.

But God's word does say ALL will be raised again in the 1st
Resurrection
And judged on their <u>works</u> and lovingly given the chance to repent
(Change their direction).
He wouldn't say **1st Resurrection** unless there be a second. So the **2nd
Death *will have no power*** over his life.
**Thus God's Mercy, Forgiveness, Love and Grace *will <u>draw</u>* ALL MEN to
Become His virgin wife.**

That's <u>not hard</u> to believe <u>knowing</u> the <u>Love</u>, <u>Mind</u> & <u>Will</u> of God <u>to</u> <u>save</u>
All men with longsuffering, mercy and Grace that directs *ALL* men to
Rise from the grave.
Some will receive more blessings than others, with some receiving **the**
Gift of life alone.
But others will receive double portions, plus some, according to the light
Their lives have shown.

The parable of the talents certainly tells of this picture.
Still being alive after we've died in this world is still in the mixture.
Paul said he *<u>died</u> <u>daily</u>*, as we're to also do, but then lived for our Lord.
If we still speak **the condemning spirit that wants people to go to Hell**,
We won't have that one accord

#95 The Candlestick of the Lord

Of the **understanding** that *only with the knowledge of our very own*
Sins being forgiven and *forgotten,*
Will we find the Grace to bear the sins of those **still lost** in which Christ
Has not yet risen and as yet **begotten**
And adopted as a child of His own through the **faithfulness** of **Christ to**
Redeem the 100th lost sheep.
God told **Jesus** He'd not lose ONE **The Father** has given Him, including
"Those **not** of this fold" He would **keep.**

The **"fold"** is the nation of **True Believers**, the **True Israel, True Church,**
True believers that also *desire*
ALL to be saved, *including* the *as yet* unbelieving fold, **even if**
Righteousness *has to* put them **through the f**ire
And **destroy their flesh IN *ORDER* to SAVE** their **self-willed**, wretched
Soul.
This is the character of God *to save*, since He's the God of the **living** *and*
Those we call **dead** from that **6' deep h**ole

That is called **"the pit"**, the **"grave"**, **"outer darkness"**, **"separation"**, as
Well as other idioms including **"Hell".**
These are all only for an **"age"**, not "forever" which is not in any like text,
And **used to redeem** the lost. So let's **tell**
The **"REAL TRUTH"** of **God's promise** that **His MERCY NEVER ENDS,** but
Is given to <u>whomever</u> and <u>whenever</u> He chooses.
<u>THIS</u> is the <u>REAL</u> **CHARACTER of God - WHO IS LOVE -** which *<u>always</u>*
<u>WINS</u> & *NEVER* LOSES ! ! !

Rich Kovatch
2-16-12

#96 Sweet Dreams and God's STILL at Work

"Sweet Dreams", my wife said as I went off to bed
With what I thought was great peace, but deep down in my head
At the R.E.M. level of sleep which takes some 4 hours to reach,
Even there, the **Holy Spirit** is active and **continues** to teach!

Right at the 4 hour mark, I had an all too common dream
Which ended up waking me after, in it, I made my wife scream
In fear from the reaction she provoked me to take
Which led to this poem, because my subconscious said: *"I'm still a fake"*

In the essence that **I'm totally at peace with how she t**reats
Me, while I'm awake - which I don't like - because it never meets
My idea of how the flesh woman is to treat her Adam and mate.
I'm still looking for my **"Eve"** to reunite with my Spiritual Adam - I still
Must wait.

This is the process of my carnal Adam mind **wanting to *FORCE* her to** see
The things she does *provokes a reaction* in me I don't *want* to be!
Like **God** gets forced to show **He *WILL NOT* A**CCEPT
This *provoking* attitude that makes the husbandman reject

The **harlot's non-compliance** with how the **"virgin wife"** must fear
Her patient and loving **Lord** in the sense of **RESPECTING** him **IN ORDER**
To stay **near,**
And not have to run and seek <u>worldly advice that gets her nowhere.</u>
The Bible teaches **she's to TRUST** His character & **not** make Him again scare

Her *back into line* and onto **the narrow path** *that leads*
To a *peaceful* and ***growing relationship*** where she always concedes
And **submits** to ***draw out*** <u>only</u> **His** <u>*peaceful*</u> side
Which wants **TOTAL** intimacy with only His **VIRGIN BRIDE.**

These poems are so long because in order to get to the point,
I have to build the foundation first from where Love first grew to anoint
That foundation which is - as shown in the poem written just before this one -
Is **<u>God's Love Before 1ˢᵗ Sight</u>**, which speaks of that provoking game to
Be **DONE.**

#96 Sweet Dreams and God's STILL at Work

And **IN ORDER** to *SEE* the **PICTURE of HOPE** as this ministry is called,
One is commanded to continually wash our brother's feet so their
Journey won't get stalled.
And when he comes in from the dirty road he's walked - the way
Through the world
Where we get dirty - the flesh man is made from dirt and must get
Hurled

Out of its mouth - like the lesson of Jonah and the whale
Which is again **God's** promise of how He deals with bad attitude and is
Not just a tale.
Jonah didn't WANT to follow **God's** directions TO *OFFER* **REDEMPTION**
To the people of Nineveh,
Which was the **capital city** of **Babylon;** which **pictures the s**in of a

Whole **nation of rebellious people** who try to build their tower UP to
God
But brought only confusion of language and separation from each other,
And into the wilderness we all trod.
Again like the **PICTURE** and **LESSON** of **Cain**, or **Lot**, or **Esau**, or **Jacob**
And **US ALL**,
But the **TRUE PICTURE** is like of **Abraham**, **Joseph** and ultimately **JESUS**
Who listened and answered **God's c**all,

And was led by the **"Good Shepherd's"** voice back into **the Father's** Hand;
And given the land of Promise...Canaan, the New Jerusalem and souls as
Numerous as all the sand
Of the entire world - **the PICTURE** of all the saved souls that can't be
Counted,
And the stars in the heavens as Love's harvest on which the truth is
Mounted.

Like **the PICTURE of Jesus** riding into Jerusalem as the servant and
Willing to die
For the sins *of the world* - so like the smaller test for us is to try
To **live** in peace with one another, with rulers and loved ones, and
Enemies and friends.
Again **the PICTURE** of how a perfect relationship with **God's GRACE**
Never ends.

#96 Sweet Dreams and God's STILL at Work

So let's finally get to the dream I had that started this all.
My wife & I were with friends watching mankind attempting to stand tall
By trying to reach into outer space with the quest to find answers
To man's problems in our relationship to find **God** - which only brings
Cancers.

It never got off the ground and a stranger couple we were talking to
Got friendlier, and the wife started befriending me, which only drew
My wife into a frenzy of jealousy and accused me of wanting to screw
The other woman, which was not true. And off the handle I flew!

I started to run after my wife, who at this point had already put distance
Between us because she knew the accusation would cause strong
Resistance
Between our relationship as being faithful companions as husband & wife.
She already knew this test would be as a stab in my heart with a knife.

So again, like I said, the **Holy Spirit** also was showing me
As like **God's** character to be long-suffering...I have to set free
The thought that *I need* to cram the written law down her throat.
Because I try to show her the beam in her eye while my own has its own
Moat .

That's why **GRACE** is the way to draw sinful man back near.
It's with *forgiveness* and *mercy* we'll show the lost sheep not to fear
As **the PICTURE** of the Shepherd's way to save is not to be scared but
With **REVERENCE**.
NOT do this or I'll get thrown to the wolves ending in a permanent
Severance

From the **God** and **Father** of **LOVE** - that FEAR message IS the *false*
Church's WAY
To scare the lost sheep back by threatening that there will come a day...
As **Hebrews 9:27** says - this Earthly time will end - AND THEN the
Judgment comes.
And if a verbal confession of **Jesus** wasn't spoken and a change shown -
INTO HELL the lost sheep plumbs.

#96 Sweet Dreams and God's STILL at Work

To continue on with this dream which **God's** word says **He'll** give as **He'll** Prove
To young men (thanks **God**, I'm 54), to show us all what we still need to Remove.
She ran to the establishment and a man came to her side.
And as she and I, and our neighbors, Keith and Maryanne drove away in My ride

He latched on to the mirror and window of my truck to watch out for Her,
Even our friend, Keith gave her $10.00 so she could leave and continue To stir
If she chose to separate again from me - Keith doesn't see **God's** way
That this chastening happening to her is what happens to all...EVERY DAY!

Keith has a love for her - but it's Earthly in nature
Not understanding the *Law of Reciprocity* - whatever you put on your Plate you're
Going to have to eat and the results will be foreknowable.
Eat the **spirit of the world**, **Devil**, and **flesh**...and the effects will be Uncontrollable.

That's why **Jesus** came to lead those who **HEAR** and **OBEY** to FREELY CHOOSE,
To walk in the **LIGHT** He gives us all to find **LIFE** and **NOT** LOSE
One precious moment in time any longer because **TIME = L**OVE.
QUALITY TIME is what **God** wants us to share by always being gentle as A dove.

So this is where I woke up, my heart beating full speed.
The *Holy Spirit* told me while I was sleeping I still have a great need
To give all situations to the **Lord** and let His timing take place.
Then in peace I will continue on as I deal with this lost human race.

#96 Sweet Dreams and God's STILL at Work

This poem, and *all* that *I'm given* is meant to encourage *my wife* and *all*
To repent - which means - **turn from one's own wisdom** & answer His **call**.
The **"Good Shepherd"** always voices the direction back home
And get back into His sheepfold from which we all do constantly roam.

It's impossible with man to be perfect, but with **God's** leading...not so.
He'll never let go of any man...**so *stop teaching* to Hell you'll go!**
That's the Devil's and carnal man's way of repaying evil with evil!
Read the **scriptures that promise ALL souls He's in the process of
Retrieval!**

Romans 8:35-39 states that **NOTHING** shall separate us from the
Love of God
And He'll eventually - even after Earthly death - give all men His nod
Of acceptance back into His glory to be one with *our Father!*
The calling to preach this **TRUTH** to which only true believers of **Christ's
Faith** will **care** to bother ! ! !

Rich Kovatch
2-18-12

#97 Love...or in Love *WITH*

There's **a difference between** loving someone & being **IN LOVE *WITH*** them.
One is just a choice; the other has a bond that shines like a gem.
A diamond is the one that's said to last forever;
Probably because it took so much time and pressure to form the rock
That will withstand stormy weather.

It shines and reflects light so beautifully it draws one in
To a dream-like state of mind that can overcome any sin.
Its commitment is forever, and like **God's Love for ALL...**
Does overcome ALL SIN He knew & allows to happen to each since we all
Do fall.

It represents **God's Love** but it doesn't speak to the **Love** He has
For His **"Virgin bride"** that's made herself clean from all this jazz
That **this world, flesh** & the **Devil** throws our way but **given GRACE** to rise
Above the selfish ways that default most from the prize.

This is because He's only **in Love *WITH*** *certain, special* souls ***who choose***
To let the sharing of each other's burdens comfort themselves...instead
Of, let's say... booze.
There are many warnings and pitfalls explained in the Proverbs of
Wisdom for the wise,
Which **differs** from **the wisdom** *of fools* which are **deceived** by their
Unrighteous lies.

People who don't allow the shepherd's staff to correct their wayward
Ways
Go through life and marriage constantly obsessed in a **LONEY DAZE**.
They wonder why their lives are **so filled with** trouble and strife
And **DON'T FEEL** THE LOVE of their God, and or husband who longs to
Give *this special gift* to his wife.

#97 Love...or in Love *WITH*

They don't see or get blessed by the companionship the **"Virgin wife"**
Will receive
Because they aren't doing their part...which is **"SIMPLY BELIEVE"**
THAT God's words bring life through death and an understanding about
Pleasure.
**This is the principle that ...the more you give out to Love, the greater
Your treasure !**

True Love will overflow like a fountain turned on
So open that it can't contain any more darkness - like each morning's
New dawn.
It will happen no matter what you say, think, do or demand.
**HIS MERCIES ARE NEW EVERY MORNING...is the word of His
Command.**

MERCY is **the GIFT** that allows growth to be made.
His sunshine as the LIGHT of TRUTH will CONQUER *ALL* and erase all the
Shade
Of any darkness of doubt of whether He or your mate's **Love** is real.
It energizes this overflowing of GIVING GRACE with an unbounded zeal !

So **MERCY** and **GRACE** are the GIFTS of God's way *that propel Love to
Grow*.
But one must be in Love *WITH* someone else for this crazy way *to show*.
Whether single or married, the "one" to whom *WITH* must be
Is the person of JESUS, who came down from Heaven, lived, died and
ROSE to set you free !

To be in Love *WITH* the person you're married to, you must SEE in your
Mate
That to die to your selfish attitudes is the path to your fate.
It may hurt like Hell, but I know it hurts like Hell way more
When one refuses to let this **true Love** live and **let JESUS open the door**

#97 Love...or in Love *WITH*

That you first have to knock on - this shows that you do have the will
To give to your **Lover** as much as you can...**and even more still !**
This abundance doesn't come from your flesh or mind, but from OUR FATHER,
Who first had to put in you the desire to even bother

To go *through* the *fires of Hell* to get to this point.
The diamond in the rough is this *Love* inside you that the **Holy Spirit** will Anoint
That will comfort and guide you through all of your tests and trials.
If you're asked to walk a mile in their shoes, you'll gladly walk two miles!

So like the Bible says...TRUE LOVE ALWAYS PUTS THE OTHER'S NEEDS FIRST.
If they're hungry, you'll feed them, and if their mouths are parched for Water and do thirst
You'll supply their need, physically, and spiritually for the water of
Baptism of the Holy Spirit to be poured upon them,
You've also fed them **"The Bread of Life"** by showing **JESUS** of Nazareth,
THE *MOST* PRECIOUS GEM ! ! !

Rich Kovatch
2-23-12

#98 Love...or in Love *WITH* - Part II

IN ORDER TO KEEP YOUR ATTENTION **FOCUSED** AND **S**HARP;
I, as God's servant have to cover this whole issue under the spiritual **t**arp
Of the tent in the wilderness - like the **PICTURE** of how God was first
Followed.
He led by day with a cloud **so their path was divinely h**allowed.   Ex.13:21

And by night as they slept, the **fire** kept them safe and **w**armed.
This, today, is how the **TRUE CHURCH** by the **fires of Hell** are formed.
He let's us rest in darkness **so the fires will** ignite
The desire to leave **the darkness of DISBELIEF** and take up the fight

To bring this **fire of *Holiness*** and ***Its Light to correct our own walk first,***
Then to the ones we **k**now
Are ***not yet*** in sync with how God wants their life to go.
And of course, the **FALSE CHURCH** will say I'm putting my big **n**ose
In someone else's business - maybe for them that's what they
Believe...but God's the one who **c**hose

Who ***I'm*** to verbalize wisdom and truth...*in love*, or **written down,** and
For sure ***lead by example***
To whoever is *now willing* to take their first bite and **s**ample
The **REAL LOVE** of the Fear of the Lord - which is TO **R**EVERE
His Laws and repercussions from evil ways so corrections will become
Less **s**evere.   Prov. 8:13

God's way is to first gently persuade, then ***if necessary***, turn up the heat,
And I know it's not my place to force the issues,
But it still hurts me, and Jesus who lives in my heart, deeply when we
See loved ones **m**isuse
The GIFT of this life OUR FATHER has blessed them with to *search out*
And *Find*   Prov. 25:2
If they'd only **TRUST** in His servant who says **"to JESUS let's bind**

#98 Love...or in Love *WITH* - Part II

Ourselves to - together - so as "ONE BODY" we'll all then walk
Rom.12:15, 1 Cor.10:17, Eph.4:4

Behind this cloud while it's still "daytime" - because the darkness of
Night does affect and stalk
Us all, and the time will come when no man will be able to work and the
Light to be seen.
John 9:4

The Bible does warn us this day does arrive for all - so it's wise to ask
Yourself - *is it being*

Shoved in your face - RIGHT NOW - by God - and is He's asking..."where
Are you?"
Like He did with Adam and Eve in the Garden of Eden when their
Relationship with Him they both blew.
Gen. 3:9

They also were HIDING FROM GOD - they saw they were suddenly naked
And deeply shaken.
Gen. 3:10

Just as He wants **"the rebel"** to see also **His TRUTH** they also have
Forsaken.

He's not going to throw you into the fire without a righteous cause !
But before **you** *step* into **it** - *He begs you to pause*
To ponder **your next step and the direction it's** headed.
Will it bring you, and even more so - someone else a blessing, or will it
Be even more dreaded

After it's been taken and **The LAW does Its t**hing?
Gal.6:7-8

Either way - the end result He desires and His WILL **IS** that you **WILL**
EVENTUALLY sing
2 Peter 3:9, 15

The praises of His Kindness of AGAPE *FORGIVENESS, MERCY & GRACE*
When you *finally* UNDERSTAND the purpose of *your* race

AT the finish line of life when your own death WILL OCCUR !
Heb. 9:27

100% OF ALL PEOPLE WILL DIE - for even JESUS - this was sure.
Heb. 9:28

SO THE LESSON He wants you to learn, NOW, is again...just TRUST
That **He Loves you dearly** and to receive Him today - you MUST

#98 Love...or in Love *WITH* - Part II

Submit yourself unto His correcting staff which brings back His lost
Sheep.   Prov. 3:12, 22:15, 23:13
Because **YOU** are the <u>**MOST** IMPORTANT **ONE**</u> in the whole world, He
And I want to keep
Safe and warm...again, under the fires by night
Which will lighten up the path to help you *SEE* what is right.

It is to listen to His preaching and pray to our Lord.
Do I want to live by **HIS WISDOM**, or DIE BY **HIS S**WORD?   Matt. 26:52
His Word is a lamp unto our feet and the Lord directs our steps.
                                                          Ps. 119:105, Prov. 16:9
What does it take to be chosen as one of His reps?

It is to SHOW **MERCY, FORGIVE** BOUNTIFULLY, **and LOVE** DEEPLY in
AGAPE Style,
NEVER FORGETTING WHAT HE'S DONE FOR US, speaking the truth
Without deceitful intent or guile
BY selling *some* truth for prideful gain or fame, **but** then finally selling
ALL OUT buying the **Pearl of GREAT P**RICE.
Visiting those in **prison**, the **Fatherless**, the **poor in spirit**, the **hurting**
And **teaching** from keeping *any* sin as a vice.

His TRULY POWERFUL CHURCH will heal the sick and give *HOPE* to the
Faithless.
Spreading the **"GOOD NEWS"** that JESUS is the savior of the ENTIRE
WORLD and an eternal Hell - **b**aseless.
Teaching all to turn form evil thoughts and to **hate sin** as God does - and
NOT THE *SINNER* !   Rom.12:17, 21
The **"Good News"** is *God doesn't want you to die **ignorantly*** or
Willingly hating Him, but as a beloved *WINNER* !

                                                          Rich Kovatch
                                                          2-24-12

#99 Destroyed for Lack of Knowledge

My people are **destroyed** for Lack of **Knowledge** is the word,   Ho.4:6
And is exactly what happens when the truth is heard
When it is ignored or refuted, rejected and refused.
Just **because** its corrective nature **hits home**...unwise people think
They're being abused.

They immediately return with loud verbal accusations of their own
Against the messenger who's only telling them they'll reap what they've
Sown.
God's word is not mocked and if you disobey...you will pay.
It was true all throughout the Old Testament **and it's still true today!**

Gal. 6 vs. 7 & 8 states that sin against the flesh comes back to the flesh
As a warning
And spirit back to your spirit which will cause an even deeper mourning.
That is of course if you have a close relationship with the one
Who came down from Heaven as God's personal messenger and
Redeemer - The SON

Of God Himself - **JESUS** - the name itself means *HE SAVES*   Matt.1:21
*His people from their sins **when** and **only when** one hears and obeys.*
This may sound as if I'm saying - if you die in disbelief...it's **Hell** for you
And that's exactly what I'm saying - but what **"Hell"** IS THOUGHT to be **is
Not true!**

I've been given a bunch of messages lately about Hell and have written
Them down.
When I've obeyed **The Word** and read it **(the Bible)** by myself, this is
What I found;
That **Hell** is the price we pay **when we disobey** the Truth...and our walk
No longer leads
To an abundant life in this world or opens the gates to Heaven when our
Heart bleeds

#99 Destroyed for Lack of Knowledge

With **COMPASSION** & **MERCY** & **FORGIVENESS** & **GRACE** for fallen Men
That seeks to cover sins like a loving and protecting mother hen.
That specific **PICTURE, JESUS** Himself gave us in Matt. 23:37 & Luke 13:34
Where He tells us that if we're scribes and Pharisees (hypocrites), He
Closes the door

UNTIL, **UNTIL**, UNTIL...ye shall say "Blessed is He who comes in the
name Of the Lord".
Thus if you're really (right now) a child of God - He's asking you if you
Can afford
To keep doing things *against His WORD* that cause division and strife
And sin against the **WRITTEN LAW** that surely brings us all **to the end of
OUR life**.   Heb.9:27

Like I said in the last poem given me - even **JESUS** Himself died. John19:30
But He did it WILLINGLY for ALL men because He never sinned or lied!!!
He always spoke the truth and **commands us** to do the same.
Admit that every day we somehow sin, but still believe in **His NAME**.

This name, again, is **JESUS**, & **it means** that ONLY IN HIM IS THE POWER
That will let all us sinners into the Kingdom when it comes to the hour
That we all die and then **SEE** and confess He's the "King of Kings and
Lord of Lords".
Here is his real mission - it is to destroy the works of the Devil when we
Daily confess and repent to gain His rewards.   1 John3:8

Child, just do a word study of **"bones"** in a concordance & find the
Secret.
A couple good ones are Prov.3:8, 15:30, and 16:24 so our yesterdays we
Won't regret,
But gain **KNOWLEDGE** and **WISDOM** and be given **a true testimony -
Through trial**
And error that physical, I and more importantly **spiritual health comes
Only when we no longer live in denial**

#99 Destroyed for Lack of Knowledge

To how we're to **eat healthy** and **think only *good* thoughts** that show
The way to bring **Heaven** to Earth & make **His Kingdom** presently grow.
It grows in so many ways to fill up the earth
Which will lead to **JESUS** bringing an end to our "Hour of Mirth".

We are deceived by our carnal nature in which we tend to be content in,
And we ignorantly ignore the way
God constantly draws us to, but we choose to listen to what **the Devil**
Continues to say.
Like **A**dam and **E**ve did in the **Garden of Paradise** - where we ought to
Dwell,
We also choose too often to eat from the wrong tree and squirm on our
Bellies in Hell.

Like **the PICTURE of Satan** told by God **he's now cursed *to eat God's***
Dust
And slither on the ground, with a flaming ***fire*** between him & the
Woman Now being a must
So mankind will not live forever in disobedience and not trusting
The **guidance** of **God's WORD** which disallows **re-entry** into **Paradise**
Without dusting

Off **the Devil**, his ways and lies, which, once again - is only **DISBELIEF**
And the spirit of it - **the man IS OURSELF** with the **#666** - good grief!
The **Book of the Revelation** of **JESUS CHRIST** is the prophecy of the way
That for **ALL** the sins of the world - done by us - only JESUS' **BLOOD**
SAVED THE DAY!!!

It's not the picture of some future day that the whole world will see on
T.V. ,
But so far individually for each person ***in God's appointed time*** when
This will be.
JESUS told us that to find our true life **IN HIM** we must first - to OUR
OWN EGO - **DIE**.
And this, again, is to turn from **the Devil's** deceptions & NO LONGER **LIE**

#99 Destroyed for Lack of Knowledge

Because **JESUS** promises that **ALL LIERS** will have *their* part in the **Lake of Fire**.
This - opposite of what the false religious church - **the Devil** - teaches is Not at all dire,
But *"The way"* God *uses* **JUDGMENT** *to burn* out dross from **His gold**
Which is you and me - we're **MOST PRECIOUS** to Him - and He's Continually told

Us all in His word - from Genesis to the Revelation of JESUS - in which *Only* is eternal life.
He doesn't accept His harlot woman, but only His VIRGIN WIFE
That has made herself clean by choosing to cover herself with **His blood.**
Again, this He's told us through **the PICTURE** of Noah's day **flood**

Where He **destroyed** all men (**with** *the* **Earth**) who **had evil** constantly On their mind
And saved only the **Family of Faith** in God's word - **8 precious souls** we Do find.
#8 is the number of **rebirth** - the NEW DAY TO COME
When we truly **believe** His word **to eventually save** *ALL* - AND **NOT JUST** SOME!!!

Because like in Cain's response to God when asked where Able was,
He denied we're our brother's keeper, and THIS also is what the **FALSE CHURCH** does!
He killed the one who gave honor to God with the 1st sheep offering Made.
Able tended the flock - like **the PICTURE** of **JESUS** who also with His life Paid

The ultimate price - His own life, at the hands of religious scoffers.
They refused to believe in the paradise life in which walking in His word Offers.
And not only offers, but promises and delivers to only those who seek.
Only they shall find this paradise - **Heaven on Earth**...He gives them a Peek;

#99 Destroyed for Lack of Knowledge

Because we can see through the glass palely at best
Until we believe in the salvation of **ALL** men and begin to rest
In **the ark** Noah built - **the PICTURE** of *the plan of God*
Who destroyed all <u>left</u> on the earth upon which they still trod.

This **"earth"** symbolizes **our flesh** - made from **the dust**.
We're to **"let it die"** - **accept** it *will*, but also to believe our spirit and soul
Continue on is what we must trust.
God had male & female of all flesh enter the day it rained - two and two.
This PICTURES that we still have the flesh nature, and this He knew.

Gen. 6:6-7 said He will destroy man from the face of the earth and
Repented.
But the new way He foreordained through the fiery sword He had
Already invented.
This now gives us **Wisdom** which had not been very active with man
Before the flood.
But after it ended, His promise not to destroy this earth shows in the
RAINBOW - **symbolizing His blood**.

This is **the PICTURE** of **God's LIGHT** for us **"first fruits"** *who see that
Light*
Consists of ALL COLORS - skins and **nations** of men *being covered by His
Might*
Reflected back off the rain that does pour on the evil and the good.
We're to preach the **"Good News"** that **He'll save ALL** men *like He said
He would*!

Even the rain is a **PICTURE** of God's blessings upon all.
Evil men **use it** to **do their thing**, just as righteous souls see it as God's call
To use their increase *to supply* **physical needs** to those in **dire need**.
This goes in the *physical arena* as well as for the *spiritual* **seed**.

The dire need of lost souls in the wilderness **is in the FAITH shown by
JESUS**;
WHO IS THE ONLY WAY TO GOD - His living body is the church and the
Whole world needs us
To bring the **UNDERSTANDING** to all that His body presently has dead
Parts
That have the minds set against God & wills set in stone covering their
Hearts.

#99 Destroyed for Lack of Knowledge

The **"stone"** covering their hearts is also God - because only on His Timetable
Does He turn our hearts of stone into hearts of flesh so I'm able
To give this message of salvation of ALL _and you can now receive it_?
It only happens *when* and *if* in this lifetime you're able to perceive it.

Rom.8:36-39 says....**even *time*** is not an obstacle over which **JESUS'** Victory hasn't overcome
And He may choose to save most souls when their lives are nearly done,
In the *last second* of anyone's life - no man knows how He works
Except the *spirit* of HOPE *which desires ALL MEN to receive Paradise's Perks*.

The **"Blessed Hope"** in Greek *means* it *is a sure thing* upon which to Lean.
Hope is what followers believe in - but hasn't yet totally been seen
Except in the true 1ˢᵗ Fruit - JESUS risen from the dead.
This is our motivation and power received from believing what He Said.

He's given ALL men a measure of faith that's been
Lost by most and **left to die** *because they chose* to continue in sin.
But in the Sower's parable - the chance to return **is always given**.
Only people who teach this "Good News" are already eternally livin'

And have **SPIRITUALLY experienced** the 2ⁿᵈ **coming** and the 1ˢᵗ **Resurrection**, and have **"The Light"** that *won't dim*.
That light is in and from JESUS and Heaven is BEING IN HIM
Serving lost mankind with *humility* and *meekness* with **AGAPE LOVE**
To the point of our passing
In the mindset that **SPIRITUALLY** we **ALREADY ARE ALSO RISEN IN TRUE LIFE EVERLASTING!!!**

Rich Kovatch
3-3-12

#100 Servant, Friend, Brother or Son

What does God call you, my **brother**
Or sister, If that be even from a different **mother**,
Because we're all children of the Spirit of Love that's **made**
All humans *to evolve out of the spirit of deception* that one day will **fade**.

We ALL will be transformed into believing souls that will see the **Light**.
Each in his own order depending on how hard & long you **fight** 1 Cor. 15:23
With the **Spirit of Love** that *corrects* each lost **sheep**   John 6:37
Because the Word says that all that the Father gave Him Jesus **will keep**.

                                                                        Gen. 1:2, 3:1
The spirit of deception has been around since BEFORE Adam and **Eve**.
Eve was deceived but Adam choose to side with her; instead of **believe**
That God would have mercy on her and correct her with **Grace**.
*This spirit of the Devil is what stops you from seeing God's **face**.*

Jesus said "If you've seen me you've seen the **Father**.
But here's the rub - Has God put in you the desire to **bother**
To seek out the truth *yourself* and **NOT TRUST ANY religion...**
*Especially the false Christian one that denies **God made the provision***

To Save ALL men **in his own order?**   1 Cor. 15:23
The teaching of an eternal Hell has crossed the **border**
Of what the *power* and *will* of **God** is **for All men**, creation, and
Especially **you**.   2 Peter 3:9, 15-16
This is what His Word says a disciple will be led to **do**.

Be like the Bereans or Colossians that looked...each on their **own**.
God has hidden the truth from some of us all...to separate the marrow
From the **bone**
With the sword of the Spirit which is the truth **revealed**
Once the flesh nature of **pride** and **selfishness** has been **peeled**

Off the bone which is hard, *And He may have to break it **first***
To test you severely *in order to* get you **to thirst**;
To drink His blood and eat His flesh because you now **hunger**;
To be taught **how to live** and *love your enemies* and no longer **blunder**.

#100 Servant, Friend, Brother or Son

When a situation arises and you feel the desire to condemn and **belittle**,
This is the beginning of when He choose to send the knife that will **whittle**
That marrow from the bone and bring the **Spirit of brotherhood** & **Light**
That *gently* helps one see his wayward way *without* a big **fight**.

Because it may not be the right timing for the other soul to **see**
Exactly how a righteous walk for him presently could **be**
Which is to repent and **turn** from the Devil and put on the **glory**
Of God's graceful leading to understand that the farther one's away the
More He

Brings conviction through the reaping of what you've sown to **be**.
If your diet is weak, your health will become weak also **so you can see**
The benefits of feeding your body, mind and spirit with food He **desires**
You to consume to *be transformed* into more of His image *before* your
Life **expires**.

This is the first step of becoming a friend, son and brother of Jesus **Christ**
Changing your **diet** in all phases **so** the old **diet** will get chopped up & **diced**.
So little by little you'll learn to throw off the **"old" man**
And live with a love for others and become their second biggest **fan**

When you see them **improve their diet, talk & walk to parallel** Christ's **ways**
Then the **Joy** you'll experience will increase moment by moment the
Rest of your **days;**
Becoming a friend, brother, and son upon which the Father can *now*
Trust in **more**
Through an increased faith in His ways which will open up another **door**

To enter another aspect of the Kingdom of Heaven here in this **life;**
Learning to put away your fleshly wrath which only brings **strife;**
Learning to be wise as a serpent and yet gentle as a **dove**
Following the example Christ set when He came down to teach the
Anointed ways from **above**.

Rich Kovatch
3-16-12

#101 What Goes In...Must

What goes in...*must* come **out**.
That's what life is all **about**.
Jesus told us the *eye* is the **key**;   Matt.6:22-23
If *it* lets in darkness, *then that's* how **your** *expressions* shall *be*.

But if it lets in the "**Light of Love**" with a *forgiving* **spirit**,
Then others will be drawn to what you say so they might personally
Hear it.   John 12:32
This is the difference of the perception of what Jesus **said:**
If you hear Him with Love, you'll live... if with contempt, you're still
Dead.

You must be born of the spirit to be able to **understand.**   Jonh 3:3-8
Will you build your house upon the rock or upon sinking **sand.** Matt. 7:24-27
When winds of tribulation come only one house will **survive.**
And if you live in that house you will endure them and **thrive.**

But *if* you're in *darkness* and *have set your anchor* in **seeds of hate**,
Especially for your enemies, with **"Hell's fire"** you'll have a **date**
That God will send you into *because* you *must be* **purified**
By Him burning the Hell *out of you* because you've just been judged
And **tried**   2 Peter 3:10

And been found wanting with no sense of brotherhood for deceived
Souls in **pain;**   Dan. 5:27
Not willing to give up your own life so their lives you may **unchain.**
This is the double inheritance Jesus was given being the first begotten
Son of the **Father**   1 Tim. 5:17
Created in order to redeem a lost world of which many wonder why God
Would **bother**   Gal. 4:5

#101 What Goes In...Must

To have created in the first place if it is to be so full of **sorrow**.
The key is to _understand_ the reasons for today with the promise of a
Tomorrow
That God has ordained to be without end and without pain, suffering or
Sin.   2 Peter 3:9-16
*But we must be consumed by this one first and be transformed for the
Second to begin*.   1 Cor. 15:53-56

THEN, we're allowed to eat again from the **"Tree of Life"**   Gen. 3:24
After we've entered as his made ready virgin **wife**   Rev. 19:27
That has cleaned herself up and endured to the **end**.
Keeping the faith that God surely is our **friend**.

Now back to the point of what enters our **body**.
We're to be good stewards of it and not let it get **shoddy**   Eph. 6:15
Or **overgr**own with weeds that will choke out a blessed **garden**.
Corporately, the body is Christ's believers, but individually our muscles
Are to **harden**.

Physically we need to work out to put a demand on them so they'll
Grow.
Mentally we also need to challenge our minds so God's wisdom will
Show.
But spiritually is the most important to insure *"Truth"* & *"Light"* enters **in**
So what we reflect out will be the *"Fruit of the Spirit"*... not **sin**.

If we neglect such a great gift we've been given, what will be the **fate?**
An **attitude** that tells others **_they're_** going to **Hell** be*cause* **_we'll_** *love* to **hate!**
By *blaming God's character* as *one that runs out of mercy* and **lets you**
Stay **lost**
Refusing to proclaim Jesus saves ALL men with *His own life* and *blood*
As the **cost;**

#101 What Goes In...Must

The propitiation for *ALL* sins the world *will ever* **commit**.   2 John 2:2
Hell is the grave, the *absence* **of life**. Without Jesus...it's the **pit**.
God set up ages for things to happen and **death has its place**.
That's how God redeems the *entire* human **race**.

What goes in, must come out is the rule of **thumb**.
To this end a follower of mankind's Messiah will keep His level **plumb;**
As our carpenter leader did, His whole life our **example**.   John 13:15
When He talked to sinners, their hearts He did not **trample**.

But He gently told them they were missing the point of **life**.
He told us "He is the Way, the Truth, and the Life" ...words that cut like
A **knife**.   John 14:6
Especially to the religious scribes and Pharisees - those that thought
They **knew**
The God of *Love* **- but demonstrated the God of** *hate* **-** as condemnation
Forever **grew**

When they proclaim the end and doom of sinners to be out of **reach**.
An eternal place of torment, because *of* the path *they* choose, is what
They **preach**!
This is the Anti - Christ spirit that dwells in *this kingdom* of *darkness*
And **hate**.   2 John :7
Disbelieving the redemption of Christ to the 100th lost sheep *denies* His
Forgiveness and **Mercy –**
Which is to *HIS* **glory...***AGAPE* **great**.

Rich Kovatch
5-29-12

#102 This World Hates Correction

This world, meaning our carnal mind, hates correction
And is constantly going in the wrong direction.
When someone is confronted that they've done something bad
They say basically...Who the hell are you? My dad?

Well, **yes I am**, as His representative **if** I'm speaking words w/ love & peace.
And you are too when you try to encourage disunity to cease.
The **spirit** that lives in this world is focused on **death** and **hate**.
This world will end someday soon - **God promised** that that **IS** it's fate.

Jesus told us this evil age will end as all others have.
And **AGAPE LOVE** is the only all-purpose salve
That can deal with the perversions of a Holy walk.
Those still blinded by God are the ones that baulk.

To make it worse, I quite often *seem* to step out of line.
And even though what I say might actually be divine,
It's taken out of context and my intent seems to fail.
And to a cross my butt people often want to help nail.

But what's right is right and the only way for evil to stop
Is when the righteous Spirit is delivered...sometimes by a karate chop.
At least in the essence that an attitude must change.
God has put His children in place to complete the exchange

And will bring down the heavy hand of the **Law** that will lead
To a quick attitude adjustment that makes a **HUMBLED heart** bleed
With Godly sorrow that leads to *repentance*...
Sometimes during and sometimes after the sentence.

But the heart and attitude that God has yet to soften
Will have to learn *the same lesson* way too often...
In OUR eyes. But in God's...it's perfectly timed and right.
When that time happens, they're READY to listen and no longer fight.

Then a blessed time of quick growth will happen all at once
And they will understand that their past life was lived as a dunce.
But was still loved and blessed by God in the wisest of ways
Because the rest of his life will become the best of his days!

Rich Kovatch
6-1-12

#103 When I Die

When I die, please **don't cry.**
But rather celebrate! And I'll tell you **why.**
It may not happen that 1st day or week, because I **know**
The feelings of emotions you must eventually let **show.**

The grief of loss is normal for **most.**
For it comes from the heart already missing me, who's now **toast.**
It can last but a moment or from days to **years**
And involve a merciful release or quickly rising up **tears.**

It can take different forms from **unbelief** to **anger;**
Or be put upon a pedestal upon which my wife can **hang her**
Resentment towards God as to why that day **came.**
But that's just the **carnal nature** which **always looks for** someone to **blame.**

Life and death are not about **us...**
But God *showing us* why we're *not suppose to* **fuss.**
If things go bad or we become **sad,**
He's always doing these things so we'll call out to **"Dad"**

And say we can't handle this world on our **own.**
The lessons we learn cut right to the **bone**
And takes away every ounce of what is called **"pride"**
To learn to trust Him as to in whom alone we should **confide.**

How will I survive *now* that my **Richie is gone?**
You must now understand...a new day is at its **dawn;**
When the Sun will rise up but you'll no longer see **me;**
Except in the spirit which I always tried to set **free;**

To live thru my flesh and bones in actions and **word.**
Too often they weren't accepted and *kicked* to the **curb**
And *discarded* as *waste* to be *disposed of* by **others**
That got *PAID* to remove them so *their* own influence **smothers**

#103 When I Die

The **"Good News"** that Christ is **"The Redeemer"** of *ALL* men.
THANKFULLY, God gave me the *outlet* to *say this* through the pen
In the poems **He inspired me** to *write down* on **paper**
Which **exposed** the Devil's **job** of **deceiving** *using* **religion's** caper.

It has its time and place so God's **"Elect"** will shine **bright.**
The world that *loves darkness* will *refute* their **"Light"**
Until it is time for Jesus to come back with **power**
To **destroy** the works of the **Devil** of which no man knows the **hour.**

But is *kept in secret* by the Father - even to Jesus himself... **unknown.**
So Romans 8:22 speaks of all creation which does **painfully groan**
Of that coming day...which for ME... has *obviously now* been **dated. (Ha)**
I was happy Jesus always loved me...**but** by the world I was **mostly hated.**

Rich Kovatch
7-26-12

#104 *Redemption* 101

There are *so many* things that *can* be said.
My *sure* future failures I used to dread.
It's *not* that I won't suffer pain from missing the mark
But **being** *condemned* from my own heart *or* others **is** *only the* **Devil's Bark**.

1 John 3:20

Because **Jesus** *said* **He** *didn't* come here to condemn us **all…**   John 3:17
But to FORGIVE and pick us back up after *each* **time we f**all.   Luke 23:43
The falls happen when we don't walk in **God's** LIGHT
And WE choose to decide what's wrong and what's right.

That's called eating from the Tree of Knowledge of Good & Evil.   Gen. 2:17
Trying to be *"like God"* by making up *our own rules* of retrieval. Gen. 3:5-6
They ALWAYS amount to be WORKS *based* and *earned*.
That's the wide path through **"Hell"** where the conscience gets *burned*

Rom. 1:24,26

And seared so completely by **God…He** *no longer* <u>will</u> **s**peak   1 Tim. 4:2
Except through the judgments that will make one so **w**eak   Rom. 1:28-32
That there will be no other conclusion but to accept **HIS w**ay!
And *it* <u>*is*</u> **that** <u>*ONLY*</u> **the** <u>GRACE</u> <u>of</u> <u>God</u> *will* "<u>save the day</u>"! Eph. 2:8-10

We're designed to be faulty and fail now and then.
He puts in **His "Elect"** the ability to **FORGIVE ALL w**hen   1 Cor. 15:22
Our brother or sister showed **PRIDE** in some way and hurt
Someone else by making them feel like they're dumber than dirt.

And **dirt is actually the** *lowest* a man can go.
And **ALL WILL RETURN to it…most 6'** <u>below</u>.   Eccl. 3:20
But in the truest sense… it's **God's** clay without **"life"** and **"Spirit"**
Taken back by **God**, who owns it all. If only all could now **hear it !**

John 18:37

#104 *Redemption* 101

The "**Spirit**" **God** has let just a few see of **TRUE LIFE** in their **heart**   Rom. 1:17
Luke 24:31
Is the **Spirit of LOVE...Who** *IS* **God...** and **Jesus** did the part   1 John 4:8
1 John 3:8
Of leaving the glory **He** had and without sin told the **s**tory   1 Peter:20
That **HE** came to die for **ALL** sins and return **ALL** back to **His g**lory.
1 Cor. 15:26, 42

His story is still evolving but Paul told us the secret and **c**lue...   Eph. 3:8-12
That sin rips apart creation but **GRACE** is the **g**lue   Rom. 8:22
That keeps **Go**d's plan together and brings an end to all **pain**   John 20:32-34
When **ALL** creation is renewed & **ALL** souls **Jesus DID g**ain.   1 Cor. 15:22-28
1 Cor. 4:21, 4:5

Not ONE lost sheep did he lose - that's us - "for **ALL** have **s**inned
1 Peter 1:24-25 Rom. 3:23
And *come* **short** of the glory" - so on **Jesus'** back alone was **p**inned
Rom. 3:10-11
The penalty of **ALL** sin and the legal redemption through the LAW.
1 Cor. 15:51-58 Matt11:18
He lived *HIS* **life** *without sin* to do just that because the end from the
Beginning he **s**aw   1 Peter 3:18

And actually planned out each detail to bring all glory to the **Father.**
Rom. 4:8, 15-16
It seems to most people, being *those* who *DON'T* believe**,** strange why
He should even **b**other   2 Cor. 4:3
To even go through the trouble & design this world of *pain* & *Sorrow.*
It's because He *KNEW* the *worse* <u>**today**</u> *is***,** the *more GLORIOUS*
Tomorrow ! ! !

Rich Kovatch
8-6-12

#105 **Pain /** _PLEASURE_

What gets my attention _MORE_ in the world I live in?
Is it the pain of obedience or **_PLEASURE_** of sin?
When making a choice, right off the get go I have to decide
On which of the two worlds designed by **God** I'd rather abide.

It's determined by my present mindset on how I see things
And the end result I'll expect to reap from what each choice brings.
Do I live in my flesh nature where **_PLEASURE_** is fleeting?
A season unto itself where that **_PLEASURE_** _seems_ to be defeating

The **lessons** that **God** is **teaching** me as I'm _chastened_ for _unwise_ choices.
Do I listen to the wisdom of foolish men or my **God**ly councilors **v**oices?
I'll be honest in saying I'm not where I desire to **be**
As to how this _present_ pain I'm in is suppose to be comforting **me**.

I get tired and _depressed when_ it _seems_ I'm drowning in sorrow
And get impatient because **God** makes me wait until **t**omorrow
Before He'll show me the blessings that **He**'s got **p**repared
After I've walked through the **fires of Hell** of which **He** told me to walk
Without being scared.

The only way I can possibly _do_ that _is because_ He's _given_ me faith beforehand
That where He wants me to go I'm to **have courage** and to understand
That to become like Christ I have to also go to the **c**ross
And **_walk my own path_** which will remove _my personal_ **d**ross.

It never feels good to be _stripped_ of **p**ride;
But when it happens it's _at THAT point_ I'll decide;
Whether to continue on walking a path where **His** best glory is not **Proclaimed**
And **His** words of correction are misheard, misspoken and **p**rofaned;

Or to _just get it over with_ and _experience_ the pain.
My many _previous lessons_ haven't made me insane,
So I won't continue doing the same things and expecting **His f**avor.
It is a _clear conscious_ and a **Holy Spirit** that I surely **s**avor.

When the expected end **I desire** has finally come to pass
It will give my motor **more power** as I **step** on the gas
And race to **MY** finish line when this carnal nature has been **removed**
And _the pain has turned to PLEASURE_ and my fragile nerves soothed.

Rich Kovatch   8-16-12

#106 S t r e s s

There are two kinds of **S t r e s s**
And I certainly will openly *confess*
That both have their effects which change its *holder*
Stress from God heats us up, from the Devil makes hearts *colder*.   Deut. 4:24

Godly S t r e s s is the "Consuming Fire" that proceeds out from **God**'s own *tongue* Heb.12:9
And always **burns the hearts** of those of us **dwell**ing upon a low, **low** *rung*   Luke 24:32
Of the ladder of wisdom; which in turn encourages an upward *climb*;
But this progression to a higher place always takes a long, long *time*.

How one views the **S t r e s s** and deals with it is the deciding *factor*.
Do you receive **His** corrections **like your field of faith** is being sowed by hand or a *tractor*?
The seed **will** get sent out <u>regardless</u> of the condition of the <u>*receiving soil*'s</u> *plot*.
Hard rocky ground, a thin layer, or deeper dirt that may be fertilized or *not*.
                                               Matt. 13:3-8, Mark 4:3-8

The seed is God's children that spread a graceful love that guides us unto a
Pure and ***Righteous act.***   Matt.13:38
Whether I **conform** & **perform or get** *transformed* determines if my faith will be *packed*
With **k**nowledge, **u**nderstanding & **w**isdom to keep my spirit calm & in *peace* Prov. 1:2-7
Or if I'll still be at a point where I'll give **God** another *fleece*

To test what He's actually doing, and *if **I'm*** the main *reason*
I might have continual **S t r e s s** and **why** it's lasting *past* a <u>second</u> *season*.
I'm *being taught* to be a *mature* follower so I can now eat some *meat*
And not just keep *sucking* **on** the **baby** milk of **His Word** & keep getting knocked
Off my *feet*

But now able to keep standing & forgo the **falling 7 times** & getting back **up.** Prov. 24:16
I'm now at the **"Bride's wedding feast"** & on **HIS BODY** & **BLOOD** I now *sup*.
                                               Luke 22:30
He's the **"Bread of Life"** and I only find nourishment now in a special *way*. John 6:48-5
It's that *I'm finding more often my flesh* being denied *while I amazingly* stay
Patient unto the *day*

When *He'll show me the* <u>*rewards*</u>, **some of which I see,** <u>**even today**</u>, that **He**
Has *planned*.
I thank **God He**'s also given me **mercy** & much **"Fruit"** to eat so the meal is far
From *bland*
But is spiced up with <u>**12 flavors**</u> I never even dreamt possible to *taste*   Rev. 22:2
So I'll know that the trials I've been through have not been a *waste*.

                                               Rich Kovatch
                                               8-23-12

#107 *WHERE* Do I See LOVE?

Where do I see **Love** ? *EVERYWHERE !*
I see it *so much* it's hard to *bear*.
What makes it hard is I know that others *don't;*
Why **God** allows *ME* to see **it** but so many others He *won't.*

I see **it** in the strangest *places.*
The easiest place is in people's *faces.*
When they smile or their eyes just sparkle and *gleam*
I know for them **God** through **Jesus** came to *redeem.*

So often I've heard the **Devil's hate**-filled *lie*
That **for ALL Jesus *did not*** come to *die...*
But only a chosen few who can hear and follow **His *voice***
Because ***their supposed will*** was wise enough to make the right *choice.*

Scripture says in John 6:44 and Romans 9:16 and many other places by
Contextual *meanings*
It's NOT of MAN'S WILL but of **God's** MERCY we receive those *gleanings*
How **LOVE *NEVER*** FAILS and what AGAPE **LOVE *REALLY*** IS.
How Ezekiel 18:4 tells us how EVERY SOUL is *His.*

I can't help but see **Love** in the light and even in the *dark*
And when words of condemnation are spoken it's only the **Devil's *bark***
Because John 3:17 says **Jesus** didn't come to condemn the *world*
But that through **HIM** the world WILL BE SAVED and **His** plan *unfurled...*

That ONLY **GRACE *can save*** so that no man can *boast;*
Like by saying "I chose **Jesus**" and "**He** might **love** all but **He loves**
Christians the *most,*
But the **love** for all is only conditional because ***YOU MUST ALSO CHOOSE***
Or that love will turn into hate, & eternal life in **Him** you'll *lose*".

Did you know that hate is not the opposite of *love,*
But apathy is because it's a total lack of compassion from *above*?
Jesus came to save the lost...which includes ALL EVER *BORN.*
The first Adam's choice affected **every soul** which makes everyone *mourn.*

#107 *WHERE* Do I See LOVE?

But in the Sermon on the Mount **Jesus** said that those who mourn will
Be comforted with peace.
Only a prideful spirit wouldn't **care** for those still **lost** and fail to cease
From the spirit "lost" Israel still has thinking **God** is exclusively "theirs"...
Which is the opposite of the truth of real Love which **bears**

The sins of the whole world which **He** created and currently has mostly
In darkness
So those **He**'s chosen will bring such a bright and vivid starkness
Between the dark and the light, from the wrong from the right
& teach others to see unbelief's wiles so they also can be strong & fight

To have a greater faith so that when crap hits the fan
To not depend on their own strength but to lean on the man
From Galilee, Bethlehem which means bread, **Who IS** the "**Bread of
Life**" "**Come down from** Heaven"   John 6:35
Whose desire, purpose and will was and is to remove all the leaven

So that a fallen creation can legally be redeemed
& experience the promised **Zoë life** w/o sin of which we've all dreamed.
There is life only in, by and through **Jesus**...the author of all
Whose plan is redemption of all after he had the first Adam fall.

Sin did not take **God** by surprise nor spoil His will
But is the vehicle designed by **God** so His GRACE ALONE will pay the bill.
His will IS to SAVE ALL, not just desire or offer a way **! ! !**
Again...only a prideful spirit will believe it's got the power to save
Oneself...**O**y **Vey ! ! !**

That **carnal pride** takes the glory of **God** & puts it smack on **man's b**ack...
As like any man...except **Jesus** himself could manipulate or even design
His own track..
A man plans his own way but **God** directs his steps.   Prov. 16:9
The way seems right to each man but are the ways of death's depths.
                                                                                Prov. 16:25

#107 *WHERE* Do I See LOVE?

But even as each man lives his own life I see how **God**'s hand works.
One's life is as a letter from **God**, individual & full of many, many quirks.

2 Cor. 3:3

We're to be content deep within our own convictions that what we
Experience is **O.**K.
Because ALL SIN was IMPUTED upon **Jesus** and **He**'s died, risen and
"Saved the **d**ay".

I intended this poem to list so many places where I see Love
But Love had me praise **Jesus** alone because I've been shown AGAPE'
Love is **a**bove
Any kind of fellowship or brotherhood or kindness through works any
Carnal spirit of man can **s**how,
And only when we've become **Jesus** freaks will this understanding
Brightly **g**low.

There's only life in **Jesus and without Him there's only death.**
And He's destroyed that "<u>last</u> enemy". He's the seed that came through
Seth
Who was Abel's replacement since Cain murdered his brother **A**ble.

Gen. 4:25-26

Moses wrote down the story of the lineage of **Christ** and it's not a **f**able.

He was inspired by the **Holy Spirit** as all the writers of the cannon **w**ere.
It is so intricate and supernatural in how many different ways it can **s**tir
An unbeliever to believe if it's his time to hear **God**'s **Spirit s**peak.
There are clues in numbers used and patterns discovered by people **God**
Has had **s**eek

The fine tuning of how the original words bring out His story
Of how Jewish idioms used and hyperboles and parables spoken by
Jesus dispel the gory
Pictures of an eternal Hell and damnation that the religious spirit still
Uses to scare
To try to get fear to do the trick of changing unbeliever's minds...so
Beware

#107 *WHERE* Do I See LOVE?

That in these "last days" evil imaginations will abound that promote a
Different gospel
Than what Paul and the other disciples taught and *warned* of that
Would be hostile
To the **GRACE of Love** that puts <u>**ALL**</u> **FEARS** to rest.
That <u>***fear in the proper light is reverence***</u> that will pass the test

So **His** small flock *that can truly hear* **His voice** *will become* a **voice** so loud
That will be bold and pure to draw true seekers out of the crowd
**Of the religious organized doctrines of demons that deny Jesus' WILL
And P**OWER.
TOMORROW IS NOT THE DAY TO PROCLAIM THIS TRUTH – BUT
<u>***RIGHT NOW***</u> **IS THE HOUR ! ! !**

Rich Kovatch
8-25-12

#108 **NO PAIN** . . . *NO GAIN*

There's a saying that body builders use all the *time*...
NO PAIN . . . **NO GAIN** ! It's not a saying that one can just *mime*
But a truth that *to receive* ANYTHING *worthwhile*
A *cost* **MUST be paid.** And from the beginning that's been **God's** *style.*

Because *one can only see* what one surely has *gained*
After *it has been lost* and **/ or damaged** as unworthy and **then** *renamed*
As a **BRAND NEW CREATION** *way better* than what has *passed*
With a promise of a Glory that for ever will *last.*

The **physical** body *was designed to regenerate* from *within*
And it would have if not for Adam & Eve and their offspring *if not for sin.*
Our **physical** body *still* re**news** _each_ **cell** (though a bit weaker); with
Some brand new *within _hours_* and _days & others taking up_ to **7** *years*!
But the **Spiritual body** of **Christ** within us is regenerated totally after
Death *and thankfully too also while* alive - with *tears*!

Tears of anguish in longsuffering, painful sorrow of repentance, or with
Shameful *fear*
Of being separated from the **Love** we seek or a heartbreaking yearning
To stay *near.*
But *that* _IS_ the lesson God also chose to experience *Himself*
By letting **His** children **die** just as **Jesus** did first - to gain the *wealth*

Of **His** *entire* creation that **must** **first** *be destroyed* in *order*
That the **NEW CREATION** can be built of **The ROCK** with **GRACE** as its
Mortar.
And **GRACE** of course is **God's Love, Christ Jesus** the **ROCK** who is
Purifying the new *container*
So *more* and *more* **His chosen ones** *will* put to death the *nature of* the
Carnal *complainer.*

All His **WILL KNOW** that with **correction MUST COME** *pain*
And **ONLY** through suffering the *strip*ping a*way* of the **carnal nature**
Comes *gain*
Because **Christ's** nature **IS** what the *VERY* BEST *IS.*
No more any of our **OLD ways** that were **selfish** and **OPPOSITE OF** *HIS.*

#108 NO PAIN . . . NO GAIN

Love means ***long-suffering*** <u>until</u> the ***true way is being*** <u>done</u>.
Then, and <u>only then</u> will we be aware of what really is *<u>fun</u>*.
It's when you **CAN SEE the Kingdom of Heaven** BEING APPLIED in *Another*
Who <u>*now*</u> *isn't any longer an enemy*...but **SEEN AS** a Christian sister or *Brother*

Who **NOW** has his or her **OWN** <u>TESTIM<u>O</u>NY</u> on how **God has *<u>worked</u>*** in Their *Life*.
The leading of the **Holy Spirit** <u>**causes**</u> pain that **cuts** like a *knife*.
He will not and ***<u>can not</u>*** ignore any **sin nature** upon whom **He** has *Chosen*.

So the whole world will see exactly who *His* FOLLOWERS *ARE*...
And ***Who's* just *posin'***

Rich Kovatch
10-4-12

#109 *NOW* ... I SEE !

I woke up this morning with this on my heart.
This MUST happen BEFORE one can even start
To really **" see "** or understand what this age is all about
And why you and I have been created for such a time as this to tout.

It's funny that immediately after arising again today
The Jehovah Witness clan was knocking at my gate to say
They have the truth as to what **God**'s plan originally was
And that He **HAD TO** put into effect **Plan " B "**...**Jesus**...because

The first **A**dam and **E**ve were given a **" free will "** which *denied*
Plan "A"...a mankind where humans would live forever...until **S**atan lied
To **E**ve and got **(** her **)** to eat from the wrong tree.
Truth is...**God** PUT IT in there...**according to plan "A"**...*SO* **man could see**

What is an even a greater glory...an aspect of our **C**reator and King
Who IS Jesus...**THE WORD made flesh** when the time was right to bring
John 1:14, Rom.5:6
The **Spirit of God** of which the **carnal nature** couldn't & STILL CAN'T
Grasp.
That no matter HOW FAR from **The Father** a man may run, He's still got a
Strong clasp

And will never let go on just the spirit level alone...because it's ONLY
THERE
Where a person can **SEE God**...who **IS** the **Spirit OF LOVE**...EVERYWHERE.
He's even in the **darkness of evil** for there is **NO difference** to **Him**.
Isa. 45:7, Rom.3:22-31
But *TO US* there is this total contrast which **He** uses to skim

Off the top of **His** golden prize upon which **He** intentionally heats up
So the **dross of sin** and **its** <u>nature</u> will be <u>removed</u> that we may sup
With **Him** at the wedding feast *after* the union with **Christ** *has* **taken
Place.**
ONLY WHEN one *UNDERSTANDS* what *TRUE LOVE IS* can one see **Christ
In** *everyone's* face.

#109 *NOW* ... I SEE !

The whole book of the Bible has such unity and splendor.
It's the picture of the "Bride of Christ" which chose to spend her
Entire inheritance on this false life and riches...which is really death
Like the prodigal son who reaches his last straw & became like a new
Seth;

The 3rd son of Adam and Eve who replaced the one killed by their 1st one
Named Cain which means "acquired"...the fruit of the first couple that
Had done
What God had told them to do and made them for...to procreate seed of
Their own kind...
People that want to be like God in their own carnal mind.

The *1st Adam* was created carnal and *flawed by design*.
The *2nd Adam* is Jesus - *the spiritual man* that does not say "mine"
But gives ALL things back to the Father just at the right time. 1Cor.15:21-28
That's when the wayward way has been exposed & one turns on a dime.

A 180° new direction where one can now face the ***fire* of Holiness.**
The guard at the gate of paradise which can allow in only a soul of
Lowliness.
The humbled heart, a servant, friend, brother and child of the Most
High.
People who followed Jesus' example *by God's WILL* to pick up their own
Cross and die

To the *1st Adam's nature which is: to disbelieve* God's lead
We also rather think it be for our good - from the Tree of Good and Evil
To feed.
THIS is the *FINEST POINT* of where *WISDOM* and *UNDERSTANDING*
Comes.
What exactly *WAS* the *1st state of Adam* and to whose drums

Did he march to...his own or God's tone and beat?
Some people believe to be back in this 1st state will be really neat.
But true wisdom asks and tells us...why would we want to go back into
The shadow   Col.2:16-17
When it is only darkness one would be in again having to battle   Heb.8:5, 10:1

#109 NOW...I SEE !

This supposed " **free will** " you'd be back in? **Jesus did ONLY the WILL of
Love** John15:-19
With power given Him from the Father because the seed in Mary was
From the **" DOVE "**
Which signifies the Holy Spirit and NOT of the 1st Adam man.
The female is the body, in which the seed is planted, grows and CAN

SEE and **DO** what the Holy Spirit leads the soul **to do in order to glorify
The Father...submit, follow, spread the LIGHT** which will horrify
The darkness...the world...those still OF it...because it's scary
To say you no longer desire to be a single soul, but want to marry

And **eat** from the purest form and ONLY true life there is...Christ Jesus
...And **walk**
The narrow path to the ONLY place life IS, and **begin to talk**
To others about what YOU CAN NOW **SEE** since the scales have been
Removed.
It's the scales of man's legalism of justice of which it behooved Luke 24:46,
Heb. 2:17

The Father to put ALL **the sins of the world upon Jesus**... 1John 2:2
The MORE PERFECT ONE than Moses was. Scripture says He's US Heb.3:2-3
Who walk in righteousness giving the Father thanks and praise.
Telling all that not ONLY a select few...but **ALL** will be redeemed and
Raised

In either **just** the 1st resurrection **OR** if judged to be so **also** the 2nd since
The 1st will only determine
Whether you'll be returned to the grave for 1,000 years or show many
Your personal sermon Rev.20:5-7
That will bring the LIGHT of TRUE PEACE to those newbies still
Clueless...that it's ONLY
**Through what Christ' successful mission HAS done - paid for EACH
Prodigal** that's so lonely

#109 NOW...I SEE !

And *SO lost he can't* **SEE** what his own hand is doing;
STILL desiring from that tree we're NOT to eat from, so on the fruit and
Consequences he's still chewing;
Which is NOT the **Tree OF Life** wherein sin and death are no more.
THIS is the knowledge THAT redeems...it's God's *UNCONDITIONAL* **LOVE,**
MERCY In JUDGMENT with supernatural **GRACE** at the **TREE OF**
FORGIVENESS' CORE.

Rich Kovatch
10-10-12

#110 Four Estates of Man

There are four estates of man and it shall be stated.

Ps. 136:23, Dan. 11:37-38, Luke 1:48, 1 Peter1:23

In this poem I'm to expose how man was created.   Gen. 1:26, 2:7

The first thing I'll say is that we didn't evolve from goo,   Gen. 2:20-23

And I'll show from God's word how the **salvation of ALL** is true.

John 12:31-32, 1 John 2:2

God is all goodness and in Him is **NO SIN**.   John 1:29, 8:46, Rom. 2:4-16, 12:17

He didn't create Satan so He'd lose & death win! Isa. 45:7, 54:16, 1 John 3:8

Not trusting in what love *can*, *does*, & *will* do **IS the spirit of DISBELIEF**

1 John 4:7-8, 10, 16, 18

He's promised in covenants He's got us *ALL* covered! What a relief!

The very first one He spoke after Adam disobeyed God's commandment

And Eve told a lie;   Gen. 3:12, 3:3

That He shall curse the ground so that Adam will now sweat to survive

And yet die;   Gen. 3:17-19

And Eve will now bear children in pain and desire Adam's position.

Gen. 3:16

THAT was then the END of man's first estate condition.

They had a choice to obey God's word and eat not the forbidden fruit.

Since God already KNEW they WOULD and suffer the consequences

Doesn't mean He's a brute;   Rom. 2:4, 3:25

But part of His plan that they then became mortal   Gen. 2:17, Rom. 14:8-9

And have a new nature to desire to sin, reap corruption and use death

As the portal   John 11:25-26, 12:24-25

To the re-creation of our souls without death any more.   Luke 20: 33-38

ALL religions that teach an existence without end...but in torture...is

The whore   Matt.18:11, Rev. 20: 10-15

That the word of God says to "Come out of her" in Rev. 18:4 and

Throughout .   Rev.17:3-7, Rev.18:4

Those He's given the faith and understanding of this are those who

Shout   1 John 5:19-20

#110 Four Estates of Man

Out the praises of the Savior of the world to the blind.
This is a tool God uses to lead back into His sheepfold those that can't
Find   Ps. 49:14, Luke 15:6, John 10:1-**16**-30
The TRUE God of LOVE who's promised to redeem ALL and cannot lie.
                                 Prov. 14:5, **1 Tim. 4:4-10,** Ps. 49:15, Rom.5:18-19
This redemption HAS occurred when a soul believes he's been
"Born Again" and will never again die   John3:3-7

But be transformed in the twinkling of an eye upon His return. 1 Cor.15:52
This is the return into the dust we're formed of which is dead & will burn
In order to purify the soul of all prideful wood, hay and stubble 1 Cor.3:12
Which used to look for life "out there" in the heavens using a telescope
Named Hubble.   I Cor. 4:3-6

This second man Adam is Christ who "makes alive" the soul of the
Walking dead.   Ps.30:5, 1Cor.15:47, Eph.2:1-5
The sleeping dead also are able to be revived from their earthly bed
                                 John 11:11-**14**, 1 Cor. 11:30, 1 Thes. 4:14
Six feet under or cremated and eventually forgotten by all except our
Father and Creator.
Again, us here and now of whom God has entered into to, repent of the
Religious harlot and hate her

Because of its deceptions and perversions of **God's ORIGINAL word.**
                                             Rom. 1:25, 28-32
Very specific in **EVERY** WORD and PHRASE used which prove how absurd
                                             Matt. 4:4, 12:36, 18:16
The perversions of such words as **judgment, destruction, hell, ever,** and
Fire are   1John2:2, Rom.5:6, Heb.2:9
Which *distort* what Love IS, salvation MEANS, and show how religious
Doctrines are SO FAR   1`Thes.5:21

From what the **ORIGINAL WORDS CLEARLY** encourage & express. 1Cor.13:4-8
Thinking one may end up being tortured without the possibility of end
Make many detest
This FALSE Jesus who failed in His purpose and a God who's a liar they
Will not follow.   **Rom.11:29-36**
When someone's word CAN'T be trusted, God's foremost, those
Promises then ring hollow.

#110 Four Estates of Man

There is a sure hope beyond this hell as professed by the false church.
Their position that they are saved because of what "they" did is the
Tallest pride perch.   Prov.8:13, 13:10, 16:18, 2Cor.3:14
God does require a humbled heart, Godly sorrow, and a repentant walk
                                        2Cor.6:16-18, 7:10, Eph.2:1-9
To even perceive the Kingdom of Heaven, of God, and the righteous talk.
                                        Rom. 14:9, 17, 23 15:9, John3:3-7

But these are not done within one's own power to change.
                                        John 3:27, Ps.94:17, Rom.14:7-9
A body made of dust and a soul apart from Christ's Spirit ALONE cannot
Rearrange   1 Cor. 15:35-55
The CIRCUMSTANCES or COVENANTS W/ God. He doesn't grade on a curve.
Those who think they can manipulate God have a misguided nerve.

Misguided from the Devil, flesh, and the world which are not true life
But are separated from the **Eternal WORD** & path of the virgin bride wife.
She's not made a virgin by her own will or desire
But by the husbandman's dowry exchange, washed in His blood, tested
And purified thru fire.   Ex. 22:17

His WORD is a "Consuming Fire". It consumes *all* that can't enter.
                                        Deut. 4:24, Heb.12:29
This *"all"* is the SIN that works in us all...***not our souls***...said our mentor.
Jesus, the WORD of truth, preached to the gentiles through His clay
Man Paul
Who was a Pharisee of Pharisees, as prideful as could be when his name
Was Saul.

The letters he wrote to the church & all in Rome & Corinth tell the story.
There are **TWO** gospels. **ONE** followed to the smallest jot & tittle by **Jesus.**
That's only **HIS** glory.   Matt. 5:18
But the **second** gospel is the one **of FAITH** with works, **not FOR**
Acceptance but **because** of it.
It's in the Heavenly places we already rest in and sit.   Eph.2:6-9

#110 Four Estates of Man

The book to the Roman church tells the whole plan of God from
Beginning to end.   **Rom.** 6:23, 7:14, 8:20-21, 34-39, **11:32**
It's NOT through works that any man can boast of except Jesus who will send
A small flock to a **darkened** world that hates Him, **THE LIGHT &TRUTH** that I profess
Along with the rest of His army that are bold enough to confess
                                        Prov.28:9, Phil.1:14, Eph.3:12, 1John 4:17-19

They're **made** *flawed* **BY DESIGN** *in order to* constantly praise our Savior.
                                        Eccl. 1:17-18, 2:9-14, 3:18, Eph.2:1-5
If we were already changed into a perfect man like Jesus then our behavior
Would never, ever be flawed or lack ANY of the fruit of the Spirit. Gal. 5:22
None...never once have even an unholy thought or desire. So NOW do
You hear it?

S*in in* OUR eyes is **NOT** too big a problem in our Father's eye - but the tool
                                        Dan. 11:32-35, Mark 9:49
Used to mold our character into one of Faith and Strength...and no
Longer of a fool.   John 4:42, 6:51, 12:47, Rom. 5:12-21
The fool is said to be wiser in his own eyes than seven wise men Prov. 26:16
Who'll either be changed in THIS world or have to wait until the second
Resurrection when

ALL will be GIVEN back to the Father, Christ's mission complete.
                                        1 Cor.15:20-**28**, 52, 2 Cor. 5:14, 19
It **will be** the time **those not raised in the first** will be pulled out of the heat
                                        James 2:13, Rev.20:10-14
Of the **"Lake of Fire"**...***Hell***...the grave; and asked once again
By Jesus; "WHO do YOU say I am"? & *answer*...**the conqueror of *ALL* sin!**

Then ***ALL*** creation will praise His name ALONE as **King of Kings**. Rev.17:14, 19:16
There will be the most glorious sound heard when the "new song of
Moses" ***ALL*** creation sings.
He's put ***ALL*** sin and death under His feet and now can give **1 Cor.15:35, 28**
EVERY SOUL back to the Father thru HIM so ***ALL*** will live. Rom.5:18, 14:11,
                                        1 Cor.15:52

NOT in a world of torture, pain & hate which has been defeated, Rom.8:21
Including even the penalty of those **who God USED** for evil deleted.
#4 is the number of the estates of women and men.
#7 equates to Spiritual Completion, Rest, Perfection; and **not IF but**
WHEN!!!
                    Rich Kovatch   10-16-12

#111 Thy Kingdom **Come**

Oh my God, what have you done?
Created ALL things thru the words of your Son.
Put mankind on this planet and let him loose to run.
Created the tempter _to test_ on how each one describes fun.

You put two trees in a garden where man was to be livin'
And gave the commandment to tend all he was given.
You gave him (and us) a choice as to from which tree he would eat...
Either **lifting _yourself_** up _**as**_ **God** or relaxing at his feet.

The woman was deceived...but the man made a choice.
Scripture **NOWHERE** says it was Eve, but Adam who heard God's voice.
Eve answered the serpent but added something God never said.
The consequence was they both lost the "**good life**" and therein that
Day they became dead.

Now we're told that **Adam lived** to be **930 years old.** Oh my!
But why was that, when God told him that in the day he ate he'd surely die
If it'd be of the tree of knowledge of Good and Evil to see
What it would be like **to _experience_ ALL** things _like a god_ from A to Z?

So he was given the path that would _**include**_ separation from life.
Did Adam do this on his own? NO. He blamed his wife!
The wife blamed the serpent, but the beast had no alibi to be said
And was punished by being **cursed above ALL** to **eat dust** and get a
Bruised head.

So the puzzle picture was thus set in motion.
What did that mean? Most have been given not the slightest notion;
But others God has given discernment to solve that mystery,
Which only happens when the **Holy Spirit of Grace** is revealed through
History.

God uses _words_ to paint us a picture.
Hebrew **idioms** and **hyperbole** become the main fixture
As to how to use scripture **to interpret scripture correctly.**
The understanding of parables is given for only the "true church" to see.

#111 Thy Kingdom **Come**

Jesus explained that this was *the reason* **he used them always;**
So the blind would stay blind *until* **the right doors and hallways**
Were in place so when opened by God the path would be clear
About how **the Kingdom** of God and Heaven aren't far off...but **near;**

And **actually within reach to touch, feel, smell, see, hear** and **eat** from.
One example that was revealed was when the Samaritan woman wanted A crumb
And **Jesus called her a "dog"**...a term used by his "own people" with **Disrespect;**
But **her** *understanding* of the King's *Grace* **to** *provide* bread **for ALL...**
Jesus did detect

And agreed with her...so the lesson was thus given:
The King has provided for ALL in God's Kingdom of the livin'.
ALL live unto Jesus...even those still dead in their sins.
The final picture shows that the Devil is defeated and Jesus WINS!

Jesus destroys sin and death and redeems ALL his lost sheep.
God's promise to Jesus is that ALL he's been given...he will keep.
So the piece of the puzzle that must be put into place
Is: **Who** is your **brother...**a *select few* or the *whole* human race?

This question was first asked to Cain after he had killed Able.
This was a historical event just as also was the **Tower** of **Babel**
When the picture puzzle was spread unto the whole face of the earth
And **the single language of all ended** and multiple tongues found its Birth

Because Adam and Eve were told to fill the whole planet and their Offspring refused
But stayed in one place using religion to reach God so they were made Confused.
I can't explain every piece of this puzzle so let me stay on track.
The **number 2 is for division** *but also better used* for **unity** - covering Each others' back.

#111 Thy Kingdom **Come**

That's why **Jesus is** _called_ the **second Adam** in fact and in picture.
The Kingdom that's come was Jesus…for one…and the spiritual mixture
That shows us that the **3rd Heaven** is to be brought down from above
Like the **"New Jerusalem"**, Jesus' 2nd Advent, and the **Holy Spirit** seen as
A dove

Of **peace** and **purity** and **love** and **hope**, and a **single focus** of eyes
Where the Kingdom of God is found in humility and confession of
Truth…not lies.
The _Spirit of God_ walked with, talked to, but only temporarily came
Inside men
Like the picture of the tabernacle in the wilderness and temples made
Were forever destroyed when

Jesus, the 2nd Adam and living temple died and rose from Hell.
God had come to earth in person in order to tell
The last chapter of the Book of Life ends with victory
With <u>GOOD</u> overcoming evil and _the blind finally being able to see_!

Death is NOT _the end of hope_ like the false church tries to decree.
Hell's only the place _where_ **sin is burnt off** and ALL _our souls set free_!
There's never been a soul besides Jesus that was righteous and pure.
Even Enoch and Elijah had to die to make Hebrews 9:27 secure
xxxxxxxxxxxxxxxxxxxxxxxxxxxxxxxxxxxxxxxxxxxxxxxxxxxxxxxxxxxxxxxxxxxxxx
With its profession that ALL men must die & then comes **the judgment** sentence.
It's for WORKS as a servant of sin or sons of Godly repentance.
Carried away in a whirlwind, or was then was not doesn't shake.
EVERY ORIGINAL word in the **Bible is true…only translations** and
Transliterations are fake.
xxxxxxxxxxxxxxxxxxxxxxxxxxxxxxxxxxxxxxxxxxxxxxxxxxxxxxxxxxxxxxxxxxxxxx
So to be able to **finish the puzzle** and _see the whole thing_
One has to be **"Born of the Spirit"** so only God's Grace will bring
ALL that he chooses back to himself - so NO ONE'S works will make do.
Only God's work through Jesus' words saying **"It IS Finished"** will ring
True.

Rich Kovatch
11-1-12

#112 In The Eye Of The Beholder

The only place where truth is found
Is **SEEN** only through the eye of what makes the world go 'round.
That's said to be **Love** because of **its power to overcome**
What may be SEEN as being evil to all eyes…except some

Who have been given the gift of **Agape Love** to suffer and endure
The means to which end will be found a life that's righteous and pure.
The end is always said to be justified by its means when **SEEN**
As the process which **MUST** take place **IN ORDER TO** wean

Whatever it is that is not pure and true to perfect Love.
This can't be **SEEN** from within the same dimension but only outside and Above
Itself of its own limitations that can't possible understand the clear
Picture and plan
Which **can only come** into **focus thru** the **EYES** of the **Son of Man.**

Only through the words spoken by **Jesus**, the only begotten **Son of God**,
Were all things created.
This includes the words of the **prophets** and **The Law** to destroy what
He Hated;
Which is disobedience and dishonor to the guiding words He's spoken
Starting w/ **Adam** & **Eve** having to die the day His Holy path was broken.

He promised them life without end as long as they should eat the right
Fruit;
But they ate from the **Tree of Good and Evil**, their own horn they
Choose to toot.
Thus iniquity was found in them exposing **Satan "The Adversary"**
Who puts oneself in the seat of God deciding for himself how to tarry.

Being **"made"** in the **"image of God"** means having the ability to subdue
And have dominion over ALL things created, out the window this flew,
When the image did not follow the instructions on what **NOT** to eat;
And the **1st Adam** created lost eternal life and went down in defeat.

#112 In The Eye Of The Beholder

But the 2nd **Adam did _not one_** thing **against** the commandments givin';
Born under the curse of death but showed the right path back by livin'
Without any corruption or decay the flesh was designed to find
Because **_it's impossible_ to please God** in the flesh alone **_without God's mind_**.

Jesus lived in a body of flesh but also obeyed 100% the Father's words.
He could have lived forever but chose to die to show us the Shepard's
Predestined path and purpose and plan for the salvation of all who are
Called to follow
The spiritual lessons He taught: that faith has substance and is not
Hollow.

Show me your faith through your works the apostle James said - but
NOT FOR redemption
But for salvation from sin so you may see Heaven's greatest invention.
It's called GRACE - _where Love provided a way where none was before_.
Jesus showed the plan for us that to find life we must go through death's
Door!

We can do it willingly like **Jesus** did if God's chosen that call for you,
Or you can die unwillingly like most of mankind will do.
Creation was made cursed under vanity so it's God who's in charge
Of the steps in your being molded into Christ's image - by-and-large.

Some clay He's made on purpose to serve sin and see wrath.
_**Wrath** is the **_correcting_ tool** used when we walk the wrong path_
That **leads to sin** and **death** and the end of your testing.
**God's elect are His children of great faith who are resting**

In that the day will arrive when sin, tears and death are no more
And every person ever born will have walked through death's door;
Some to find themselves at the 1st **Resurrection** and the **Wedding Feast;**
Others, when shown this light, **will reject it and follow the Beast.**

#112 In The Eye Of The Beholder

This is not something that means damnation of some **Lake of Fire**
Without end.
Eternal means an **"age"**, which may or may not end, but only send
Condemnation and **consequences** upon **all who refuse** to give grace
To the people sent before us to **_test our gift_** of **_SEEING_** God in each face.

Jesus said: "Unto the _least of these_ you do _also unto me_".
The Kingdom of Heaven becomes visible only when one can **SEE**
That the person in sin is no different than all ever made.
It's _just_ that that person _doesn't yet understand Love_ and carries a failing
Grade.

He hasn't yet become the **"teacher's pet"** and **given the ability** needed
And the compassion and gentleness you were shown when the **Good Shepherd** greeted
YOU back into the sheepfold, protected and free to bathe in the glorious Light
Of the **Spirit of Mercy, Forgiveness, Grace, Joy, Peace** and **Truth** of
What's right.

God's WILL _IS_ the _salvation_ and _redemption_ of **_ALL_ men...NOT merely**
_A_ DESIRE.
The message _is_ that Love CONQUERED death,
Love USES death, and Love USES FIRE
To burn off the impurities of the sin nature and leave only Spirit.
You must leave the carnal mindset plane & dimension to **SEE** & **HEAR** it.

Without leaving _that_ dimension it's like looking into a mirror
In which **you'll** _only_ see yourself - you must be transformed to **SEE** clearer
That **God's plans** for you are **GOOD** and consists of bringing **_ALL_** back to
The **Garden**
Of Paradise to tend and keep it...this time without the sinning nature
Which does harden

#112 In The Eye Of The Beholder

The heart, which is where God lives, into one made of stone.
The Law was written in stone & doesn't change, but from it we can hone
Out the pattern that it wasn't to **"earn"** redemption, but to show us
What's right.
**God didn't create sin and darkness by mistake**, simply overcomes it
With His might!

The **1st day** began with **darkness and proceeded into the Light**.
Subverting your strong, unbending faith in the **Mercy of God** is the
World's fight.
He who loves this world does not the will of the Father - **for this world
Lives in hate**
And your return back to our Father has a place, hour and date

Already known by our creator...not one detail you can possibly change.
You may think you can but every dimension there is He did arrange;
And that's so we'll forever find more glorious and wonderful things
About Him to find
When we've been humbled by His power to say, "Mold
Me into **YOUR IMAGE**...not the one of my foolish mind"!

Rich Kovatch
1-16-12

#113 It's *NOT* Earn...But *APPLY*

I heard *a beautiful woman* say under her breath
That *IF ONLY* she had blonde hair and a big bountiful breast
Like a certain rich and famous and sexy country singer starlet
She might *"EARN"* her lover's adoration as a **Queen instead of a *harlot*.**

And this expression of *unbelief* hurt me down to my innermost core
That **she's *STILL* DECIEVE**D by the **D**evil that she's seen as my chore
**Instead of the beautiful *and* sexy, loving *and* charmingly sweet piece
Of Fruit she IS**
Off the **Tree of Life** - NOT the tree of knowledge **unto death** - gee whiz!

And *could it possibly be a coincidence* that today was seen
By many that because of the Mayan calendar it will mean
That a new eon will begin where **Venus** will align with **Mars**
As the 70's song proclaimed - **The Age of Aquarius** when **"Love will
Guide the stars"?**

Now...I certainly don't trust in the Zodiac per say...
But only in Jesus' message - that over and over refers to "if" and "a day"
That **when one becomes "Born Again"** of the **Spirit the "Light"** *will* turn *on*
That you've been washed by His **water** - His **blood** - and so today is the
New **dawn**

Of the day when the **darkness (*DISBELIEF*)** is **OVER** and the sun **(Son)**
Has risen.
The **gates of Hell haven't prevailed** and she and we are released from
Prison.
Freed from the *bondage of the Law* which *only revealed* our own sin.
But n**ow we** *CAN* live **in** Jesus - who was *MADE* SIN *FOR US* - and begin

To experience the **liberty of Freedom** which the **Grace** - which **His
"Light" reveals.**
This happens **not when blinded by law but** to the remnant Its Truth and
Power *is what* appeals.
Our apostle Paul told us to "work *out* our own salvation"...**Yoo Hoo!**
He **didn't** say work **"FOR"** it which only Jesus **already** *DID* DO!

#113 It's *NOT* Earn...But *APPLY*

With **Wisdom**, who **IS J**esus, comes an understanding that we may now apply
This "Great salvation" from the power of sin & death which only says to **"try"**
To **EARN** your redemption **yourself** and deny what Jesus proclaimed
In His very last words spoken as a man. THE Man - who <u>ALONE</u> is named

King of Kings and **LORD of Lords** - the *ONLY ONE* found *<u>worthy</u>* to begin
To open the scroll & loosen its seals, or even *look at* the **judgment** on sin
Which **He** <u>ALONE</u> could see & not die; but then *CHOOSE* to do so that day
To have The Father **IMPUTE** our sins upon <u>HIM</u> so He <u>ALONE</u> could pay

And be the *propitiation* for the sins of the *entire* creation.
The ecclesia being the first fruit after Jesus to profess with elation
*That the **first** Adam's **fall** was but **the way it was planned**.*
There's no other way **God**'s glory could have been *<u>shown nearly as grand</u>*

As the **Spirit of God** showing **His** character through Jesus - to serve & die
For the pinnacle of **His** creative works - MAN - who **He's** lifted up high
Above all other things created so in **God**'s image man could create
Even more children with which to share the *pleasure - done intimately*
With*in* a *wife*...h*is* m*ate*.

*For **Love's** desire is to **share** and reveal **its** character to all.*
God is the **Spirit of Love** - most gloriously unseen - until creation's fall
And rebirth with the way made sure - with suffering, death and victory
Through Jesus' life, death and resurrection of which some 500 did see

And thus came into the written record - **HIS story** now *history*
Told unto all especially around Christmas time and Easter - the *mystery*.
Paul wrote it down in his letters but only a few ever believe.
He wrote it for ALL men - *this redemption of ALL*, but only the ecclesia receive

The **whole understanding** which leads to the greatest character of all...
The *<u>ability</u>* to **FORGIVE** our ENEMY *after* and *even during **their*** *fall*.
That is called *AGAPE LOVE* which Jesus explained to Peter.
It's also called *GRACE* - undeserved merit, **the overcoming by LOVE.**
Nothing sweeter ! ! !

Rich Kovatch
12-21-12

#114 Come Unto Me

"**Come unto me**" are the words of **GREATEST POWER** !
Only when one does that will The **Comforter** shower
The **TRUE** <u>seeker</u> with blessings of the **Kingdom** itself and *its*
Unimaginable **wealth**   1 Cor. 2:9
Which has provided room for EVERYONE and described abundant
Health.   John 14:2

The **wealth of the Kingdom is: to KNOW the Father and** Jesus.   John 17:3
The **plan of redemption** is **NOT** to torture us forever in **Hell...but to**
Please us.   Jer. 29:11
Hellfire was *not* **made** <u>*for*</u> **man** but *the Devil* and *his messengers* Matt. 25:41
Who ignorantly voice the spirits of "Free Will" and "Pride", but they will
Come out less and less in yours   Luke 16:13

Because the **King**dom of **God** HAS BEEN SHOWN TO YOU as continual
Daily **b**lessings   Matt. 25:34
When you share what's been given you with the hungry, thirsty, naked
And those with prison **d**ressings;   Matt.25:35-36

Blinded and *afflicted* by the *Prince of this world* who has *corrupted*
ALL since Adam and Eve.

He's the one given power by Jesus to *blind and confuse* us all and to
This very day **d**eceive.   2 Cor. 4:4

BUT, unto those that <u>*hear*</u> & obey our **she**p**herd**'s <u>*voice*</u> to *"Come* **unto me"**

We won't be as scattered sheep being *devoured by wolves* because
We'll be able to see.   Matt. 10:16-22
Like the happy antelopes wearing night vision goggles in the funny

Commercial *laughing* at the *hungry lion*   1 Peter 5:8
We'll be **able** to **see thru the darkness** so to perceive how the **"Light"**
Illuminates from **Z**ion.   Mic.4:2

#114 Come Unto Me

The *wiles* of the Devil will no longer effect our walk as it certainly once did.
Eph. 6:11

The armor of **God** has been put upon us his *deceptions* are no longer
Hid
But open for us to see and avoid; & better yet *to* **teach** others **by our walk**
Luke 22:27-30

So **God** might finally open their *ears* as to: **ALL ARE BEING SAVED** being
The "Good News" we **boldly t**alk.
Eph. 6:19

Jesus himself said he came to rescue the sheep that have *strayed* & far
Away they've *foolishly* wandered.
Matt. 18:14

Of a **God of LOVE** *being pleased* with souls being tortured *without end*
Have you never pondered?

He has *NO PLEASURE* in the **death** of the *wicked* but that they turn from

Their *wicked* ways and live.
Eze. 18:32, 33:11
Only a perfect sacrificial offering could be accepted by our just **God** - so
That's what Jesus came to give.

He lived the perfect life without a single sin so a **P**ure and **H**oly justice
God could serve
2 Cor. 5:21
And the **judgment upon** *sin* could be imputed unto him in our place -
Which we rightfully **d**eserve.
Rom. 4:6,8
To HIM ALONE we can give glory as our mediator, advocate and **M**essiah
From **Hell's** fire
1 John 2:1, 1 Tim.4:5,Heb. 8:6

The 2nd Adam that came to destroy *the works of the Devil;* and no
Other man will ever be lifted higher.
1 John 3:8

"Come unto me" are words a **little child** will **gladly b**elieve.
And unless **we do** that **as one** _with_ **faith** too we'll be *unable* to retrieve
Luke 18:17
The blessings he promised at the Mount of Olives to one & all.   Matt.5:3-12
The *rewards he desires* to give *us* **NOW** will only go to those who
Respond to his **c**all.
1 Cor. 3:11-15

#114 Come Unto Me

We are the ecclesia who **God** has drawn **out of the darkness** which is
The Carnal nature of PRIDE.
He shows the way which is through suffering and death and a sharing,
Willing servitude to guide   Luke 22:27-30
Whomever The Father also gives you to be an angel to*: to show God's*
Merciful Light.   John 16:15
We give ALL the glory to Jesus who **HAS** SAVED US **ALL** whether we do
Wrong **OR** right   2 Peter 3:9, 1 John 2:2

Because *"works based"* faith upon what <u>WE</u> <u>DO</u> is the darkest *"lie of*
Satan"   Eph. 2:8-10
And when we tell others to not worry about your sins it's US the false
Church will be hatin'.   John 17:14
THAT will be the cross we're to carry as Paul did - Christ said its burdens
Are light   Matt. 11:30
Because Jesus did it ALL: created ALL life which became disrupted SO it
MUST end and be resurrected in incorruption...

THAT'S RIGHT !!!   Gen.1:2, 1 Cor. 15:53

                                                    Rich Kovatch
                                                    12-25-12

#115 Woman, Where are your accusers?

There is a huge difference between an *evangelist* and a *proselyte*.
One professes the *"Good News"* of what's **BEEN** DONE and the other
Says *join us. We're right*.
The **evangel** *is* that Jesus *is* the propitiation for *ALL* **of God's wrath.**
The *proselyte* says follow me and *I'll show you* the path.

The **evangel** points to **the one** who PAID the FULL PRICE to redeem *ALL*
From the penalty of sin.
The *proselyte* Jesus said lead the blind to **a** *double* **judgment** because
They were all blind kin.
How can there be judgments worse than others if *Hell* be the **cost?**
That's a *Hell* as taught by the *"religious" zealots* who enjoyed being
Called **"master"** by the *lost*.

Jesus said he came for only the "Lost Sheep of Israel" according to their
Clock.
But he also said he has sheep that aren't of this flock.
This means his evangel was directed towards **His** *"Chosen People"*...
Those who've had the closest relationship which may now lead today's
Religious **sheeple.**

But the problem with these people and organization is they think
They're holier than thou
All because *they* "believed" or "confessed" or "repented" after taking
Some vow.
These **all** *came under the heading of "self-works" and* **blind** *pride*
Thinking: what *they've* *done lets them in* **and others stay forever**
Outside.

Jesus did say for a fact that no man comes to The Father **but through**
Him.
That's totally true for sure and here's where their light quickly goes dim.
They *refuse to acknowledge* that He *came to save* one *and* ALL
Because we're ALL in the SAME condition of not seeking God after
Adam's fall.

#115 Woman, Where are your accusers?

Every man goes his own way *and screws up royally.*
No man **besides the 2nd Adam** *ever* *walked* *perfectly* *and loyally*
To do what the **Father** of **Love** and **Mercy** and **Grace** speaks every
Second and every hour.
God alone chooses to whom & when **He** gives this understanding of
Power

It's the power to overcome temptations - not to *not* sin - but trust
In their own righteousness that determines for everyone whether it's
Heaven or bust.
And this righteousness HAPPENS only when they've shown some
Outward religious sign
And show a *continuous* lifestyle & character that they're towin' the line.

Once again the **subtle lie** of **disbelief** puts the **onus** upon EACH SOUL
And THEY have to put enough in the offering at the alter to pay their
Own toll.
Completely ignoring what **C**hrist's crucifixion means for ALL mankind.
They can't grasp they've got billions of souls that will live and die but
Not yet find

The *pure comfort of understanding* that God's **Will** *IS* to SAVE *ALL* !!!
It's not just an "OFFER" or legal description to be accepted or you'll fall
Into the **"Lake of Fire"** as described by *THEIR* DOCTRINE *which imposes*
Only fear.
They **deceive the lost** *into* *believing* that the God **of ALL** is **Not near!**

But they'll be separated forever **without ever being** forgiven &
redeemed.
And it fits perfectly with their doctrine which easily seemed
To be in perfect harmony with a judgment of reaping what one sowed.
But we'll all pay what we owe - death for a segway to life bestowed

#115 Woman, Where are your accusers?

Upon us by our Christ who told that adulterer woman that got set up
He *does not* accuse her of *that* deed but to forget it and get up
For **HE HAS PAID** the price he knew it would take to cover her
Transgressions
Of the Law that DOESN'T lead to life but shows us what should be our
Own confessions.

Condemnation comes from the Devil & **His spirit** shows in many ways.
The worst way is he comes as an **"angel of light"** & covers truth with a
Haze.
In the **P E R V E R T E D** Christian **doctrine** is *where* the deception *surely*
Happens...
You're still on your way to **Hell** until YOU do something that somehow
Dampens

The flames in the **"Lake of Fire"** & extinguishes them w/ **His Holy** blood.
This pattern of flooding the problem area is just like Noah's flood;
Saving ones numbered 8 which is *the # for rebirth & a new beginning*
In whom were found grace and came out of the ark grinning

Thankful to the Will of God to save ALL mankind through the family
That believes.
Corruption grew again and this *will be dealt with through fire* which
Receives
The power needed to consume all impure elements tainted with the
Curse of sin
And renew *ALL* things and give it back to The Father after **His** win

Over the ill effects of unbelief and distrust and **HE** sits upon the throne
Seat
At the right hand of **G**od to **judge** ALL CREATION as needing **GRACE** to
Meet
The strictest of strict requirements to live forever in the **3**rd **Heaven's**
Realm.
A place and existence unimaginably blessed without sin and the **K**ing of
Kings at the helm!

Rich Kovatch
1-2-13

#116 LOVE'S Vantage Point

The **LORD** finds ways to make me *laugh every day!*
So if I should ever think "I've got it down" *He*'ll find a way
To make me contemplate what **HE HAS** done and *currently* doing
In ME - most importantly - in order to correct my tainted viewing

Vantage point & biases which influence beyond measure how I see things.
Receiving the **GIFT of WISDOM** and *AGAPE LOVE* enables *Joy* to be
Found in what *He* brings
To my table for me to eat and drink so to have our relationship build.
He directs everything that happens to me as **dirt** and **clay** being tilled.

Having prepared for certain seeds to be planted, watered, and
Harvested when ripe;
There's a long growing season and pruning *necessary* which early on
Made me gripe
But now-a-days I don't have the energy to get upset or depressed and
Worry.
I've learned *He*'s been here every day of my life so there's no need to
Hurry.

His timing will be perfect but I do pray for a *super human-like* mercy
Towards me
Because I don't have it down quite yet to be totally content with what I
See.
I'm a child of *God*'s *Love* and so thankful that my **life is in HIS hands**.
He doesn't do things like throwing stuff in the air JUST TO see how it
Lands.

His LAWS and *WILL* - ALONE determine how everything and every life
Will begin and end.
Life is : *praise* to our Father and Creator, **alone**, for the solution **He**
Foreknew **He** would send.
This is the 2nd Adam who **LEGALLY** and **LOVINGLY** redeemed ALL from
The 1st Adam's fall.
ALL SOULS *WILL* RISE TO BE WITH HIM when our dead bones respond to
His call.

#116 LOVE'S Vantage Point

Risen immortal because the sinful carnal nature of our bodies was
Defeated.
That goes for ALL born in Adam, not just a prideful group of believers
Totally conceited.
All things will conclude in the season decided by *God* that will glorify
HIM the most.
Mankind is saved ONLY BY GRACE - so that no man can ever boast!

This makes its sharpest cut to beliefs when it comes down to *God gives
Them over* or "free Will".
The bottom line is *when pride demands* one must **"CHOOSE" to
"Accept"** the **FREE** gift still.
This "choice" is of *God*, *not us*, to be called a **"child of God"** in this
Wicked age.
This **"choice"** *to believe* is considered IDOLATROUS by *God* as a most
Vile "**religious**" wage.

People think they **"W**ork for *God*" by doing *"good things"* while being
Even **MORE blinded by pride.**
He knows who's doing what and why and *He* removes more dross when
We're tested and tried.
The **first picture** *He* gave us was **baptism** by *WATER* being **drowned** in
LOVE and *rising anew*.
The **final picture** is that of *FIRE* which **destroys ALL** creation on
The Father's cue.

Fire's purpose is to purify and **remove** *all* that *can't* survive *Love's*
LIGHT.
Love defeats *ALL* enemies, *never fails*, and is the driving force that
Shows us *God's might*.
God has *no* <u>pleasure</u> in the **destruction** of the **wicked** & is ALSO *GOOD*.
<u>So</u> it must be <u>good</u> that **wickedness be destroyed** & *ALL* redeemed like
He PROMISED *He* would.

#116 LOVE'S Vantage Point

While we were yet sinners *God* sent the change to happen.
This is the AWARENESS of our own self-righteousness being the reason
To dampen
The *hope* we could ever redeem ourselves...because a sinner can *NOT*
Satisfy
The NECESSARY LAW OF SALVATION...A *PERFECT* OFFERING, & that is why

Jesus had to come to save *His* people by being the "fall guy" for Adam
And Eve.
HE is the *ONLY ONE EVER* who was given by *God* the faith to obey and
Believe
Everything **the *Father* and *Spirit of LOVE*** told him to do and say.
And Paul is who *God* sent to tell us all will be O.K..

His gospel is for the uncircumcised, not Israel and it is diametrically
Opposite
Of requiring works of faith *to show* the world where one does sit.
It is in the hand of *God* - The shaping of one's future;
If YOU believe YOU'RE deciding for or against *God* suits your

Innermost understanding of the plan of *God* to give us a life without End.
God resists the proud and *lifts up the humble; so...*to depend
On your ability to even **"choose"** light...when surrounded by **darkness...**
And not even desiring to be in the *Body* of *Christ shows* this complete
Starkness.

It is *ONLY* by *the power* and *choice* by *God* to open eyes and hearts to
The "*LIGHT*".
The "*LIGHT*" of the world is *JESUS* so we no longer have to fight
Against the wiles of the **D**evil that influence our beliefs in *God*'s might.
They become STARVED to **DEATH** because The *Holy Spirit* has us **IGNORE**
Disbelief's bite.

Rich Kovatch
2-1-13

#117 Happy 40th Birthday Joy

God has given you **14,610 days**

And **He has proven He Loves YOU** in **that** many **ways.**

Each dawn you receive Mercy, Compassion, and **Grace.**

When you open your eyes He wants you to SEE HIS FACE

In people you talk to and friends you will **meet.**

He'll appear instantly **if** with a **BIG SMILE** you **greet**

Each and every soul you gaze upon, **ESPECIALLY** in the **MIRROR,**

Because of the **"one"** you **"see"** there, He Loves NONE DEARER!

The **"eyes"** I speak of **are known** only to **spirit**

Which means when **God "Talks"** to you… you **"HEAR IT"**

And it always ends with: **"TRUST ME,** put your fears in their **place,**

It's **MY STRENGTH** that will pull you through, as is always the **case.**

For **I live within you.** I'm called **Faith** and **Love.**

I'm also called **Wisdom,** not of this world but **above.**

These are the **keys to life** and they're **in** your **hand.**

Now after 40 years, GO RECEIVE the BLESSINGS

I've ALREADY PLANNED !!!"   Rich Kovatch

2-28-16

#118 Thank You Joy

Roses are **red**

Violets are **b**lue

There's fresh **Joy** in **my** head

Since **I've** met **you** !

I'll keep this short

Because **words** <u>won't</u> <u>**do**</u> the trick.

Life is a **contact sport** .

I Thank God your latest one is called **Rick** !

Rich Kovatch

Spring 2016

#119 My Bubble Of JOY

Such wonders my life exposes me to,
Like my new "**Bubble of Joy**" that's come into view.
So beautiful, yet so delicate, drifting alone in the air
The temptation is to touch it, though do I dare ?

Compassion and **Love** have told me that **this** is a **test**,
For as this **bubble** is floating alone, it is **at rest**
Being touched by nothing except the "**Winds of Change**".
Selfish reasons raise concerns it may drift out of range.

So once again the choices are mine…
Do I show it how I **turn water** into **wine** ?
How I see life is full of miracles on which to dine ?
And the "**Gift of Sharing**" – I see as **DIVINE** ?

For only **when my mind is open** and **my heart as well**
Can peace rule my soul and **Harmony**'s Winds **dwell**
So this bubble will drift near enough for me to enjoy.
Wisdom says it **WILL** … **IF soothing calm vibes I do employ**.

And employ means not work; for this **GOODNESS comes out** naturally…
When called
And **TRUTH** is never so far behind that **Love**'s **Wind** current will be stalled
By crosswinds of fear or pressures – however conceived.
For **FAITH** to **WORK** , **WORDS** must be **SPOKEN** that **WILL** be
BELIEVED !

"**ASK and you SHALL find**" is sage advice for sure.
Trick is to **ask** the **right teacher** and for the **purest cure**.
Cures we usually need only because we get so far out of balance.
The **RESTORATION of PEACE** in the **PRESENT** & **JOY** for the future
Are Love's greatest talents !

Rich Kovatch

5-22-16

#120 "That's *Impossible*"

Deep inside each & every soul
There is a conflict which takes its toll.
How high or how low one sets a goal
Determines how joyful ones *"Rock"* will roll.

This *"Rock"* is ones force field...the *"Source"* inside
From which ALL THINGS seen and unseen cannot hide.
Universal & Absolute LAWS exist <u>IN ORDER</u> for TRUTH to MANIFEST.
How our lives are at this moment proving what we like the best.

Just remember that *each snapshot frozen in time*
Cannot tell ones story with PROPER rhythm or rhyme.
This will sound like a total contradiction
Without the highest comprehension of fact & fiction.

We are Co-Creators *designed to show God's glory*
Written miraculously & INDIVIDUALLY in EACH soul's story.
God is more than anyone will ever figure out and all we can say is
"Who Knows" ?
Yet this **"Spirit of LIFE"** *appears* with splendorous grandeur *as **our**
Understanding **grows**.*

When someone is kind and demonstrates the **"Golden Rule"**
OPENED eyes will see Love using a human tool
Through choices made and vibes sent out.
SURELY this energy to HEAL exists – when there is NO DOUBT.

For UNBELIEF is the "sin unto death"... *in this way...*
Growth can **NOT** happen when PEACE says **"Move", and yet you stay.**
This **FEAR** of the Unknown is **NOT** in harmony with **LOVE.**
For **LOVE** is courageous as a lion, yet gentle as a dove.

#120 "That's *Impossible*"

The **"roars"** are meant to **DISEMBODY** FEAR from *your* heart.
It HAPPENS when you *remember whose* you **ARE** from the start.
You are one with **LOVE**, thus no worries should come near
When the **"roar"** quickly fades and it's the dove's cooing you hear

Grateful that the Lion was really the King.
His **PEACE** & **JOY** is what He has to bring
To the dinner table – when you are then calm enough to eat
Because His **"roar"** sent ALL *negative* spirits into retreat.

This **Spirit wants to share ALL** that is **good.**
It's **WILLING** to do this **NOW, but waits** till it **should.**
It's when the darkness of cold **is transformed** by the **LIGHT** of Life's **FIRE**
Ones feet can't stay planted in the earth, but **YEARNS** to **RISE HIGHER !**

This **signifies carnality** and **selfishness** as spirits **that kill.**
When **LOVE** drives the ride the *JOURNEY* becomes one miraculous thrill
To SEE what wonders CAN, WILL and DO appear as if out of nowhere,
You'll realize God's not somewhere far off *when you MAGICALLY*
START TO DARE!

LOVE has **NO** limits but it **DOES** have its **LAWS.**
An un**WILL**ingness **to FORGIVE** is among **hate's** sharpest claws.
For *WHY* is there darkness **TO** contrast the Light ?
It's for **EACH** moment's **PERSONAL CHOICE** to submit or fight.

There are actions that kill life on the **path** full of **worries** and plans
Restrained
Or bring such a **NEW LIGHT** and **GOODNESS** to our dreams our **joys**
Can't be contained.
ALL is working for the good – QUICKER for those who **"Believe".**
Just constant opportunities forsaken for those unwilling to conceive

#120 "That's *Impossible*"

That we **MUST** be conscious *for a higher glory.*
We're BEINGS on a level on which we **can't SEE** the *WHOLE* story.
It's (by **FAITH**) we live; from (thoughts) our "LIFE" is born – so to speak.
Life's purpose is to show ourselves where it's strong or weak.

The Serenity Prayer has a most UNIFYING spirit.
Glory be to God the day EVERY SOUL DOES HEAR it !
Using **Strength, Courage,** and mostly **WISDOM** ... *to follow*
THRUTH'S WAY
THE WORDS **"That's Impossible"** will be *UNUSED* in the **LIGHT** of this
NEW DAY.

Rich Kovatch
8-24-16

#121 God's <u>Light</u> <u>Blossom</u>

You and I are a **"God _Light_"** blossom.
When one's light gets **"turned _on_"** life becomes awesome.
The current now flows out of darkness & creates what we see,
What we feel, what we do, what we hear about who we might be.

With **God** nothing's impossible**,** so with this power of thought
Electrical signals bring **vibrations _to create_** what is sought.
A **picture** immediately **_forms_** in the **mind** of what to cast.
The process begins with the first not being the best, but the last.

This is known as the **_"Law Of Grace"_** which allows **Hope** to **grow.**
WHAT an amazing world _we will see_ tomorrow...The image of
What we sow.
The unity of Spirit to _let love bloom_ through _each_ petal, _each_ face.
**Every** flower has _**its**_ season _**to flourish**_ and _**its own special**_ place.

The **lilies of the field** have _**no**_ worries or **stress.**
We also need not worry of what to eat or how to dress.
We have _**no**_ lack, _**no**_ problems, _**no**_ dead ends. **ONLY ANSWERS.**
So in unison, but as individuals upon this wave we are the **dancers.**

**Such a thrill to live** wit _h_ in this **Wa**v**e** of **change.**
What we **"_will_"** to be, we can **re-arrange**
Our cells on a molecular level, but the body as **one.**
Each **"cell"** means _**your enemies being transformed thru love**_
When it's all said and **done.**

Love God and Love your neighbor is how Heaven works.
This makes us UNIQUE with our own special quirks
That show a **facet of God** _only displayed through you._
**So let's go see what you can do ! ! !**

Rich Kovatch
11-9-16

#122 What I CAN Do

The **HARDest** thing I have **to** discover
Is how to *"let go" of a previous lover.*
"Takes **time"** I'm told. **I hear that a lot.**
I'm not totally sold on the **new life** I've got.

I do understand that this is all for my **goo**d.
Feel my heart's been **stabbed** with a **knife** made of **wood**
And **I'm** a **vampire** with **eternal life - under one condition...**
All my *unhealthy* **pains** and *unhealthy* **baggage** be *put* into *remission,*

Never again able to pull me into **Hell's deep** abyss
When *self-pity* leads to tears *feeling denied a hug and a kiss.*
It takes two to tango, but *that* dance partner *departed.*
To let **TODAY'S NEW** opportunities **BE SEEN** I need only **get** *started*

EVERY morning **GIVING THANKS** in *every way* that **I** *can***!**
I **know** I **still** have *lots to give,* and that's in God's *plan***!**
ALREADY RECEIVED The **GIFT of LIFE** **TODAY** upon *waking***!**
There's **NEW** *JOY* to **uncover** from this **darkness** **I'm** **shaking!**

My very **next breath** of **air** and **life** is **surely a miracle.**
Then it's best to **exhale and relax** knowing **life** is also *satirical.*
Give **thanks** to **our Creator.** Don't let **ANYTHING** get you down.
Life causes one to **SHARE HAPPINESS,** so I'll go act like a clown!

LAUGHTER is the *KEY* to mello out one's **HARD**ened **heart.**
Those *VIBRATING* in *HARMONY* get the attention of **Cupid's dart.**
Sharing laughs brings **Super-Charged** oxygen with **its clarity** and **focus**
To our **very center.**

My **perfect partner'**s **smiling face** *will then* be *seen* when
True Love **IS our MENTOR.**

Rich Kovatch
11-15-16

#123 I KNOW God (STILL) Loves Me

Thank God! **I *KNOW*** I'm (still) Loved.
I no longer feel pushed and shoved.
There is this glorious energy ready and willing.
Clarity given why my ***joy***ful dreams I was actually killing**!**

I love sharing words and songs so very much.
My current way of a connecting touch
On a much deeper level than just through your eyes, ears and skin.
The power of OPTIMISM will tune up every atom within.

The scope of imagination is far beyond any barrier.
The creative power words: **"*Let* there be"** is certainly a carrier.
Words vibrate out and organize despite complexity and size.
"***ASK*** and ***you SHALL* receive"** is Spirit that **nature will then harmonize.**

"Good" lives in my heart and lives to be shared.
There is no worry of **"mistakes"** of which to be scared.
Choices just set WHAT I may learn and HOW to play
Knowing serendipity appears, when I'm looking, every single day.

I only need to focus and set my sights on joy.
God is Creator, I AM the vehicle and the Universe my toy!
Every time I awake from a peaceful rest and even every blink
I observe MY present reality of how I really think.

So ***NOW*** to think ***THIS*** is where I ***WANT*** to be**?**
Through all I saw as hardships, I finally see I'm free
Of worrying and giving ANY power to what others **(MIGHT)** think of me
Giving myself room to bloom and share my **GIFTS** for all eternity.

#123 I KNOW God (STILL) Loves Me

I set my intentions high and this is what **"LIGHT"** shall be emitted.
I'll stay happy and thankful in this present present – that I'm quick-
Witted
And am guided so often to give words of life and hope
To troubled souls thinking they're drowning like; "Raise your periscope!

You're in a self-created vessel submerged and lost in confusion.
Everything you see and experience is just your flow's current illusion.
It's a stormy sea of brainwashing with condemnation and negativity.
So friend, just **re-boo**t & **re-pro**gram **your par**adigm **w/ joy**ous Creativity.

Say; **_"Let there be"_** to whatever dreams you desire.
LOVE is everywhere to help you raise your sights higher.
Thoughts lead to actions - usually VERBALLY 1st, so when you're wise
In what you SAY.

No matter where you're at today, your best is _NOW_

With EVEN _BETTER_ ON _THE_ WAY !

Rich Kovatch
12-23-16

#124 It Happened *When* I Decided ((*Garden of Eden*)

It hap**pened** faster than a blink of my eye.
The moment I decided I no longer had to try
To **MAKE** my dreams come true exactly as imagined ... and **TODAY**.
When my mind slowed down to neutral & parked. **THIS is what I finally
Heard Spirit say.**

"The work has ended; your dreams have been made known.
Now, there's a plan already in progress with only details to hone."
It was amazing how quickly I'd put stumbling blocks in my way
By my negative thoughts I'd unwittingly harbor and worse, what I'd say.

I had it all backwards as most people still do.
I'd sweat all the details and worry, then my attitude would turn blue.
I thought I had to keep it all together all by myself and by force.
Be the pilot & co-pilot, air traffic controller and maintenance man too,
Of course.

All that did was put my big nose where it didn't belong.
I thought that being a man meant I had to be real strong.
Being an instructor I got used to running the whole show
But micro-managing is **God's** job. I'm just the pilot. I didn't know.

Now that I have the rolls switched back in proper **WORKING** order
All I do is **AIM** my dream and let **God** be my manager and porter.
Now here's the best part, my inward blues turned to **violet**,
The **color of Kingship** – when I **"Turned on"** my **"Auto-pilot!"**

The reason the details are no longer my **FOCUS** and **"Home Port"**
Is that I haven't yet decided **WHICH** beautiful creative **form** to **court**.
The *sensuous WOMANLY* kind is definitely highest on my list
With only making music topping it, & **then** *probably* only till I get *kissed!!!*

Then it won't be limited to my pen or voice or piano and guitar
The **music** I'll be making will somehow be **WAY BETTER by far.**
She'll have musical skills to harmonize on instruments to me yet unknown,
And looks that invite my cells to synchronize with hers. Right down to
The *merry* **bone!**

#124 It Happened *When* I Decided (*Garden of Eden*)

Together we'll **create** venues that bring people *Joy*
Through music, art and service. **All** will be **our** pl**oy**.
Life will then enthusiastically show it's very **BEST** to all
When we know how to *stay positive* and "Life" *becomes* a "Ball!"

And not only the party kind where laughter and dancing take place,
But maybe picture this point or sphere growing endlessly in what we call space.
Exponentially faster in every direction. No corners or pits to get trapped in
Like religious fear tactics of an eternal torture because THEY say you sin.

No obstacles to stop it and *IT IS* the creative process in motion.
So now *I've made my choice to grow Love here* right next to the ocean
Where INVISIBLE FORCES are stronger and **DEEP** CHANGES the norm here.
Ones that *HEAL* the body, *FREE* the spirit and *rid* the soul *from FEAR!*

Meaning the **Spirit of Life** and **Love** has only more of *itself* to *share*
And there is no place of death (even in THEIR Hell) where *God's Spirit*
STOPS TO CARE!
The **River of LIFE** flows **EVERYWHERE** with 12 trees from which to be
Feedin'.
Unlimited fruit – *God's GRACE, PEACE & LOVE.* I'm already *IN*
"My Garden of Eden!"

Rich Kovatch
12-25-16

#125 What's to Value?

So many things we think *about.*
Some make us sing and some cause a *shout.*
Does it depend on how or where one grows *up*
Or how one **RE-FILLS** their "LOVING *CUP*"?

I'm led to believe that the answer constantly *varies*
According to what *personal values* one *marries.*
What drives your **soul,** makes you smile *inside*
And ***do you have others*** to whom you can *confide?*

There are **places so deep** *inside* our *hearts*
It makes us wonder <u>where reality *ends*</u> and **imagination** *<u>starts.</u>*
It seems to me we always get hung up on the concept of *time*
Whenever we contemplate the realm of the *Divine.*

There are times when time seems <u>to stop</u> or *<u>fly by</u>*
And other times when the **very** best thing to do is *cry.*
It happens to me <u>when</u> I <u>imagine</u> possibilities for *good.*
We would do **SO** many things **IF** we <u>BELIEVED</u> we *COULD!*

Like ridding the world of hunger and *pain…*
If we did this would it be **Heaven** we *gain?*
Now get ready because here's where it really gets *deep.*
Who do **you** **"hang-out"** with, *creative **god-like beings*** or **beguiled**
Sheep?

The company you keep *effects* the *life* you'll *live.*
Some people can't find enough to consume, yet others to *give!*
Stupid sheep can't think for themselves, thus are led to *slaughter*
Stuck in a manifestation paradigm that is purely selfish *fodder.*

#125 What's to Value?

There is **no point** in God's HEART that has a **lack** or *need*.
It **WILL CREATE** whatever is **IN ORDER** and it always makes **OURS** *bleed.*
A picture that gives life...blood flowing from a broken *heart*
But being captured by **BRAND NEW** veins to be returned to its *start.*

These new veins are the paths created by positive *thought.*
The cells have circulated throughout the body and brought back
Whatever they have *caught;*
A positive energy that shares **ALL** – thus **CREATING** MORE *blood*
Or **defeated & broken** down **shadows** of themselves all covered in *crud*

Which physically clogs the arteries and causes many invisible spiritual
Scabs to *form.*
A **LOSS OF ZEST** for life and happiness, then all manners of morbidity
And **death become** the *norm.*
I see MY body as The **Christ of God** in this present sensory manner
Called *NOW*
Anointed with the very **best** of **LOVE & MERCY, JOY & GRACE** *somehow.*

What I value most is not money and material and carnal *things*
But the happiness and **JOY** that my peaceful presence *brings*
To others **that can SEE** I'm **not** _always_ at my _best_
But allow me to be me - TO FIND _MY_ VALUE through _MY_ TEST.

I haven't yet figured out why curiously I was named R*ich*
When NOT having a lot of money to share seems to be a *bitch*
To me because despite all my *"riches"* I KNOW OF, I'm still *complaining.*
Obviously I have another lesson or two to learn yet waning. **HA.**

Rich Kovatch
1-7-17

#126 In The Hands Of God

I live in the hands of God, **I SEE.**
I am growing strong wings and my spirit is now flying free.
I can lift my desires into the winds that blow over the Sea of Eternity.
Knowing I'm to glide, not rush. I feel a sense of maternity.

A new me being born every morning when I awake.
The 1st thing I **do is *THANK GOD I DID*!** For Heaven's sake!
I'm given the mantra of *L.O.V.E.* as my functioning acronym.
Living One Vibrational Experience. My consciousness within.

I have grown for the better through processing all my yesterdays.
Fresh clarity arriving daily allowing me to see thru the thick haze.
Picture the nature of clouds made on purpose with two views to
Ponder.
Either from above or below forming antipodal places for my mind to
Wonder.

It's actually a GREAT place to go — say today's no-nonsense preachers.
Quite the opposite of the chastisement I got from my elementary school
Teachers.
"Get your head out of the clouds — or you're going to 'Get IT'!"
Geez! That's EXACTLY what I WANTED and they'd FORBID it!

<u>It's where inspiration is born and champions are made.</u>
Old ways torn off and new foundations laid.
There is no place where I'm really alone and far from home.
God's hands hold me up and is happy with how I've grown.

I TRUST the Spirit of LOVE in ways before untested.
Being shown new ways for **my "riches"** to be invested
Where my dreams will have backing and support and I constantly gain
New friends.
So my **R.O.I.** will power a wave of prosperity that never ends.

#126 In The Hands Of God

And prosperity actually means simply a " **Good path"**. That is all.
And not only for me but for any who hear the Spirit of *Joy*'s call.
THAT'S the message I KNOW I'm called to write, sing and sometimes
Maybe roar.
And since I now have wings plus momentum at my back, it's time for
Me to soar.

Huh. What has wings to soar and yet might roar like thunder?
I picture the Cherubim guarding the Ark of the Covenant we're under.
Only pure hands could touch and handle its Holy power.
Meaning its laws cannot be broken or your taste for life will sour.

God has set laws in place that keeps ALL in ORDER so that life not end.
They will not break but some somehow strangely seem to be allowed to bend.
This is WHAT the le-way in GRACE – by definition – IS.
So I'll leave questions raised by this poem as today's little quiz.

THAT'S the GREATEST BEAUTY of God to me of all that I see.
Questions are generators that power ideas of how today can be
Better than yesterday but not nearly as grand as tomorrow.
And _AS_ I get "there", I'll have no need or reason to borrow or sorrow.

Rich Kovatch
1-9-17

#127 The *Kiss* Of Life

Oooooooh Mmmmmmmmy Goooooodneeeesssss sake!
I had to make a double-take!
Did my *dream girl* just walk into *my view*?
I'm THINKIN' she JUST DID when I SAW *YOU* !!!

The split-second **you** appeared I thought; "<u>Act</u> upon THIS whim! **I'm Takin' my shot!"**
So here's my beautiful soul mate, now where the heck did I dock my Yacht?
I figured **"my babe"** just **appeared** to unleash my most **intimate** desire,
So nothing stopping THAT from manifesting too, since **"RIGHT NOW"**
You've got me so much higher

Than I've ever been in this lifetime, and who knows...maybe ALL
I *MIGHT* have **EVE**R HAD.
If **THIS** is how close to perfection **I FINALLY AM, I will** *never again*
Experience the feeling of **"sad"**.
All outside distractions disappeared when my *dream princess* turned
My head around,
And *on a journey* through the **"Gates of Heaven"**... *I KNEW*... I was *now*
Bound

Because the very next place **my concentration** and **focus** was drawn
Was to *your alluring eyes* that looked like <u>*my*</u> **Heaven's morning Dawn**
So open they allowed me to *see deeply* into your **sweet** and **sensuous Soul**.
Somehow, someway this *MAGICAL* **View** made my life instantly **whole**.

#127 The *Kiss* Of Life

Then **like a magnet** we were **drawn together** towards friendship, then
Intimacy and *BLISS*.
Our two positIVe life-forces synchronized when we enjoyed our first
Passionate KISS.
I knew there'd never be any carnal-based issues like jealousy or trust.
We **instantly connected to the deepest levels** and **you & I became US!**

This **KISS** got started - in **MY head** at least - **way** before **our lips** *met* to
Touch.
Already, I had imagined **KISSING every inch** of **your body** – many times
OVer and **oVer this much...**
That my **heart** started *pounding SO HARD* and my **CreatIVe Juices**
Started flowing,
My mouth started watering, and my eyes as well, as **your whole being**
Was now glowing

With a *radiance* that exceeded even the brightest noon-high Sun's**!**
I saw *your inviting smile a mile wide pleasantly* contrasted by your
*Cute Tiny buns***!**
I was really hoping you also had a great sense of humor
When I told you I**'ve** always been a super-late bloomer.

Born in the evening on **the _long_est** day of the year in **'57**
I always thought I was growing up somewhere in **Heaven.**
I was surrounded by **Love** and security and family and friends
Believing this is how life *can be* lived - where happiness never ends.

#127 The *Kiss* Of Life

But all too quickly I became aware – that I was **very** blessed.
That the majority of souls today are **hampered by fears** and **extremely
Stressed.**
I got caught up in that **"Rat Race"** too to a large degree
Until I was finally led to proclaim this liberating decree;

That **I'm** *MEANT* to be *HAPPY* and <u>bring *special* JOY</u> into <u>someone</u>'s life!
Be a **peace-maker** bringing harmony to our **ears** and **hearts** and ending
Our strife.
I do it with face to face words of encouragement and *now also in poems
And music*
Spreading the **"Good News"** how words are great but <u>actions</u> <u>complete</u>
This **MAGIC.**

Getting back to **MAGIC** actions, I was talking about **our very first KISS**
One to be always **remembered** and **embraced** so *its feelings* we'll
NeVer MISS.
Wholeness of Life doesn't come by constantly *HAVING* it **"all"**.
It GROWS with **TRUST** and **FREEDOMS** to answer our soul mate's call

In the way **WE CHOOSE** *each precious opportunity* to be spontaneous,
Intimate and dear.
SLOWLY enjoying *"Our time"* because time disappears when **WE'RE
THIS NEAR.**
I get to *see your beauty* and *smell your aroma* and hold you like my
Precious delicate flower,
Then hold you tighter and tighter, giving you more freedom as you give
Me this sacred power

#127 The *Kiss* Of Life

To unleash the **Creative PASSIONS** *you've* been building up inside *your* Tender soul

Reaching ever-increasing creSCendoS to its *CLIMAX* when you give Up *Control*

And let love's security through my strong hands allow your *DEEPEST* **Relaxation** through *stimulating* **vibrations.**

And when we're through, all we'll have for **God, life** and *each other* will

Be the *highest* **possible** *salutations* !

Rich Kovatch
1-24-17

#128 Twinkle Twinkle Little Star

Twinkle, *twinkle* little star
How I wonder what you are
Up above the world so high
Like a diamond in the sky.

That short kid's poem does this one thing right.
It gets young souls to enjoy the night.
It's natural to ask questions about nature and God. That's what we were
Taught.
Still have questions why your life didn't quite turn out like you'd thought?

Maybe it's because we *lose those inhibitions* to disCover,
Especially when *it comes* to finding *Peace* & *Joy*; & now for me; a new *Lover*.
We get programmed to believe being wrong ever is NOT all right.
This pretty much quells most people's inspiration to rise to a higher height.

It's much safer and easier to just go with the flow.
Don't buck the system when you find a whistle that **needs to blow**.
It usually has to do with someone's almighty dollar
Because *to improve means losing power* which makes people holler.

The **concept of *Joy*** I now believe in is - *simplicity at its best*.
Do what I can now and let <u>*God do*</u> all the rest !
It's merely **my INTENTIONS (that <u>WILL</u>)*** get things done
And it happens when one is merely **WALKING with God, not** *"on the run"*.

This awareness is that there's really nothing to **fear**.
No matter where you **"think"** you **"are"**, *LOVE IS ALWAYS NEAR*.
The twinkling of the stars in the dark suggests this **peace**;
That **the "thought"** we <u>*have*</u> to **"earn"** – anything – should cease.

#128 Twinkle Twinkle Little Star

This shows *we're to understand* the <u>concept</u> of contradictions.
Science can't actually prove anything but only makes qualified predictions
Based upon what the past has repeated so often
To suggest a "New Way" starts closed-minded people scoffin'.

Even a thing is that seems to be **the tiniest change means "Brand New".**
The world turns and with each second the **night's black sky** turns to **morning's**
Bright blue.
Black & **blue** are colors that usually happen when our flesh fights with nature.
I'm going to suggest right here and now that you'll be wiser to bate your

Fishing *"line"* in the **"Pond of *Your* Dreams"** with *words* of *Joy* and *Gratitude.*
We live where miracles happen when we own the **BEST ATTITUDE**
That's **<u>open</u>** to changes, because ***that's*** what the twinkles <u>*ARE*</u> !
Ideas are **God-Light flashes** that propel us forward. Maybe to even *visit THAT*
Star !

Positive vibrations get emitted when ideas **"come to light".**
I can let go of everything *knowing* **LOVE's holding me t**ight.

RELAX and ENJOY the tremendous blessings I now choose to perceive **. . .**
I'm Adam in <u>MY</u> "Garden Of Eden" & already enjoying sharing its gifts with
<u>My</u> *"Eve".*

That's the vibration **I** <u>choose</u> to send out
And to not **"have her"** now" I will not pout.
She's so near to me now *but only invisible.*
<u>God seems to always tease me</u> in ways that make me miserable.

But I **KNOW** it's <u>really **His Way**</u> to tell me
That **to** finally **find** her I'll have to see
That when the time is **PERFECT** I'll visit "My Twinkling Star"
And find out <u>for myself</u> – what <u>you</u> really ARE ! ! !

*(contemplate upon <u>*Will*</u> & *all highlights, as constantly suggested)* *

Rich Kovatch
1-25-17

#129 Just Hold My Hand

Just **hold** my **hand**. That means **SO M**UCH.
It's the signal to our worlds that we want to **t**ouch
And connect at the friend level while we do our **t**hings.
Just walking and talking & en**joy**ing what being near each other **B**rings.

Two **Joy**ful **hearts** is what then becomes apparent to **a**ll.
Just this *act of union* with another at **ANY** level is a **b**all.
Butt, **to actually touch** *this part* of **our bodies** that is **used** *to create*...
And *when we* hold **BOTH HANDS** together . . . *oh*, the *pleasures* we
Initiate !

To **hold both hands** at once brings **this power** to **full f**orce.
And everyone **KNOWS** what **THAT** means**, of course !** *!!*
A *position* we **hold each other** where we **lie** to **see e**ye to eye
And **every cell** of our **beings start vibrating** at a rate **so incredibly h**igh

Time and **space** and **ALL outside distractions** quickly **d**isappear.
There is **no division** betwe**en us** when **we unite** this near.
We then *deeply* **penetra*te*** each **other's** bodies, mind, heart, **spirit** &
Soul
Freely and WILLINGLY with *no hol*ds **barred** we release - to the other -
Control.

Now, in this **united state**, the partner *"has the reins".*
Freedom to pump our spirit **up** *then* **drain** our weary **v**eins
Of any & **all energies** & **vibes** just **itchin'** to *be released* & *"scratched"*.
& pleasures of ***UNCONDITIONAL LIBERTY*** just waitin' to be *snatched* **!**

Rich **Kovatch**
1-30-17

#130 Love WINS

I find it funny where my conscious thoughts have ventured.
But I still believe our lives work out best when we're actually indentured
Slaves unto **RIGHTEOUSNESS,** which means this to **me;**
From the moment of *my creation* I was **"Born to Live FREE"!**

I'm free to love whoever, whenever, wherever and however I please.
That includes times when I choose to withhold or give & times to **tease.**
That's how creation works - as **God** has so brilliantly designed.
He gives each soul - *EVERYTHING* - and <u>in its **zenith**</u> it gets refined

To a **"Picture of Hope"** in which **God's face** is seen as *GOLD so PURE*
One can see right through it – into where we can *FIND EVERY CURE*
To whatever might ail our troubled hearts and soul.
When we **"REALLY *BELIEVE"*** this – our lives BECOME *WHOLE!*

The **MAGIC of LIFE** is so simple when found.
The answers to everyone's questions are all around.
They're **INSIDE** the person sharing a moment with **me.**
It's the **Ultimate Question God** asks; **"WHAT DO *you* SEE?"**

A world and universe we've now **CO - C**REATED
Where **every** other **soul** is either **loved** or berated!
Might we **CHOOSE** the vibes we create our **OWN** realities near 100%?
Individually it wise to decide whether each thought is worldly and carnal
Or **"HeaVen sent".**

#130 Love WINS

Their origination will eventually become crystal clear
When listening inside your head if it's **God**'s voice you **hear**.
It will always say; **"Do what's BEST for one a**nother**",**
This way the other soul will be treated like your mother or **brother**.

Mother-wise; as with the utmost love, respect and **unity**.
Brother-wise; with the camaraderie and **WISDOM** to **see**
We all have the same original **M**other and **F**ather – however that
Transpired - thus we're all family.
Trees produce fruit only of its own kind and we should **"Let them be".**

If the **fruit** is **GOOD,** *your slice of the pie* **will** *taste* *de*licious**.**
If it *still needs* **time to mature –** it will be **m**alicious
Towards something **"out of ba**lan**ce"** either outside or within our own **skins.**
When PEACE of Mind is obtained & HARMONY is RESTORED...

THAT's when Love WINS !

Rich Kovatch
1-30-17

#131 The **FAKE** Religious **Smile**

Oh, the hypocrisy on a **FAKE** *RELIGIOUS* smile.
I can spot one from about a quarter mile.
It will always appear in a religious cult's church building, for sure
Because a **new relationship** with *YOUR WALLET they yearn to procure*!

It's SO EASY to see WHO's "In it" for the money.
They'll preach a disposition that acknowledges things only light & sunny.
Proudly smiling (to your face) while describing **what** we **all** *should see*
As **"God's Light".**
But when questioned about evil & dark things they'll always start a
Fight.

This way they **end the inquiry** as to **"How** that could be?"
There **MUST** be **darkness;** *for where else CAN Light be used "to SEE"?*
IF **ALL** WAS **LIGHT** THERE'S BE **NO CONTRAST TO** *RELATE TO.*
THIS **CONTRAST EXISTS EVERYWHERE** ELSE & today it would equate to

Playing a basketball game in which the baskets meant **dittle.**
Can't say you won a game when different scores become *just a riddle.*
And one **WITHOUT** AN ANSWER that **WILL WORK** *for the WISE.*
I'll now **ask** some questions and leave it up to you to surmise

How they can even *USE* the *descriptive* terms **"Bad" & "Good"**
When no matter what transpired; it happened **"Like it should".**
Say a woman pastor or child gets *raped & murdered* and left for **dead.**
No EVIL power exists; so if you've got *problems* with it, they're all in
Your head.

#131 The **FAKE** Religious **Smile**

Apparently _**YOUR**_ child's life was just meant for this to happen.
The kid brought it on him or herself so _don't_ let that dampen
Your _SUNNY SMILE_ when YOU GO TO your church **to learn:**
"How IT Works".
But most visiting folks quickly get eager to walk away thinkin' "You
People are jerks"!

It's **GOOD** that you'll need to learn to balance from one point of view.
That's exactly what they do saying **"I REFUSE TO DISCUSS IT"**. And leave
The questioning on that cue.
That's CRAZY. Denial didn't STOP your kid from **EVIL** and **GREAT PAIN.**
COME WALK THROUGH OUR DOORS. **All is good. Let us explain.**

Of course, this takes classes that will cost lots of money.
P.S. We also teach to give **them** money JOYFULLY & BLES**SINGS** directly
Relate to how you give. **FUNNY!**
JESUS didn't "charge" to **ENLIGHTEN** the troubled. Got PISSED at THOSE
That DID.
I know for sure that **those** that **can discern TRUTH** stay far away from
That grid.

I told you it would be hard for **ME** to try to understand or explain
There's only 1 power & 1 God that _also_ operates _through the **insane.**_
So acts of violence or random events are only accepted as Good lessons.
And I agree, in time. But out of both calmness or tragedies can come
Blessin's.

Jesus and **James** said the tongue _**HAS POWER**_ to **give life OR KILL!**
So do "bad" or sinful **thoughts** that come to fruition just for the thrill.
They taught this 2,000 years ago and only the spiritually blind can deny
**If you preach only "Good" exists; it'd be OK & "Good" if I poke out your**
**Eye?**

#131 The **FAKE** Religious **Smile**

Yeah. **It's "Good"** that you brought it on too.
Gets tougher & tougher accepting that point of view.
It's crazy & irrational to just **deny evil** is **_par_**t of **God's** plan to use pain
Spirit says it's just another **tough tool used** by the **Law to explain.**

Come join our classes. They _don't_ cost _lots_ of money.
Jesus & Buddha & Gandhi never CHARGED to enlighten. Funny.
Some lesson you scored **"Bad"** on just changed your whole outlook.
Hope you see **NOW** how new people might see **YOU AS A CROOK.**

Send money our way with **Joy** & **blessings** will return in some manner.
Usually not in the same way but they still hold up the **"Give cash"**
Banner.
We were told money will just appear like **"Magic"** so never you mind.
Heard pulpit preachin' that money **WILL "appear"** in mom's mailbox
Right at the **LAST** MONENT... or the same as **"RIGHT ON time".**

Of course blessings won't always mean monetarily back.
God is good. **You DESERVE** to be _in your position_ of lack.
It's to learn to do **"GOOD"** and **not "BAD"** the next time you give;
And all things will work out for you. **Be happy just to LIVE.**

Have gratitude you're **near starving** & **sleeping** in your **truck.**
But **don't** stop by **"To SEE"** if we _back up our words_ or they're just
Muckity-muck.
I had a **serendipitous opportunity** to **share** exuberant **JOY** with our
Group.
Asked for permission to share **a BRAND NEW poem _spot on_** with
Today's sermon. A NO-GO. **OH POOP!**

#131 The **FAKE** Religious **Smile**

Two minutes was **"too long"** & it **wasn't** **"approved"** beforehand.
DAMN! *How could it have been* if I just realized **God's** timing and plan?
"What's to Value" – the name of my poem *exactly*!
Apparently the **"Spirit"** **doesn't** **"work"** from the crowd when *IT* desires.
It works with leaders *only* from the pulpit **contractually**.

"I get PAID to lead this church & I'll bring this place to WHOLENESS"
"Remember, we teach God is present in *every* soul's face. No need to
Guess."
No matter their religion, or beliefs, or where they're coming from
Just DON'T ASK ME TO actually do *WHAT I CAN* for you – that's **dumb.**

We're just here to teach but not relate to or respect your tough spot.
Again – **they teach "What goes around, comes around". You'll GET
What you've got.**
So again, your kid must have been really **bad,** not **"good"**? Maybe
Hampered by **FEAR?**
STILL NOTHING TOTALLY EVIL IN, OF, or AROUND the perpetrator as a
"Spirit energy" had *anything* to do with losing your kid. Some day **you'll
HEAR.**

Such bull crap excuses for not giving a hand.
I only asked for **friendship** and **compassion** – not a flippin' house or a
Grand.
I'm fine **where I AM** for now & actually **quite HAPPY** to be **HERE.**
Takes time to get over a divorce, you jerks. Like maybe a year?

#131 The FAKE Religious Smile

Just WAIT till YOU LOSE YOUR IDOLS that YOUR SECURITY LIES IN.
God does surely Loves & lives inside you too – so these lessons are on
Your horizon.
The Laws of TRUTH are neutral so through personal choices we DO
DECIDE
In which energy side – light or dark – do we confide?

Here's the part that I will never tolerate & let stay hidden;
Is when "religious" people only care about THEIR "business". Hard
Questions are forbidden.
If YOU were hungry and hurtin', being taught "How to overcome it –
Someday" would be enough?
I heard: "Here's a list of Big Brother government support. If you can't
Find any help FOR TODAY...TOUGH!

I'M NOT SET UP TO SUPPLY WHAT YOU NEED".
EXACTLY. It's takes KINDNESS & BROTHERHOOD. NOT SELFISH GREED.
HOW CAN YOU SAY YOU DON'T HAVE ENOUGH WHEN SPIRIT PROVIDES all?
Did you forget that The Spirit of Compassion and Kindness for
Somebody else MIGHT actually CALL

On provision to appear instantly (from what YOU'VE already been
Blessed with)?
I'm suppose to be your brother, neighbor, friend and child. I was totally
Messed with.
Jumping to conclusions driven by FEAR & PRIDE.
Huh. The two bad things religion - from TRUTH & PEACE - can't hide!
One guy in need may not turn into 100. Even so, what if it DID?
Could you dare?
No? You can't envision a vision of "WHOLENESS" meaning you help me
Get started over again and I'll take it from there?

Rich Kovatch
2-8-17

#132 BALANCE and HARMONY. . . God's E.Q.

One thing anyone **"of TRUTH"** *WILL* agree *upon*;
God *IS* **"The *KEEPER*"** *of DIVINE ORDER*... not *confusion*.
Laws are the canvas our lives get described *by*.
Rules, Laws, and guidelines set **"*HIS* PEOPLE"** **FREE** but make slaves to
Religion's *cry*.

How this gets brought to our attention *varies*.
It all <u>depends</u> on how *our* **UNDERSTANDING** of *GRACE* & *LOVE*
Grows or *tarries*.
These rules apply across **HIS E.Q. board** which **FINE *TUNES***
Each **soul,** each **MUSICIAN** in **God's orchestra** of **princes** and *goons*.

The vocal *seek* **HARMONY, RHYTHM, RESTS, & RUNS** using many a *note*.
MORE Creativity to incorporate minds **"on the fringe"** is what we *tote*.
God...human consciousness of **HOW** things *CAN* work *out*
If we continue to communicate *without* the <u>spirit</u> to *pout*

When things don't seem to manifest exactly WHEN we *DESIRE*.
THAT's when our **EGO's** vocal chords tighten so our understanding
Comes out *higher*.
The **"Wise"** often tighten up so tightly they stop ALL *output*.
Fools speak loosely without *Love's* filter that leads to their big *foot*

Ending up in their mouth quite often, so to *speak*
Because stresses and laws and rules make them *weak*;
Whereas leaders en*JOY* the challenges set before *us*.
We discover *UNCONDITIONAL LOVE* leads us to sing, but the frustrated
To *cuss*.

#132 BALANCE and HARMONY...God's E.Q.

Extreme *highs* and *lows* on God's E.Q. board have great *influence*
But to those musically "**Tone deaf**" they absolutely make no *sense.*
These "**Notes**" are "**Callings**" – people and situations are our
"**Spice of Life**".
We learn to balance our Highs & Lows and avoid overly complicated &
Unfruitful *strife.*

Life is **WILD, EXCITING,** always **NEW** and **UNPREDICTABLE,** a *bit;*
But never to the point we can't get all the *"NOTES"* to *"FIT"*
Using a "Rock-n-Roll or Jazz , or a Folk or Blue's style *emotion*
Finding measures and beats to employ **ALL POSSIBLE COMBINATIONS** is
Love's *Potion.*

Notes, scales, modes, balance, movement, rests and pauses, timing,
And fluctuating volume are all *part*
Of **HOW** you and I can use **music** & our **LIVES** to TOUCH **God's HEART**...
Stay basic and simple – get along with your neighbors and *"Live"* The
"Golden Rule"
So when you look in the mirror every morning and every night, you'll
SEE a **_WISE_** soul...not a *fool*!

Rich Kovatch
2-10-17

#133 The OPPOPSITE of LOVE

The **OPPOSITE** of **LOVE** is **NOT HATE**.
It's _**APATHY**_ that gives room for this ineluctable fate;
Loneliness, frustration, anger, confusion and **fear**
When you let negative emotions to pour out; few even care enough to
Come near.

Only persons & organizations that **Love _or_ Hate** will even pay attention
To your struggles or handicaps. So now let me again mention
The fact that **APATHY** - _**not giving a damn**_ is _**WAY WORSE**_ than **HATE**.
HATE at least breeds conflicts _which will eventually set up a date_

**To discuss** the issues at hand; _opportunities_ _**to treat the other as your**_
**Brother** and be _thankful you can_ relieve his need.
Ask helpful questions about **attitudes** and **character, charity** & **greed**.
What is the "**reason**" or "**Power**" that drives apathy?
Selfishness, greed, pride & fear that "**change**" _means_ "**loss**" is _HOW_
THEY _**SEE**_.

Change IS CONSTANT. **But when doctrines over-ride LOVE – LOOK OUT!**
Somewhere down the road you're gonna cause someone to shout
Loudly and directly in your face because that's what vibe you emit.
God's not always subtle in the way **He'll** get you to quit

Thinking you will ONLY serve humanity in ways comfortable and
Conforming
To the "**Bird's of a feather**" **church** flock **set on** **their** **way** of reforming
Human contact to only **SPIRITUAL** TEACHINGS; & other things "**heady**"
But find you**self** _in_ _a_ _moment_ _**to PROVIDE** something_ _quite_ _**different**,_
You're _**never**_ _ready_

#133 The OPPOPSITE of LOVE

To stretch out your hand, walk on water, so to speak.
Open up your arms to hug because <u>**connections**</u> **is what they seek**
To another human being **that has *MORE* THAN ENOUGH.**
To **RUDELY TURN THEM AWAY** because that's **"Not <u>*WHAT*</u> we DO"** is tough

And **100% <u>*NOT*</u>** *LIVING*, so now that **KARMA** will return
And in <u>*your own idea*</u> of <u>*HELL's FIRE*</u> you're about <u>to burn.</u>
LOVE and life puts situations in all our lives so we'll **LEARN.**
God is very sweet and gentle, **but when we** <u>*refuse*</u> **to** <u>*SHARE*</u> **HIS LOVE,**
HE tends to get stern!

He'll **TAKE** your stuff *(idols)* away – **THAT'S "How IT WORKS".**
ALL OUTSIDERS can ***SEE*** if a church is **full of LOVING** persons or **JERKS!**
<u>**Just go ask them**</u> that you *might* **"Receive"?**
They'll say; "We DON'T provide <u>*THAT*</u> – IT'LL COME SOON...JUST
"Believe"!

SYMPATHY and **EMPATHY** are **MILES APART** when it comes to <u>***ACTION.***</u>
Sympathy may cry for and with you *but it brings no satisfaction.*
EMPATHY has ***"BEEN THERE"*** and ***KNOWS*** <u>HOW</u> IT <u>***FEELS***</u>
When you go to a **"church"** to be fed eatable food in the carnal, not
Spiritual MEALS !!!

APATHY IS PATHETIC when it comes to **SHARING.**
"You're getting what you deserve" – look out – that's a **Red Herring**
That **"FOOLS"** and the **"Wise"** <u>interpret</u> **LOVE** *exactly* the **OPPOSITE!**
ON *WHAT SIDE* OF **God's JUSTICE SCALES** do **you** believe **YOU** sit?

#133 The OPPOPSITE of LOVE

Are YOU ready to NOW RECEIVE *the way* that *YOU* GIVE?
If you should lose everything TODAY, *HOW* WOULD YOU LIVE?
Do you have family or friends or a "church fellowship" to "take you in"
Or *turn you away because* they say "You're in sin"?

They may even *PREACH* that there *IS NO* EVIL POWER.
ALL *is EXACTLY* AS IT *SHOULD* BE THIS DAY AND THIS HOUR;
BUT TO **DENY** EVIL POWERS *EVEN EXISTS* **IS** BLINDNESS **and EVIL ...**
HERE'S H*OW*.
I'M *JUST ME*, *HERE* & *NOW*, NOT 100, that was *just looking* for a
"LITTLE HELP"... and *YOU TURNED ME AWAY ! ! !*   *OW ! ! ! ! ! ! ! !*

Rich Kovatch
2-10-17

#134 WHAT I DESIRE

The **POWER OF LIFE** starts with **POSITIVE *INTENTIONS*.**
I DESIRE not correction but *improvements* in my **contentions;**
Starting with this very first line written just **now.**
LIFE'S POWER doesn't "**START**" anywhere; but just "**IS**" *somehow!*

Alpha. Omega. No Beginning. No End. CanNOT be destroyed, only **CHANGED.**
THE Word...IS...CREATION from **ALL** there "**IS**"... just *re-arranged*
Into the reality I **DESIRE** which **WILL come** to *be*
Because **MY SPIRIT OF LIFE** inside *my* MIND IS **ABLE** to *SEE*

THE SAYING; "With **GOD ALL** Things **ARE POSSILE**" is more solid than a *Rock.*
A rock is just a collective manifestation of mankind. So is a *"Clock".*
This means with **God – ALL** that there "*IS*" & "*IS*" means **Ying / YANG.**
Where my soul **DESIRE**S to **BE** *this instant* is giving me my *biggest* "*Bang*

For my buck"; the *understanding* of *"Luck".*
Why I've so often waddled in the muck; which generated a verbal
Outburst... usually *"Yuck"?*
Ha. Just kidding. A *different*, more *forceful* and *fuming, rhyming* word I
Frickin' *used.*
So stay with me here and don't get **confused.**

That emotion I released was negative on the **surface;**
But in reality what it DID WAS SERVE its intended **PURPOSE;**
To bring to the FRONT of my MIND how I saw MY **LIGHT.**
MY CREATION WAS NOT in **HARMONY** with PEACE – so I had to *fight*

#134 WHAT I DESIRE

The only way I knew **HOW** TO – at that **time**.
Today – that attitude has "Turned around on a **dime**".
I **CHOOSE** TO re-arrange again the sour lemons my life is giving me and
Adding a **lime**.
NOW , what **I SEE** and **HAVE** at my fingertips is totally **SUBLIME**.

For instance, just now, I double checked on this word's **meaning**.
What a PERFECT Word God gave me has me brilliantly **beaming**
With this energy I KEEP GETTING – I BELIEVE it's my **FAITH** becoming
Substance.
The definition of **sublime** – material things changing into vapor then
Re-appearing in a **instance**

Of "PERFECT TIMING" by God – I LOVE LIFE SO **MUCH**
I DESIRE every **sense** of **sense** I have to **touch**
MY female counterpart I KN**OW** I WILL **FIND**.
Like me – she'll love the fact she's also "ONE of a **KIND**"

As special in her own way to me as I am to her.
The energetic spirit of sharing will continue to stir
Her DESIRE to EXPERIENCE INTIMACY with my soul
OUR P**I**CTURE of two delicate bubbles meeting, touching, and gloriously
MELDING into ONE **WHOLE**.

This happens when two vibrations of intention are SO **CLOSE**.
The **ULTIMATE "THING"** we could **POSSIBLY DO** is en**JOY** another **DOSE**
Of **sweet LOVE-MAKING,** in the flesh and **even stronger** in our **spirit**.
The GLORY of God I experience **gazing gleefully** into your **sultry eyes...**
SEEING YOUR SENSOUS SOUL... I DESIRE TO BE NEAR IT ! ! !

Rich Kovatch
2-11-17

#135 To Touch My SOUL

Being a **Human BEING is to me a *MIRACLE.***
The amount of HAPPINESS & *JOY I EXPERIENCE* is pure *empirical.*
What I decide to call a "Fact" is actually *subjected*
To the **UNDERSTANDING** for **THAT LEVEL ONLY** or else be *rejected*

As being unrelated to the issue at *hand.*
"One man's junk is another man's treasure" is the law of the *land.*
Ha. And it must be found then dug up first, then ***become*** acclimated to
Its NEW EXISTANCE;
While discovering *its* **MOST GLORIOUS FUNCTIONS** we encounter
Strong *resistance*

From this **HU*MAN* CONDITION** that **HAS** to **KEEP** SURVIVAL its *#1 GOAL.*
"CHANGE" means my present comfort level just *lost control*
Of "**HOW** LIFE WORKS" because this *NEW* **UNKNOWN** *is* **NOW** *PART*
Of this **very moment** and **HOW IT** *might* **EFFECT** **MY** **HEART.**

EMOTIONS are the GATEWAYS to the **DEEP**EST spots *within*
Our **MINDS** & **SOULS** so this *NEW* EXPERIENCE will now *begin*
To V**IBRA**TE at a speed sponsored and directed by *CREATION.*
It can drag one's spirit into the depths of depression & despair **or**
Lift you up with *UN*CONTROLLABLE *ELATION !*

INTENT & **CHOICES** determine each path we *walk.*
The **MOST IMPORTANT** & **RELATIVE** concept of **CREATION** is: *it 100%*
MATCHES *our TALK.*
INTENT is OPPORTUNITY & CHOICES that lead to ACTION.
ACTIONS & HABITS BECOME OUR CHARACTER . Hopefully of one **to our**
Own *satisfaction.*

#135 To Touch My SOUL

Without satisfaction, **HAPPINESS** & *JOY* are like grains of *sand*
That no matter **how _hard_ I _try_ to _hold_ _it_ _ALL_** tightly, it *slips* through
My *hand*.
The **LESSON IS; Whatever UPLIFTING or deflating energy & spirit I
CHOOSE to** *express*
My THOUGHTS AIM my HANDS, FEET, and TONGUE *towards* **what I**
Want **to** *impress*

Upon **MY CREATED** world and most importantly with **SOULS** I share
L.O.V.E.
Living One Vibrational Experience is the comprehension a level *above*
What most people can *deal with*, much less *CARE about*.
The **"Butterfly Effect" happens** on levels that reach throughout the
Universe is true, but to what *degree* ?
Always comes back to *how I treat you* and *"SEE"*

The **miracle of sight.** Nearly 8 billion people and *counting*.
That's **what** I SEE and stresses are *mounting*
Upon the collective consciousness of US *ALL*
EFFECTING *COMMUNICATIONS* between _us_ to the point it will *stall ;*

Thus *division* occurs **because** a **fence** *suddenly* *appears.*
When movement *doesn't* occur, The fence becomes a WALL of
Disrespect, then *nobody* *"Hears"*
Any other *brother's* opinion or voice of the **heart** & **soul** they speak
From.
To me & others where **LOVE's 528 VIBRATION** rate RULES our hearts,
That's just plain old *dumb*.

#135 To Touch My SOUL

But _understood_ and _put_ "in _its_ place".
I **CHOOSE** TO **EMIT** vibrations that **bring SMILES** to your _face_.
A _SMILE_ is the BEST thing this person can _wear_
As long as _it's_ **REAL** and _its proof_ will be in **HOW I** _CARE_

To **SHOW** you through my **ACTIONS which** I tell you are from _LOVE_.
I'll help **FEED** you, and **CLOTH** you, keep you **SAFE & WARM** and _shove_
Any _thoughts_ of **negativity** and **doubt** whether **I CAN** or even _SHOULD_
Right back _out_ that _damned_ **door**
I call the "**Religion of FEAR, HATE & PRIDE, and The APPOCALYPTIC HARLOT And** _WHORE_.

The **SPIRIT OF THE UNIVERSE** I BELIEVE _LOVES_ _ALL_
And has _constant_ opportunities for us to arISE and HEAR LOVE's _CALL_.
Like everything else, the more **LOVE**- led instructional practice we get in
Any _endeavor_
We **WILL** be **BLESSED** when we push _PASSION's_ button and _GRAB_
LOVE's LEVER

To **send us** on a journey of **JOY** to **discover God's** _GOODNESS_.
After nearly 60 years of this I'm **HAPPY TO** _CONFESS_
The LIFE & L.O.V.E. I've **SEEN** has Opened up my _eyes_
Ever wider than before **so more LIGHT MIGHT ENTER and re-**_size_

My **HEART** to such a GLORY that even FORGIVENESS _changes meaning_.
It **blends** or **HARMONIZES** its vibrations with this _miraculous gleaning_.
Proverbs states that _KNOWLEDGE WITH UNDERSTANDING_ is the
BEGINNING of _WISDOM_.
WISDOM was FOUND when _CHOICES_ made **our DREAMS COME TRUE,
NOT** _FIZZED UM_'!

#135 To Touch My SOUL

So the question I desire to answer for myself and *others*:
"Have I acted WISELY consistently enough that any *brothers*
Or sisters and the whole world SEES that I'm still doing *O.K.,*
Even if the **DUES** I think it *might* take to help another out, I DON'T HAVE
MONEY TO *PAY* ?

But money is not the only way in which I can SHARE MY ***RICHES****.*
I've CREATED 134 displays. NOW HEAR THIS; My *pitch is*
THIS BOOK OF POETRY **IS MY** *MIRACLE* **COME TRUE.**
When I got **really HAPPY** or **DEPRESSED,** *THIS* IS WHAT I'D *DO* !

Write poetry to God and MYSELF to *express* my **LOVE** and *FEELINGS*.
I'm the summation of **ALL MY past decisions** and their *revealings*.
I'm sometimes *OVERWHELMED* by the **BLESSINGS I** *RECEIVE*.
Still seems a bit crazy to me *HOW* my *Inefficiency* to **SHARE**
UNCONDITIONAL LOVE makes me *GRIEVE*.

But as I've written over and over and over again and **I HOPE YOU**
NOW *SEE*
LIFE *IS* TO ME GOD ENJOYING **HIS LIFE** *THROUGH ME*;

Even **things** that SEEM **EVIL** or **negative** at their first point in *TIME,*

LONG AFTER **God**'s **Touched My SOUL** and the LESSONS
Are *LEARNED*,
They make EVERY MOMENT of Life's JOURNEY SO
SUBLIME ! ! !

Rich Kovatch
2-13-17